F&I LEGAL
DESK BOOK
5th Edition

DEDICATION

To the memory of Teresa Rohwedder,
our friend and colleague,
who never knew the meaning of the word "quit."

1963 – 2006

MEET THE AUTHORS

Here are the authors and editors who prepared 362 things you need to know about auto dealer finance. They are among the dozens of attorneys at Hudson Cook, LLP, a law firm with hundreds of years' aggregate experience in consumer finance.

Thomas B. Hudson
Phone: 410.865.5411
Email: thudson@hudco.com

Michael A. Benoit
Phone: 202.327.9705
Email: mabenoit@hudco.com

Catharine S. Andricos
Phone: 202.327.9706
Email: candricos@hudco.com

A. James Chareq
Phone: 202.327.9711
Email: jchareq@hudco.com

Patricia E.M. Covington
Phone: 804.212.1201
Email: pcovington@hudco.com

Lisa C. DeLessio
Phone: 410.865.5437
Email: ldelessio@hudco.com

Anne P. Fortney
Phone: 202.327.9709
Email: afortney@hudco.com

Michael A. Goodman
Phone: 202.327.9704
Email: mgoodman@hudco.com

Daniel J. Laudicina
Phone: 410.865.5435
Email: dlaudicina@hudco.com

Nicole Frush Munro
Phone: 410.865.5430
Email: nmunro@hudco.com

L. Jean Noonan
Phone: 202.327.9700
Email: jnoonan@hudco.com

Alicia H. Tortarolo
Phone: 401.884.0154
Email: atortarolo@hudco.com

F&I LEGAL DESK BOOK

5ᵗʰ Edition

362 Things to Know About Auto Dealer Finance

AUTHORS

Catharine S. Andricos, Michael A. Benoit,
A. James Chareq, Patricia E.M. Covington,
Lisa C. DeLessio, Anne P. Fortney,
Michael A. Goodman, Thomas B. Hudson,
Daniel J. Laudicina, Nicole Frush Munro,
L. Jean Noonan, and Alicia H. Tortarolo

EDITORS

Michael A. Benoit and Thomas B. Hudson

CounselorLibrary.com, LLC

ISBN: 978-0-9779501-8-8

Discounts are available for books ordered in bulk.
Inquire at CounselorLibrary.com, LLC,
7250 Parkway Drive, 5th Floor, Hanover, Maryland 21076
or 410.865.5420.

Printed in the United States of America

Project Director: Marlene K. Locke
Production Manager: Jean E. Heckhaus
Cover and Jacket Design: Christopher A. Pearl
Book Design: Lisa A. Allen
Printer: Sheridan Books, Inc.

ACKNOWLEDGMENTS

We should take this opportunity to comment on, and thank, the lawyers of Hudson Cook, LLP, who took time out of their busy practices to contribute chapters to this book—chapters that address the laws and regulations they know so well, but in a format that speaks to the F&I Professional. We also owe a special thanks to Peter Cockrell and Judy Nixon of Hudson Cook for their efforts in providing the materials the authors needed to update their chapters.

We also were graced with the support of Marlene K. Locke and Jean Heckhaus, whose proofreading, design suggestions, cajoling, "second set of eyes," and other guidance through the tasks necessary to finalize any such project served to keep us on track.

And, because no project starts without some inspiration, we also thank David Robertson, Executive Director of the Association of Finance and Insurance Professionals (AFIP) in Colleyville, Texas, for encouraging us to consider this project as a way to develop a textbook for AFIP's formal Certification Program for Finance and Insurance Professionals.

The result is a superb desk reference for F&I Professionals. (That's just what we were after.)

Michael A. Benoit and Thomas B. Hudson

CONTENTS

CONTENTS

CONTENTS

EDITORS' PREFACE

Good Decision?

You bought this book. Or, you're considering the purchase. Good decision? We think so. Here's why...

Then and Now

The car business, originally designed to fill basic transportation needs, has seen a lot of change over the years. Once upon a time, you went down to the neighborhood car lot, kicked some tires, and talked to your friend and dealer, Joe. You spotted a shiny new beauty. You and Joe agreed on a price. You forked over some green. Then, Joe gave you the keys, and you drove your new car off the lot and onto a country road. Yes, car life used to be simpler. Your right foot was leaded, but so was the gasoline. Fiberglass was for surfboards, not auto bodies. Plastic was what toys were made of, rather than bumpers.

Today, we have catalytic—what?!

Were those better times? We don't know, but they were simpler. Then, cars got smaller and much more expensive. Margins narrowed. The alphabet changed, and acronyms like TILA and UDAP crept in. States followed federal trends, and not to be outdone, they amassed regulations, sometimes as motor vehicle laws, sometimes as financing laws. Suddenly the federal Truth in Lending Act and Unfair and Deceptive Acts and Practices had regulatory neighbors extending from sea to shining sea.

These laws brought new complexity. Even experts had to specialize; they couldn't know everything. Such complexity spawned a new generation of organizations formed to help.

Epiphany

One morning, confronted by a desk layered with car legislation, I experienced an epiphany. *We need a guide,* I thought, slamming the heel of my hand to my head. *A guide to* <u>*what we need to know*</u>*! More personal than that, a guide to* **Everything You Should Know** *about financing and leasing cars.*

I got up from my desk and walked down the hall to run the idea by my esteemed colleagues. Turns out we have a history with this. After producing **CARLAW®**, we realized that there was an audience in the car business for a short, quick reference book.

Author! Author!

Who should write such a book? Who better than the author of **CARLAW®** and the other lawyers at Hudson Cook, LLP, who specialize in advising clients on consumer finance regulation? After all, what other law firm has dozens of lawyers with that combination of consumer finance experience in one place?

So, we began writing, and here we are. We have, and now so do you, a new guide to what you need to know about financing and leasing cars. We're calling it **F&I Legal Desk Book.**

And the initial response was quite positive: The Association of Finance and Insurance Professionals endorsed our **F&I Legal Desk Book** and built its Certification Program around it. We're proud of that. We're also proud that the book won an Axiom Business Book Award.

But mostly, we're glad to offer you some help, so we all can have time again to go look for those simpler things—like a twilight drive along a mountain road, the purr of a well-functioning engine, the gleam of sunshine on chrome—they haven't gone away, but we didn't have the time to enjoy them. Now, we will.

A Book, and More... (How to Use this Book)

Sometimes a book is just a book. Sometimes a book comes with a few bells and whistles. This one has the bells and whistles.

Often, a discussion of a law or regulation isn't enough, and you or your lawyer will want to look at the actual law or regulation. This book contains a number of routing links to original materials and relevant links that may be helpful. We will post these materials at www.dealerdeskbook.com, the **CounselorLibrary** companion website to this book. The website also will contain occasional "Messages to Readers" regarding topics in the book. Surf there anytime. If you sign up to receive them, we also will alert you when changes occur, as part of our service to readers.

For problems or questions about the links, just contact dealerdeskbook@counselorlibrary.com.

Tom Hudson
for the Editors

Chapter 1

An Introduction to F&I Compliance

By Thomas B. Hudson and
Michael A. Benoit

The retail automotive industry is one of the most highly regulated in the nation. In the areas of sales and finance, dealers and dealership employees must navigate more than a dozen federal laws and find their way through the many state and local laws that impact their operations. In our years of involvement with dealerships and the law, we have found that there are two types of people who travel these dark roads: those who are informed about industry rules and regulations and those who are not. Generally, the ones who are informed fare better as they maneuver toward the bright lights and litigation-free streets of Good Compliance City.

Those who are fortunate get good training on the laws that govern this industry—much like having a GPS in an unfamiliar place. They receive formal compliance instruction, obtain a compliance certification, and are provided with the tools they need to keep their dealerships on the right side of the law. These folks make a strong effort to stay on top of changing laws, and they try to create a culture of compliance in their dealerships. In the end, their preparation and dedication to "doing it right" will pay off for their dealerships in distinctly positive terms: less concern over enforcement, more operational efficiency, a better overall reputation, and, ultimately, greater customer satisfaction. Not to mention, less money spent on cleaning up messes.

Those less fortunate receive no formal training. Instead, they are turned loose to learn as they go, zig-zagging through a course laden with rules and regulations and confused by a roadmap mixed with myth, hearsay, and legend. Ultimately, they find themselves deep in a minefield of mistakes.

These untrained "compliance specialists" are *unaware* of the significance of their actions. Some forms they use are correct, while others are not. Sometimes, their information is correct, sometimes not. Sometimes, their procedures are flawed, sometimes not. And even when the forms, the information, and the procedures are in good order, a dealership's employees may use them improperly.

Where compliance is concerned, the uninformed dealership's effort may be partly correct and partly incorrect. Rarely, if ever, is it completely correct. Not only do these "compliance specialists" *not know* the correct protocol, but also, *they don't know what they don't know.* Nor do they realize what they need to know to follow the rules. Furthermore, without proper training and tools, they have no way to figure it out. These folks—and their dealerships—usually learn the hard way on the receiving end of a subpoena.

Even as some dealers fail to ascend the compliance curve, others are eagerly climbing it—and by now, the curve has become a complex legal landscape. Knowledge becomes the harnessed weapon of determined consumer advocates, wily plaintiffs' lawyers, and persistent opponents of the retail automotive industry. They do their homework, publish books and materials, and construct manuals, which serve as "how to" instructions for nabbing dealers who don't walk the compliance line.

Sad but true, today's dealers face a hostile environment, with serious threats that sting far more than a slap on the wrist. The stings have lasting or endangering consequences. These threats come in numerous shapes and sizes, including:

Class Action Lawsuits

These claims by groups of "similarly situated" plaintiffs can result in large and potentially fatal (to the dealership) settlements or verdicts. In the past, these cases have run the gamut from claims of discrimination to payment packing and failure to make proper disclosures. A class action lawsuit can take a dealership out of the game.

Big Verdict Non-Class Suits

Such suits often result in large punitive damages awards, designed to "punish" a dealer for his or her behavior.

Federal Trade Commission Enforcement Actions and Penalties

The federal enforcement agency that regulates a significant number of car dealers can pack a punch. Because the FTC's relatively small staff has its hands full, its style is to hit violators hard to make an example of those who fall short of regulatory requirements.

Consumer Financial Protection Bureau

Those dealers who are not regulated by the FTC are regulated by the Consumer Financial Protection Bureau (CFPB). The CFPB is a well-funded organization with a laser-focused mission—to protect consumers when they engage in financial transactions.

State Attorneys General

Typically in charge of enforcing state laws and regulations, they often like to pick on car dealers. In the eyes of the AGs (a.k.a., "Aspiring Governors"), car dealers are particularly desirable targets. After all, there are far more customer/voters out there than car dealers.

Federal Legislation

Ever changing, such laws pile more and more obligations on dealers.

State Legislation

These laws create nuances (often significant) in a dealer's compliance obligations, which vary from state to state.

State Consumer Credit Officials

Often thorns in some dealers' sides, these officials remain inconsistent where competence is concerned: some are good and some are bad. Usually, these folks don't understand the car business, yet dealerships often find they have to answer to them.

Public Opinion Battles

Last, but certainly not least, unfavorable publicity can cause substantial harm to a dealer's name and standing. While there may be no direct legal penalties from unwanted newspaper, TV, or other media exposure in such battles, the impact on the dealership's reputation can be devastating. No dealer wants to be the featured topic in the next exposé by a news program that is trying to earn ratings points with its viewers.

For all these reasons listed as threats, listen up. Remember this: ***Responsibility for compliance starts with you.*** Dealerships that want to survive and prosper in today's hostile environment must take their compliance efforts up a notch. Here's why:

- ***The dealer is the creditor in a typical credit transaction.*** The dealer owns the transaction documents. In a typical credit transaction at the dealership, the dealer originates the sale and finance documents—the dealership is a party to these contracts! It is the dealer that is responsible for making proper disclosures. Not the bank. Not the finance company. Not the forms or DMS provider. Not the vendor. *The dealer.*

- ***The dealership is responsible for employee compliance.***
  The *dealership* will be sued for the violations of its
  untrained people, its careless people, and its bad actors.
  The *dealership* will have to pay the bill for its lawyers, and
  if it has violated the law, for the plaintiffs and their lawyers
  as well. It is the *dealership's* image that will be sullied by
  the media when the news of a lawsuit hits. In most cases,
  the *dealership* will be held responsible for the illegal
  actions of its employees and will be subject to civil or
  criminal penalties for their actions.

- ***The dealership cannot rely on vendors to assure
  compliance.*** Sure, companies that provide services, such
  as insurance and GAP for dealers to sell to car buyers,
  have a stake in making certain that the dealer follows the
  law in the sale process, but they also have an interest in
  selling products. While many vendors advise dealers on
  sales compliance and promise their forms are in
  compliance, the *dealership* ultimately is responsible for
  compliant sales, procedures, and forms. Furthermore, the
  dealership typically will not be able to rely on the forms
  and advice provided by its vendors as a defense when the
  regulator comes knocking or when the lawsuit papers
  are served.

- ***The dealership employee simply must comply with
  applicable state and federal law.*** Employees are the voices
  and faces of the dealership. With the role of employee
  comes responsibility. The employee has the day-to-day
  responsibility of ensuring that the dealership conducts
  operations correctly and compliantly. It is the employee's
  face that will show up on the five o'clock news if caught
  by an undercover news camera while gouging a customer,

but again, the *dealership* often will bear the ultimate responsibility for misdeeds.

- **The consequences of employee non-compliance are hefty.** If you hang around this industry long enough, you'll hear stories about undercover police officers conducting "sting" operations in which they snatch up some dealership's finance employees for engaging in fraudulent behavior and throw them in the clink. We bet you would sleep much better at night if you knew with a high degree of certainty that you were doing your job the right way.

- **You don't always know what you don't know.** Unfortunately, ignorance of the law won't shield you or your dealership from heavy penalties, lawsuits, or prison time. We meet with many dealers and dealership employees. All too often, we are confronted with a shocked, "deer in the headlights" gaze from an employee when we talk about a basic, fundamental rule or law. If you don't know what you don't know, you certainly will not be able to fix it.

Here Comes Help!

Fortunately, you've got a serious arsenal of experience on your side.

In this book, we've pooled top legal minds from our firm, Hudson Cook, LLP (the smartest folks we know!), to write about the legal topics that they know best. As we go to press, the attorneys at Hudson Cook have several hundred years of combined practicing experience. That being said, don't take this book as a substitute for your legal counsel. This is a reference tool, not legal advice. The "legal" answer to virtually all compliance issues turns on the specific facts of a given situation, so be sure to talk to your own lawyer for legal advice regarding your specific circumstances.

With this book, we arm you and your dealership with the tools necessary to take charge of reducing your compliance risks. We cut through the legalese mumbo-jumbo to deliver the things that we think every dealer should know.

No scare tactics. No broad-brush commentaries. Just a serious "what to know" guide for folks who care about running a clean and compliant operation.

But This Book Is Just the Beginning

While this book is a great tool to set you on the right path to running a compliant operation, there are plenty of other resources out there, so don't stop here!

One of the best things a new (or old!) dealership owner, manager, or employee who has any interaction with sales or finance operations should do is to become certified with the Association of Finance and Insurance Professionals (AFIP). You can obtain the certification online, and additional information is available at www.afip.com. In fact, this book also is designed as a study guide, or textbook, for the AFIP Certification Program.

Another good idea is to plug in to any resources available from your state auto dealer association or independent auto dealers association. These associations often have helpful training or compliance materials for free or at a nominal cost. Also, don't forget about the National Association of Automobile Dealers (NADA) or the National Independent Automobile Dealers Association (NIADA), which both provide great resources for dealers.

Check out the Federal Trade Commission's website at www.ftc.gov. There, the Commission has materials on the federal Used Car Rule, about federal "Do-Not-Call" compliance, on the FTC Privacy Rule, and about federal advertising guidelines, to name a few. Much of the information on the FTC website is written as a "how to" guide for business and will put you on the path to compliance with FTC rules.

And don't forget the CFPB's website, at www.consumerfinance.gov. The site is new, and so far is of limited usefulness, but we expect that the CFPB will be adding to it quickly. It is possible it will develop into a useful compliance resource.

Get up to speed on your state's laws. Go to the websites of your state's Attorney General, consumer protection agency, and motor vehicle administration (your state may have different names for these organizations) and check them out for free information.

Go to industry conferences, particularly those sponsored by the national and state dealer associations, the National Automotive Finance Association, Leedom and Associates, and the National Alliance of Buy-Here, Pay-Here Dealers. Most of these have legal education programs.

Consider joining a twenty-group. This collection of dealers, which meets periodically to discuss their individual business practices, may be of help. You will benefit from learning about what works and what does not work in other dealerships.

There are professional trainers who make money teaching compliance procedures to dealers—some are very good, some aren't so good. Do your homework. Get references. Be wary of any professional trainers who have not received formal compliance or ethics training.

Consider having a legal compliance review. A compliance review can give you a "snapshot" of your compliance risks and let you know where your problem areas lie. The devil you know is better than the devil you don't know!

Consider subscribing to these publications—**Spot Delivery®**, **CARLAW Counselor,** and **CARLAW®** (not the book, but the monthly subscription service by the same name). These are all available at www.counselorlibrary.com. **CARLAW®** (the book) and other useful titles also are available at that site.

Be advised: It is a dark and treacherous highway of auto lingo, legalese, and legal action out there. So, as you make your way to Good Compliance City, grab the best GPS you can get—knowledge. Now, start your engines and start reading!

Chapter 2

The Truth In Lending Act & Regulation Z

By Thomas B. Hudson

Twenty-Four Things a Car Dealer Needs to Know About the Federal Truth in Lending Act

The federal Truth in Lending Act, or "TILA," has been around since the late 60s. It's the "granddaddy" of the federal consumer protection laws that Congress enacted in response to perceived abuses by companies offering credit to consumers. TILA has some real teeth, and TILA claims against car dealers are common.

It's important to understand TILA's role in regulating consumer credit. TILA is primarily a disclosure law that applies to loan and credit sale transactions. It does not apply to lease transactions—those are covered in Chapter 3.

TILA does not impose maximum finance charge rates, late charge limits, and the like. State law is responsible for those kinds of restrictions, and generally, in most states, they can be found in a Retail Installment Sales Act or a Motor Vehicle Retail Installment Sales Act.

As far as TILA is concerned, you could charge an annual percentage rate of 100% and a late charge of $1,000. TILA doesn't care about the amounts; TILA is only concerned with how these and other credit terms are disclosed.

With that brief background, here are 24 things that we think dealers need to know about TILA.

1. What is TILA?

The federal Truth in Lending Act, or "TILA" is a federal law. It was passed by Congress to require creditors (for example, like car dealers who sell cars on credit) to make disclosures to consumers about the cost and terms of credit. Only Congress can change TILA.

2. Does TILA have an accompanying regulation?

Yes. Congress directed the Federal Reserve Board (FRB) to draft regulations implementing TILA's provisions. That authority was transferred to the Consumer Financial Protection Bureau on July 21, 2011, for all creditors except some car dealers who were expressly exempted from the CFPB's jurisdiction. Exempted dealers—those who sell all of their credit contracts and leases and who have a vehicle servicing capability—will remain subject to the FRB's rulemaking authority. The regulation is called Regulation Z (or "Reg. Z" as we lawyers like to call it). The FRB and the CFPB have the power to change Reg. Z, but they cannot change TILA (we repeat—only Congress can change TILA). The FRB staff has issued something called the "Official Staff Commentary" to Reg. Z. This "Commentary" is the staff's explanation of what it believes TILA and Reg. Z require. The CFPB has also adopted the Commentary so it applies to dealers under the CFPB's jurisdiction too.

3. Where can I find TILA, Reg. Z, and the Commentary?

Sometimes it helps to look at the law. That said, you can find TILA at www.dealerdeskbook.com/resources/tila/, Reg. Z at www.dealerdeskbook.com/resources/regz/, and the Commentary at www.dealerdeskbook.com/resources/tilacommentary/. For anyone having trouble sleeping, a textbook on Truth in Lending is available from the American Bar Association. Titled **Truth in Lending** (catchy title, no?), it is edited by our partner Robert A. Cook, our former partner Elizabeth A. Huber, and the Executive Director of the Conference on Consumer Finance Law, Alvin C. Harrell. The book is available from the American Bar Association, 750 North Lake Shore Drive, Chicago, IL 60611 (see www.dealerdeskbook.com/resources/tilbook/).

4. Describe TILA, Reg. Z, and the Commentary.

TILA, Reg. Z, and the Commentary address different kinds of credit in different ways. It is important to understand some basic distinctions before wading into the actual laws and regulations themselves. So, let's look.

First, TILA and Reg. Z treat "open-end" credit, like credit cards and home equity lines of credit, differently from "closed-end" credit. Typical car sales at dealerships, using retail installment sale contracts, are closed-end credit. Because auto financing at dealerships is rarely offered as open-end credit, we do not address TILA and Reg. Z provisions dealing with open-end credit in this chapter.

Next, TILA and Reg. Z treat "loans" differently from "credit sales." A "loan" transaction occurs when a *lender*, such as a bank, exchanges *money* for a *borrower's* promise to pay. The *borrower's* promise to pay in a *loan transaction* usually takes the form of a *promissory note*. A "credit sale" transaction occurs when a *credit seller,* such as a car dealer, exchanges a *vehicle* for a *buyer's* promise to pay. The *buyer's* promise to pay in a *credit sale transaction* usually takes the form of a *retail installment sale contract.*

TILA and Reg. Z have different rules for "variable rate" transactions, in which the rate of the finance charge can vary during the term of the consumer's obligation, and "fixed rate" transactions, in which the rate doesn't vary. Because there are very few variable rate car finance programs offered by banks and finance companies, this chapter does not address them.

Finally, TILA and Reg. Z impose additional requirements when a creditor takes real estate as collateral. Because typical auto financing at dealerships does not involve real estate as collateral, this chapter will not address vehicle financing secured by real estate.

In a typical credit sale of a car by a dealership to a customer evidenced by a retail installment sale contract, the credit involved is a closed-end, fixed rate credit sale secured by the motor vehicle. Those parts of TILA and Reg. Z that deal with open-end credit and real estate-secured credit don't apply to these transactions. As a result, we don't discuss some fairly large parts of TILA and Reg. Z in this chapter.

5. OK, what parts are left?

TILA and Reg. Z impose the following broad requirements on car dealers:

Finance Charges

TILA and Reg. Z specify what fees and charges imposed in a loan or credit sale transaction are finance charges; they direct how the creditor must calculate the annual percentage rate, or "APR"; and they require that the APR be calculated using the actuarial method.

"Finance charges" are defined as "the cost of credit as a dollar amount." In addition to the "interest" that is collected during the term of the credit sale transaction, they can include charges by persons other than the dealer, if the dealer requires the use of the third party as a condition of, or incident to, the transaction, even when the buyer can choose the third party, or the dealer retains a part of the charge.

Some third-party charges, such as credit insurance and credit insurance charges, can be excluded from the finance charge, provided that the dealer makes certain disclosures and follows special rules. Taxes and fees paid to public officials for determining the existence of, or for perfecting, releasing, or satisfying, a security interest also aren't included in the finance charge, nor are government-imposed taxes on retail installment sale contracts or other security instruments.

TILA and Reg. Z expressly exclude some charges from the finance charge. For example, late charges are not finance charges under TILA and Reg. Z, nor is "any charge of a type payable in a comparable cash transaction." This latter exclusion is particularly useful (and common). For example, if you charge a $100 documentary fee in both cash and credit transactions, that $100 is not included in the finance charge for TILA and Reg. Z disclosure purposes.

The banks and sales finance companies you sell retail installment sale contracts to will have you program your forms-completion computers to calculate the finance charge and the annual percentage rate according to their instructions. Note, however, that the responsibility for making these calculations accurately is yours, not theirs, even if they instruct you how to do it.

TILA and Reg. Z recognize that in many transactions, calculating an exact APR is difficult, if not impossible. Therefore, they provide you with a little wiggle room in your disclosure. As long as the disclosed APR is within 1/8th of 1% of the actual APR, you'll be OK for TILA and Reg. Z purposes.

Disclosure Content Requirements

The dealer must give TILA and Reg. Z disclosures clearly, conspicuously, in writing (special rules apply to electronic disclosures), and in a form the buyer may keep. In loan and credit sale transactions, the terms "finance charge" and "annual percentage rate" must be more conspicuous than other disclosures. "More conspicuous" means that when other terms are in regular type, these terms have to be in capitals, or underlined, or in bold type, or appear as type of a different color, or in larger type.

Some disclosures must be grouped together and segregated from everything else (that's why a dealer's retail installment sale contracts contain the so-called "federal box"). The federal box cannot contain anything not "directly related" to these "segregated" disclosures. Finally, the "itemization of amount financed" must be separate from the other required disclosures. TILA and Reg. Z disclosures are both complex and lengthy and must include the following:

- The creditor's identity.

- The "amount financed," along with a brief description of the term, such as "amount of credit provided to you or on your behalf," calculated as directed by Reg. Z.

- Either an "itemization of the amount financed" or a statement that the consumer has the right to one, with a space for the customer to indicate whether he or she wants one (most retail installment sale contracts include an itemization of the amount financed). The itemization must show amounts paid to the consumer, amounts credited to the consumer's account with the creditor, and amounts paid to others by the creditor on the consumer's behalf, identifying those persons.

- The "finance charge," using that term, with a brief description such as, "the dollar amount the credit will cost you."

- The "annual percentage rate," using that term, with a description such as, "the cost of your credit as a yearly rate."

- The consumer's payment schedule, including the number,

amounts, and timing of payments required to repay the obligation.

- The "total of payments," using that term, with a description such as "the amount you will have paid when you have made all scheduled payments."

- The "total sale price," with a description such as "the total cost of your purchase on credit, including your downpayment of $XXXX.XX. Note that the downpayment may not be a negative amount. If there is no cash downpayment and the customer owes more on the trade-in than the amount of the trade-in allowance (so-called "negative equity"), the downpayment must be shown as zero, and the amount of negative equity must be disclosed in the "itemization of amount financed" section. If a customer with negative equity also has a cash downpayment, you have a choice of showing the cash as a cash downpayment or applying the cash to reduce or eliminate the negative equity (referred to as "netting").

- A prepayment statement. When the contract includes a finance charge computed from time to time by applying a rate to the unpaid principal balance (an interest-bearing contract, sometimes called a "simple interest" contract), the disclosures must contain a statement indicating whether there will be a penalty if the contract is prepaid in full. When the finance charge is calculated in some other manner (such as, for example, using a "precomputed" calculation), the disclosures must contain a statement indicating whether the customer is entitled to a rebate of any finance charge if the contract is prepaid in full.

- Any dollar or percentage charge that may be imposed

before the maturity of the contract due to a late payment, other than a deferral or extension charge.

• The fact that the dealer has or will acquire a security interest in the vehicle being sold or in other property by item or type.

• The disclosures required to exclude the cost of insurance and debt cancellation contracts from the finance charge and to exclude from the finance charge certain fees prescribed by law, to exclude certain security interest charges from the finance charge.

• A statement that the consumer should refer to the appropriate contract document (usually a reference in a retail installment sale contract to "the rest of this document") for information about non-payment, default, the right to accelerate the maturity of the contract, and prepayment penalties and rebates.

As a practical matter, the banks and finance companies to which your dealership sells retail installment sale contracts will either provide you with retail installment sale contracts that they have prepared or they will permit you to use approved "generic" forms such as those produced by Bankers Systems® and Reynolds and Reynolds®. Your dealership should complete these forms as instructed by the bank or finance company that is to buy the contract from you. But again, remember that the responsibility for the forms' compliance with TILA and Reg. Z resides with your dealership.

Disclosure Timing Requirements

The dealer must give TILA disclosures "prior to consummation" of the credit sale. "Consummation" is the term used in TILA and Reg. Z, but the term is not defined in federal law. Instead, federal law directs us to look at state law to determine exactly when consummation occurs. An agreement that binds the car buyer to certain stated credit terms would almost certainly be consummated when the customer signs it. Currently, the Federal Reserve Board staff says that consummation does not occur when a customer in a credit sale transaction becomes committed to buy goods, but occurs only when he or she agrees to buy goods *on credit.*

Disclosure Delivery Requirements

TILA and Reg. Z disclosures must be given prior to consummation and in a form the buyer can keep. The FRB staff says in the Commentary that this can be accomplished by handing the completely filled in, but unexecuted, retail installment sale contract to the buyer. While the buyer has control of the contract, he or she can read the contract (thus receiving the required TILA and Reg. Z disclosures in a form he or she can keep) and sign it, assuming he or she decides to agree to the terms of the contract. There are likely other permitted ways of satisfying TILA and Reg. Z timing and delivery requirements, but this is a tricky area, so be sure to consult your lawyer.

If the disclosures are provided to the customer electronically, the customer must be required to access the disclosures before the transaction is consummated (roughly speaking, before the customer becomes obligated to buy the vehicle on credit). A link to the disclosures satisfies the timing rules if the customer can't bypass the disclosures before becoming obligated.

Electronic disclosures are permitted under Reg. Z, provided you follow the requirements of the federal Electronic Signatures in Global and National Commerce Act (ESIGN). These requirements are somewhat straightforward, but if you want to do a fully electronic retail installment sale transaction (for example, one where the buyer will not get written disclosures prior to consummation), check with your attorney for guidance on how to implement the ESIGN requirements.

6. What should I use as the basis of my disclosures?

The disclosures should be based on the terms of the legal obligation between the parties. Disclosures may be made on the assumption that the customer will pay all amounts due on the dates they are due and in the required amounts due.

7. Can I use estimates?

Yes, but if you do, the estimate must be based on the best information that is reasonably available to you at the time, and your disclosures must clearly state that it is an estimate. There are special rules for making estimated disclosures.

8. What happens if my disclosures become inaccurate after I give them?

TILA and Reg. Z disclosures are essentially a snapshot in time. The disclosures have to be accurate as of the time they are given. If an event occurs after the creditor delivers the required disclosures (we lawyers call this a "subsequent occurrence"), causing the disclosures to become inaccurate, the inaccurate disclosures don't violate TILA or Reg. Z.

9. What happens if I give the buyer his or her TILA and Reg. Z disclosures and then must re-contract at a later date?

You should re-contract the transaction as of the date of re-contracting, recalculating all deal terms and disclosures as if the re-contracting were a completely new transaction. This isn't a "subsequent occurrence," but is rather the creation of a new credit transaction that requires new disclosures.

10. Does TILA apply to all of my credit transactions?

No. Actually, many transactions aren't covered by TILA and Reg. Z. They do not apply when you sell a car on credit to a business entity, such as a corporation, partnership, or association. That's the rule even when the car will be used primarily for personal, family, or household purposes. They don't apply when you sell a car to an individual, and the car is to be used "primarily" for purposes that are not personal, family, or household in nature. "Primarily" means at least 51% of the time, and you may rely upon the buyer's representations about the intended use of the car.

In most instances, TILA doesn't apply when the "amount financed" (note that in most cases this is not the same thing as the price of the car) exceeds $53,000*. A few states (for example, California) impose a *state law* requirement that creditors must make TILA and Reg. Z disclosures even when they don't apply, so be careful with this exemption. There are some other exemptions to TILA and Reg. Z coverage, but they usually don't apply in a typical dealer credit sale of a car.

---

*The Dodd-Frank Act increased this threshold amount from $25,000, effective July 21, 2011, and provides that the threshold will be increased annually based on the rate of inflation.

11. How do I handle non-TILA transactions? Do I use the same documents I use for TILA transactions?

You can. The prevailing practice among dealers is to document non-TILA transactions on the same forms used to document transactions that are subject to TILA. There is little danger in this—simply providing TILA and Reg. Z disclosures in a transaction to which they do not apply will not make the transaction subject to TILA.

12. Do TILA and Reg. Z permit a consumer to rescind a car purchase transaction?

No. A consumer has a right under TILA and Reg. Z to rescind certain real-estate-secured transactions, but not your typical retail installment sale transaction involving the purchase of a motor vehicle.

13. What must I do to make sure my advertisements comply with TILA and Reg. Z?

If your advertisement states credit terms, it can state only those terms you will actually arrange or offer. If your advertisement states a rate of finance charge, it has to state the rate as an "annual percentage rate," using that term or "APR." You are not permitted to use other methods (such as the add-on method) of calculating the APR appearing in your advertisements.

After that, things get a little tricky. In regulating advertising, TILA and Reg. Z use the concept of "triggering terms." If certain specified terms appear in your advertisements, they "trigger" further disclosure requirements.

The "triggering terms" are:

• The amount or percentage of any downpayment;

- The number of payments or period of repayment;

- The amount of any payment; and

- The amount of any finance charge.

If a "triggering term" is used, your ad must then contain the amount or percentage of the downpayment, the terms of repayment, and the annual percentage rate, using that term or "APR." If the rate can be increased during the term of the obligation—rare in car financing—other rules apply. When you offer a range of possible credit terms, it's OK to use examples of typical transactions, as long as the examples contain all the applicable required terms.

Special rules apply to catalogs or multiple-page advertisements. If such an advertisement gives information in a table or schedule in sufficient detail to permit the reader to determine the required disclosures, it will be considered as a single advertisement. The table or schedule has to show all appropriate disclosures for a representative scale of amounts up to the level of the more commonly sold higher-priced cars offered.

If you do electronic advertising (for example, on a web page), essentially the same rules apply, but with some minor differences to accommodate the realities of the Internet. For example, if you use any of the "triggering terms" described above, you would need to link the triggering term to the additional information Reg. Z requires to be disclosed with such triggering term.

14. What is an "advertisement" anyway?

The FRB says that an advertisement is "a commercial message in any medium that promotes, directly or indirectly, a credit transaction." It provides the following examples:

- Messages in a newspaper, magazine, leaflet, flyer, or catalog
- Radio, TV, or public address system announcements
- Internet messages
- Direct mail
- Exterior and interior signs
- Point-of-sale displays
- Telephone solicitations
- Tattoos on salespeople (We're kidding—the FRB didn't really say that, although it would be correct if they had. We just wanted to make sure you were still awake.)
- Price tags with credit information
- Letters to customers as part of an organized solicitation of business

What isn't an advertisement? Direct personal contacts, follow-up letters to customers, oral or written communications relating to the negotiation of a specific transaction, and a few other things. Unless you're certain, treat it as an advertisement until your lawyer says you don't need to.

15. What happens if I violate the advertising rules of TILA and Reg. Z?

There is no "private right of action" in TILA or Reg. Z against a creditor who violates the advertising rules. This means a private party (such as a consumer or business entity) can't sue you for violating these rules. However, that doesn't mean that there is no consequence for a violation. The Federal Trade

Commission (FTC) enforces TILA and Reg. Z requirements against car dealers. Initial violations are subject to the FTC's "cease and desist" actions and a subsequent violation of the C&D Order can expose a dealer to fines of up to $16,000 per day, per violation. CFPB penalties would apply to dealers subject to the CFPB's enforcement authority. In addition, plaintiffs' lawyers have argued, sometimes successfully, that a violation of a *federal law or regulation* is an unfair or deceptive act or practice under state law. We address these state laws in a later chapter, but they tend to come with very stiff penalties.

16. Must I use the term "annual percentage rate" in oral disclosures?

In an oral response to a customer's inquiry about the cost of credit, only the annual percentage rate can be stated. If a simple annual rate is applied to an unpaid balance, you can state that rate along with the annual percentage rate. An example of this would be a simple interest retail installment sale contract with a "prepaid finance charge." The prepaid finance charge (like points in a home loan) would make the APR higher, and you would be permitted to state the APR and the simple annual rate that is applied to the unpaid balance.

17. What language must be used for disclosures?

In general, disclosures required by TILA and Reg. Z may be made in a language other than English, provided that the disclosures are made available in English upon the consumer's request.

18. What are the TILA and Reg. Z recordkeeping requirements?

You must maintain evidence of compliance with TILA and Reg. Z (other than the advertising provisions) for two years after the date disclosures are required to be made or action is required to be taken.

19. What do I do if my state's laws are inconsistent with TILA and Reg. Z?

State law requirements that are inconsistent with TILA and Reg. Z are preempted by federal law. A state's law is inconsistent if it requires you to make disclosures or take actions that contradict TILA or Reg. Z. A state law is contradictory if it requires the use of the same term to represent a different amount or a different meaning than TILA or Reg. Z. For example, a state law that defines "finance charges" to mean something different than what it means under TILA and Reg. Z would be contradictory and inconsistent and, therefore, preempted by TILA and Reg. Z. A state law that requires a different term from that required by TILA and Reg. Z to describe the same item (for example, a law that required you to disclose the "finance charge" as "interest") would also be preempted. Simple, huh?

There is a process by which a creditor, state, or interested party may request the Federal Reserve Board to make a determination of inconsistency. After the FRB makes such a finding, creditors may not use the inconsistent form.

20. Are some states exempt from TILA and Reg. Z?

Yes, but odds are your state isn't one of them. Maine, Connecticut, Massachusetts, Oklahoma, and Wyoming have received exemptions from parts of TILA and Reg. Z. If you are operating in these states, ask your lawyer for advice on which provisions of TILA and Reg. Z the exemption covers.

21. What is the penalty for violating TILA and Reg. Z?

There are criminal and civil penalties for violating TILA and Reg. Z.

If you "willfully and knowingly" give false information or inaccurate information, or fail to provide information that TILA and Reg. Z require you to give, or if you use a chart or table not authorized by the Federal Reserve Board to determine annual percentage rates, or if you otherwise don't comply with TILA and Reg. Z requirements, you face a criminal penalty of not more than $5,000 or a year in the slammer, or both. Don't do the crime if you can't do the time. Better yet, don't do the crime!

Criminal actions alleging violations of TILA and Reg. Z are as rare as hen's teeth. Our jails are not filled to overflowing with TILA and Reg. Z violators. It's the civil action liability, often in the form of a class action lawsuit, which makes TILA and Reg. Z lawsuits so dangerous.

If you violate TILA or Reg. Z and you are sued in an individual (as opposed to a class) action, your potential liability consists of the following:

- The plaintiff's actual damages

- "Statutory damages" of twice the finance charge (but not more than $2,000* or less than $200*)

- The plaintiff's reasonable attorney's fees and court costs

*The Dodd-Frank Act increased these amounts from $1,000 and $100, respectively, effective July 21, 2011.

In a class action, the formula changes a bit. You would be looking at the following potential liability:

- The plaintiff's actual damages

- "Statutory damages" of "such amount as the court may allow," except that in class actions, there is no minimum recovery, and the creditor's maximum liability is capped at $1,000,000* for any class action or series of class actions arising out of the same failure to comply by the same creditor

- The plaintiff's reasonable attorney's fees and court costs

For the most part, the "statutory damages" mentioned in both formulas are available only for the violation of certain parts of TILA and Reg. Z. The disclosure violations giving rise to statutory damages include those dealing with the following:

- The finance charge

- The total of payments

- The number, amount, and due dates or periods of payment

- The total sale price

- The descriptive explanations required by Reg. Z for the amount financed, the finance charge, the annual percentage rate, the total of payments, and the total sale price (including a reference to the amount of the downpayment)

---

*The Dodd-Frank Act increased this amount from $500,000, effective July 21, 2011.

- The statement that a security interest has been taken in the vehicle being purchased

- Any late payment charge

As a practical matter, it is often difficult for a plaintiff to show actual damages in a case alleging TILA and Reg. Z violations, so if an alleged disclosure violation doesn't fall within this laundry list, the case can often be disposed of at an early stage.

22. *Are there any defenses to a civil claim for a violation of TILA or Reg. Z?*

Yes. There is something called the "bona fide error" defense. A creditor claiming this defense must show by a "preponderance of the evidence" that the violation was not intentional and resulted from a bona fide error even though the creditor maintained procedures reasonably adapted to avoid such an error. TILA gives examples of bona fide errors—clerical and calculation errors, computer malfunctions, programming problems, and printing errors. Note that an error of legal judgment doesn't make the list.

There's also a "safe harbor" for a creditor charged with violating TILA or Reg. Z if the creditor relied in good faith on "any interpretation or approval by an official or employee of the Federal Reserve System authorized by the Federal Reserve Board to issue such interpretations or approvals under such procedures as the FRB prescribes." The safe harbor applies even if a court or some other authority later determines that the interpretation or approval was invalid.

23. If I violate TILA or Reg. Z, can I remedy the violation and avoid civil liability?

Yes. Within 60 days of discovering an error (and before you are sued for the error), you can notify your customer of the error and make those adjustments to the customer's account necessary to assure that the customer will not be required to pay an amount in excess of the charge actually disclosed or the dollar equivalent of the APR actually disclosed, whichever is less.

24. What is the statute of limitations for a TILA and Reg. Z violation—how much time must pass after the violation before a consumer is barred from bringing a suit against me?

A consumer must sue you within one year from the date of the occurrence of the violation (usually the date that you gave the consumer the disclosures). However, TILA and Reg. Z place no time limit on when the consumer may raise the violation as a defense or in recoupment (a reduction in the creditor's damages because of a demand from the consumer arising from the same transaction) or a set-off in a collection action.

CHAPTER 2

The Consumer Leasing Act & Regulation M

By Thomas B. Hudson and
Daniel J. Laudicina

Twenty-Three Things a Car Dealer Needs to Know About the Federal Consumer Leasing Act

The Consumer Leasing Act (CLA) has its origins in the federal Truth in Lending Act, or "TILA." The CLA, like TILA, has its own accompanying regulation—in the case of the CLA, that Regulation is Reg. M. We won't bore you with a lengthy recitation of the history of the CLA and Reg. M. For our purposes, it's sufficient to start our discussion with the last major revision to the CLA in 1996, and the issuance of "new" Reg. M, effective October 31, 1996. The CLA and Reg. M were the federal government's responses to perceived abuses by companies offering leases to consumers. Like TILA and Reg. Z, the CLA and Reg. M have some real teeth, and CLA and Reg. M claims against car dealers are common.

It's important to understand the CLA's role in regulating consumer leasing. The CLA, like TILA, is primarily a disclosure law. The CLA doesn't impose maximum lease charge rates, maximum bounced check fee limits, maximum lease terms, and the like. Those sorts of restrictions, when they appear, are imposed by state law through either Article 2A of the Uniform Commercial Code, or a state law that regulates leases in the way a typical Retail Installment Sales Act regulates credit sales of vehicles, or both.

As far as the CLA is concerned, you could charge any lease rate, excess mileage rate, or bounced check fee you wanted to charge. With a couple of important exceptions, the CLA doesn't care about the amounts—it is only concerned with how these and other lease terms are disclosed.

A few quick, but important, notes on leases and lease agreements include the following paragraphs.

The "lessor" is the dealer or the leasing company that owns the car and that permits the consumer to use it for a specified time period. The "lessee" is the consumer who is leasing the vehicle from the lessor. Note that the lessee has only the right to use the vehicle for a specified time. Except for the right to use the vehicle and a purchase option, if any, the lessee has no rights to the vehicle and may not sell it or trade it without the lessor's permission, or use it as collateral for a loan.

In a typical lease contract, the lessee agrees to abide by all of the terms and conditions of the lease agreement, to return the vehicle to the lessor without damage or excess wear and tear, and to keep the vehicle in good mechanical condition.

Lease agreements usually provide that the lessee bears the risk of loss if the vehicle is stolen or damaged in an accident. The lease agreement usually requires the lessee to maintain insurance against these risks. As with a financed vehicle, if the leased vehicle is destroyed and the insurance company's payment is insufficient to pay the lessee's lease balance, the lessee usually must pay the difference between the amount of the insurance proceeds and the lease balance ("usually" because some lease agreements provide that the lessee is not responsible for the shortfall).

A typical lease contract will also contain an agreed-upon mileage limitation; if the lessee exceeds the agreed-upon mileage, the lessor usually charges for the excess miles.

Leases may contain a purchase option permitting the lessee to buy the leased vehicle at a price, or using a price formula, set forth in the lease. Sometimes the option permits the lessee to buy the car before the lease term ends, while other leases permit the option to be exercised only at lease end. Some leases contain options that permit either early or end-of-term purchase. If the lease contains no purchase option, the lessor may nevertheless sell the leased vehicle to the lessee, but is not bound to do so, as would be the case if the lessee had a purchase option. If the lessor in such a situation elected to sell the vehicle to the lessee, the sale would be a totally new transaction, the terms of which would have to be negotiated at the time of purchase between the lessor and the lessee.

Leases may be for any period agreed to between the lessor and the lessee. In recent years, the terms for leases have tended to be shorter than the terms for retail installment sales and loans.

With that background, here are 23 things that we think dealers need to know about the CLA.

1. What is the Consumer Leasing Act?

The Consumer Leasing Act is a federal law. It was passed by Congress to require lessors, like car dealers who lease cars to consumers, to make disclosures to consumers about the cost and terms of the leases. Only Congress can change the CLA.

2. Does the CLA have an accompanying regulation?

Yes. Congress directed the Federal Reserve Board to draft regulations implementing the CLA's provisions. The FRB's regulation is called Regulation M (or, "Reg. M," as we lawyers like to call it). The Consumer Financial Protection Bureau (CFPB) took over rule-writing authority for all dealers except those expressly exempted from its authority; Reg. M rule-writing authority for the exempted dealers will remain with the FRB. The FRB and the CFPB have the power to change Reg. M, but they cannot change the CLA (only Congress can change the CLA). The FRB staff has issued something called the "Official Staff Commentary" to Reg. M. This "Commentary" is the staff's explanation of what it believes the CLA and Reg. M require.

3. Where can I find the CLA, Reg. M, and the Commentary?

The CLA is available at www.dealerdeskbook.com/resources/cla/. Reg. M and its Commentary are available at www.dealerdeskbook.com/resources/regmandcommentary/. To our knowledge, there is no generally available textbook that covers the CLA and Reg. M.

4. Describe the CLA, Reg. M, and the Commentary generally.

The CLA, Reg. M, and the Commentary address different kinds of leases in different ways. It is important to understand some basic distinctions before wading into the actual laws and regulations themselves. Let's look at a few basic distinctions that the CLA and Reg. M make.

First, the CLA and Reg. M treat "open-end" leases differently from "closed-end" leases. Typical car leases at dealerships are closed-end leases. Reg. M says that an open-end lease is "a consumer lease in which the lessee's liability at the end of the lease term is based on the difference between the residual value of the leased property and its realized value." Reg. M says that a "closed-end" lease is a consumer lease "other than an open-end lease." Most auto leasing at dealerships, in our experience, is offered in the form of a closed-end lease.

Dealers need to determine the sorts of lease programs that they are offering, because they will need to describe these programs to potential lessees accurately. For example, in a typical closed-end lease, the lessee has no liability at the end of the lease term except for excess wear and use charges and excess mileage charges. By contrast, a lessee under an open-end lease typically is obligated at the end of the lease term for the difference between the vehicle's residual value and its "realized value." That's an important distinction, and one that dealers offering open-end leases (also known as "finance leases" or "participating leases") need to know about.

5. OK, what do the CLA and Reg. M require?

The CLA and Reg. M impose the following broad requirements on car dealers:

Disclosure Content Requirements

The dealer must give CLA and Reg. M disclosures clearly, conspicuously, in writing (special rules apply to electronic disclosures), and in a form the consumer may keep. The disclosures must be given to the lessee in a dated statement that identifies the lessor and the lessee. The disclosures may be made in the lease document itself or in a separate statement that identifies the lease transaction. Alternatively, some disclosures may appear in the lease itself, while others may appear in a separate statement. Certain disclosures must be grouped together and segregated from everything else (that's why a dealer's leases from various leasing companies and banks all contain the same general tabular layout). Generally, the forms provided to dealers by various leasing sources will contain the disclosures (or spaces for the disclosures) as required, but remember that the dealer in most leasing programs is the original lessor and is responsible for the accuracy of the disclosures.

Electronic disclosures are permitted under Reg. M, provided you follow the requirements of the federal Electronic Signatures in Global and National Commerce Act (ESIGN). These requirements are somewhat straightforward, but if you want to do an electronic lease where the lessee will not get written disclosures prior to consummation, check with your attorney for guidance on how to implement the ESIGN requirements.

Note that all of the disclosures and contract terms are important. It is not a good practice to attempt to highlight some of the disclosures, and not others, in explaining the terms and conditions of the lease to the lessee.

The CLA and Reg. M disclosures are lengthy and complicated. Most forms that you get from your finance sources who buy leases from you will contain the appropriate disclosures (or have spaces that can be completed with the data that varies from lease to lease). All of the forms you use should contain the following, as applicable:

- A description of the leased property sufficient to identify it to the lessee and the lessor.

- The "amount due at lease signing or delivery," itemized by type and amount, including any refundable security deposit, advance monthly or other periodic payment, and capitalized cost reduction. In a motor vehicle lease, the lessor must itemize (in a form substantially similar to model forms provided in Reg. M) how the amount due will be paid, by type and amount, including any net trade-in allowance, rebates, non-cash credits, and cash payments.

- The number, amount, and due dates or periods of payments scheduled under the lease and the total amount of the periodic payments.

- The total amount of other charges payable to the lessor, again, itemized by type and amount, that are not included in the periodic payments. These other charges include the amount of any liability imposed on the lessee at the end of the lease term, but in an open-end lease the charges don't include the potential difference between the residual value and the realized value of the vehicle.

- The total of payments, with a description such as, "the amount you will have paid by the end of the lease." The total of payments is the sum of the amount due at lease signing (other than refundable amounts), the total amount of periodic payments (less any part of the periodic payments paid at lease signing), and other charges. If the lease is an open-end lease, this disclosure must be accompanied with a description such as, "You will owe an additional amount if the actual value of the vehicle is less than the residual value."

- A mathematical progression of how the scheduled periodic payment is computed in a format substantially similar to the model forms provided in Reg. M.

- The "gross capitalized cost," which must also set forth the "agreed upon value of the vehicle," using the phrase, "the agreed upon value of the vehicle [$XXXX.XX] and any items you pay for over the lease term (such as service contracts, insurance, and any outstanding prior credit or lease balance)." The lessor is required to either provide an itemization of the gross capitalized cost or provide the lessee with a statement informing the lessee that the lessee has the right to obtain such an itemization. If the lessee requests it, an itemization must be provided before consummation of the lease.

- The capitalized cost reduction (similar to a downpayment), with a description such as "the amount of any net trade-in allowance, rebate, non-cash credit, or cash you pay that reduces the gross capitalized cost."

- The adjusted capitalized cost, with a description such as "the amount used in calculating your base [periodic] payment."

- The residual value, with a description such as "the value of the vehicle at the end of the lease used in calculating your base [periodic] payment."

- The depreciation and any amortized amounts (essentially the difference between the adjusted capitalized cost and the residual value) with a description such as "the amount charged for the vehicle's decline in value through normal use and for any other items paid over the lease term."

- The rent charge (the difference between the total of the base periodic payments over the lease term minus the depreciation and any amortized amounts) with a description such as "the amount charged in addition to the depreciation and any amortized amounts."

- The total of base periodic payments, with a description such as "depreciation and any amortized amounts plus the rent charge."

- The lease payments, with a description such as "the number of payments in your lease."

- The base periodic payment (calculated by dividing the total of the base periodic payments by the number of payment periods in the lease). The base periodic payment is made up of the monthly estimated depreciation and the monthly lease charge.

- An itemization of any other charges that are part of the periodic payment.

- The total periodic payment, which is the sum of the base

periodic payment and any other charges that are part of the periodic payment.

- A statement of the conditions under which the lessee or the lessor can terminate the lease before the end of the lease term and the amount, or a description of the method for determining the amount, of any penalty or other charge for early termination, which must be reasonable. A notice substantially similar to the following, warning the lessee of the costs of early termination, must be given: "Early Termination. You may have to pay a substantial charge if you end this lease early. The charge may be up to several thousand dollars. The actual charge will depend on when the lease is terminated. The earlier you end the lease, the greater this charge is likely to be."

- A statement of whether the lessor or the lessee is responsible for maintaining and servicing the vehicle; a brief description of the responsibility; a statement of the lessor's standards for wear and use, if any, which must be reasonable; and a notice about wear and use substantially similar to, "Excessive Wear and Use. You may be charged for excessive wear and use based on our standards for normal use." The notice must also state the amount or method for determining the amount of any charge for excessive mileage.

- A statement of whether or not the lessee has the option to purchase the vehicle. If the purchase option applies at the end of the lease term, the purchase price must be included. If the purchase option applies to early termination, the lessor must disclose when the option may be exercised, and the purchase price, or the method for determining the purchase price.

- A statement that the lessee should refer to the lease documents for additional information on early termination, purchase options, maintenance responsibilities, warranties, late and default charges, insurance, and any security interests, if applicable.

- A statement of the lessee's liability, if any, at early termination or at the end of the lease term for the difference between the residual value of the vehicle and its realized value.

- If the lessee's liability at early termination or at the end of the lease term is based on the vehicle's realized value, a statement that the lessee may obtain, at the lessee's expense, a professional appraisal by an independent third party (agreed to by the lessor and the lessee) of the value that could be realized upon the sale of the vehicle. The appraisal is final and binding on the parties.

- If the lessee is liable at the end of the lease term for the difference between the vehicle's residual value and its realized value, several disclosures are required. The first is the rent and other charges paid by the lessee and required by the lessor as an incident to the lease transaction, with a description such as, "the total amount of rent and other charges imposed in connection with your lease [state the amount]." The second is a description of a rebuttable presumption that, at the end of the lease term, the residual value is unreasonable and not in good faith to the extent it exceeds the realized value by more than three base monthly payments (there's a formula that approximates that amount when payments are other than monthly) and that the lessor cannot collect the excess amount unless the lessor brings a court action and pays the lessee's reasonable attorney's fees, or unless the excess of the residual value over the realized value is due to unreasonable or excessive use of the vehicle, in which case, the presumption does not apply. The final disclosure is a statement that the lessor and the lessee are permitted, after the termination of the lease, to make any mutually agreeable final adjustment regarding excess liability.

- If insurance is provided by or paid through the lessor, the types, amounts of coverage, and cost to the lessee. If the lessee must obtain the insurance, the types and amounts of coverage have to be disclosed.

- All express warranties and guarantees made by the lessor or the manufacturer regarding the vehicle must be identified.

- The amount, or method of determining the amount, of any penalty or other charge for delinquency, default, or late payments. These charges must be reasonable.

- A description of any security interest (other than a disclosed security deposit) held or to be retained by the lessor, with a clear identification of the property to which the security interest relates.

- If the lessor provides a percentage rate in an advertisement or in documents evidencing the lease transaction, a notice stating, "This percentage may not measure the overall cost of financing this lease." Use of the terms "annual percentage rate" or "annual lease rate" are prohibited.

Disclosure Timing Requirements

The dealer must give CLA disclosures "prior to consummation" of the lease. "Consummation" is the term used in the CLA and Reg. M, but the term is not defined in federal law. Instead, we must look to state law to determine exactly when consummation occurs. An agreement that binds the lessee to certain stated lease terms would almost certainly be consummated when the customer signs it. If the disclosures are provided to the customer electronically, the customer must be required to access the disclosures before the transaction is consummated (roughly speaking, before the customer becomes obligated). A link to the disclosures satisfies the timing rules if the customer can't bypass the disclosures before becoming obligated.

Disclosure Delivery Requirements

CLA and Reg. M disclosures must be given in a form the buyer can keep, prior to consummation of the transaction. In the context of loan and credit sale transactions, the FRB staff says that this can be accomplished by handing the completely filled in, but unexecuted, promissory note or retail installment sale contract to the buyer. While the buyer has control of the contract, he or she can read the contract (thus receiving the required TILA and Reg. Z disclosures in a form he or she can keep) and sign it, assuming he or she decides to agree to the terms of the contract. It's a pretty good bet that you can use the same process in the context of a lease transaction and satisfy the CLA and Reg. M timing and delivery requirements. In any event, this is a tricky area, so be sure to consult your lawyer.

Remember, the requirement that the Reg. M disclosures be provided in a form the lessee can keep prior to the consummation of the transaction applies to electronic disclosures as well. If you're planning to do purely electronic lease transactions, be sure to check with your attorney about how to do it in a way that meets the requirements of the ESIGN Act.

6. What should I use as the basis of my disclosures?

The disclosures should be based on the terms of the legal obligation between the parties.

7. Can I use estimates?

Yes, but if you do, the estimate must be based on the best information that is available to you at the time, and your disclosures must clearly state that it is an estimate. There are special rules for making estimated disclosures, and they may not be used to circumvent or evade any disclosure requirements of the CLA or Reg. M.

8. What happens if my disclosures become inaccurate after I give them?

The CLA and Reg. M disclosures are essentially a snapshot in time. The disclosures have to be accurate as of the time they are given. If an event occurs after the lessor delivers the required disclosures (we lawyers call this a "subsequent occurrence") causing the disclosures to become inaccurate, the inaccurate disclosures don't violate the CLA or Reg. M.

9. What happens if I give the buyer his or her CLA and Reg. M disclosures and then must re-contract at a later date?

You should re-contract the transaction as of the date of re-contracting, recalculating all deal terms and disclosures as if the re-contracting were a completely new transaction. This isn't a "subsequent occurrence," but rather the creation of a new lease transaction that requires new disclosures.

10. Do the CLA and Reg. M apply to all of my leases?

No. Actually, many transactions aren't covered by the CLA and Reg. M. The CLA and Reg. M do not apply when you lease a car to a business entity, such as a corporation, partnership, or association. That's the rule even when the car will be used primarily for personal, family, or household purposes. The CLA and Reg. M do not apply when you lease a car to an individual and the car is to be used primarily for purposes that are not personal, family, or household in nature. "Primarily" means at least 51% of the time, and you may rely upon the lessee's representations about the intended use of the car. Most lease forms contain a box for the dealer to check indicating the purpose for which the vehicle is being leased. Checking the box is important—if the lessee later claims a CLA violation and the lease is not primarily for personal, family, or household purposes, the checked box can be an important defense for the dealer.

The CLA and Reg. M don't apply when the "total contractual obligation" exceeds $53,000*. Note that the total contractual obligation is not the same thing as the price of the car, nor is it the same thing as the total of payments under the lease. The total contractual obligation includes non-refundable amounts a lessee is contractually obligated to pay the lessor, but excludes residual value amounts or purchase option prices as well as amounts such as taxes, license, and registration fees collected by the lessor but paid to third parties.

Finally, the CLA and Reg. M do not apply to leases for a term of four months or less.

---

*The Dodd-Frank Act increased this threshold amount from $25,000, effective July 21, 2011, and provides that the threshold will be increased annually based on the rate of inflation.

11. How do I handle non-CLA transactions? Do I use the same documents I use for CLA transactions?

You can. The prevailing practice among dealers who don't do a majority of their leases to businesses is to document non-CLA transactions on the same forms used to document transactions that are subject to the CLA. There is little danger in this—simply providing CLA and Reg. M disclosures in a transaction to which they do not apply will not make the transaction subject to the CLA.

12. Do the CLA and Reg. M permit a consumer to rescind a vehicle lease transaction?

No. There is no right under the CLA and Reg. M to rescind a lease transaction.

13. What must I do to make sure my advertisements comply with the CLA and Reg. M?

Your leasing advertisement may state that a specific lease of a vehicle at specific amounts or terms is available only if you usually and customarily lease, or will lease, the vehicle at those terms or amounts. It's OK to advertise terms that will be offered for only a limited period of time, or terms that will become available only at a future date, but you may not advertise terms that are not, and will not be, available.

Advertising disclosures have to be made clearly and conspicuously. If you provide a percentage rate in a lease advertisement, that rate cannot be more prominent than any of the other required lease disclosures, with the exception of the notice referred to earlier in this chapter that is required to accompany the rate. The terms "annual percentage rate" and "annual lease rate" may not be used.

After that, things get a little tricky. In regulating advertising, the CLA and Reg. M use the concept of "triggering terms." If certain specified terms appear in your advertisements, they "trigger" further disclosure requirements. The "triggering terms" are the amount of any payment or a statement of any capitalized cost reduction (or that none is due) prior to or at consummation or delivery (if delivery is later). If one of these "triggering terms" is used, your ad must then contain the following:

- A statement that the transaction is a lease;

- The total amount due prior to or at consummation or delivery, if delivery is later;

- The number, amounts, and due dates or periods of scheduled payments under the lease;

- A statement of whether a security deposit is required; and

- A statement that an extra charge may be imposed at the end of the lease term where the lessee's liability (if any) is based on the difference between the vehicle's residual value and its realized value.

When you offer a range of leased vehicles, it's OK to use examples of typical transactions, as long as the examples contain all the applicable required terms. Examples must be labeled as examples.

Special rules apply to catalogs or multiple-page advertisements. If such an advertisement gives information in a table or schedule in sufficient detail to permit the reader to determine the required disclosures, it will be considered as a single advertisement. The table or schedule has to show all appropriate disclosures for a representative scale of amounts up to the level of the more commonly leased and higher-priced cars offered. If a triggering term appears elsewhere in the catalog, it must clearly direct the consumer to the page or location where the table, chart, or schedule begins.

If you do electronic advertising (for example, on a web page), essentially the same rules apply, but with some minor differences to accommodate the realities of the Internet. For example, if you use any of the "triggering terms" described previously, you would need to link the triggering term to the additional information Reg. M requires to be disclosed with such triggering term.

14. What is an "advertisement" anyway?

The FRB says that it is "a commercial message in any medium that promotes, directly or indirectly, a consumer lease transaction." It provides the following examples:

- Messages in a newspaper, magazine, leaflet, flyer, or catalog

- Radio, TV, or public address system announcements

- Internet messages

- Direct mail

- Exterior and interior signs

- Point-of-lease displays

- Telephone solicitations

- Skywriting (We're kidding—the FRB didn't really say that, although it would be correct if they had. We just wanted to make sure you were still awake.)

- Price tags with lease information

What isn't an advertisement? Direct personal contacts, follow-up letters to customers, oral or written communications relating to the negotiation of a specific transaction, and a few other things. Unless you're certain, treat it as an advertisement until your lawyer says you don't need to.

15. What happens if I violate the advertising rules of the CLA and Reg. M?

For violations of the advertising rules under the CLA and Reg. M, wrongdoers are liable to the consumer for:

- Actual damages;

- 25% of the total amount of monthly payments under the lease (but not less than $200* nor greater than $2,000*) in an individual action, or the lesser of $1,000,000**, or 1% of the lessor's net worth in a class action; plus

- Attorney's fees and court costs.

In the case of a class action, courts are instructed to consider, among other factors, the amount of any actual damages awarded, the frequency and persistence of the failure to comply (which could be quite frequent in the case of advertising to the general public or in a large scale mail campaign), the number of people adversely affected by the violation (once again, might be quite high), and the extent to which failure to comply is intentional.

---

*The Dodd-Frank Act increased these amounts from $100 and $1,000, respectively, effective July 21, 2011.

**The Dodd-Frank Act increased this amount from $500,000, effective July 21, 2011.

As a practical matter, it is difficult for a plaintiff to show actual damages in a case alleging violation of the advertising rules under the CLA and Reg. M. The plaintiff must show that it relied on the advertisement and that, but for the violation of the advertising rules, he would not have entered into the lease. That's a very steep hill to climb. In practice, plaintiffs typically recover only statutory damages, as detailed previously.

That isn't all. As with TILA and Reg. Z (discussed in Chapter 2), the Federal Trade Commission enforces the CLA and Reg. M requirements with respect to car dealers. Initial violations are subject to the FTC's "cease and desist" (C&D) actions. Subsequent violations of that C&D order can expose a dealer to fines of up to $16,000 per day, per violation. Also, as we mentioned in regard to TILA and Reg. Z, plaintiffs' lawyers have argued, sometimes successfully, that a violation of a *federal law or regulation* also is an unfair or deceptive act or practice under *state* law. We address these state laws in a later chapter, but they tend to come with very stiff penalties.

16. What language must be used for disclosures?

Disclosures required by the CLA and Reg. M may be made in a language other than English, provided that the disclosures are made available in English upon the consumer's request.

17. What are the CLA and Reg. M recordkeeping requirements?

You must maintain evidence of compliance with the CLA and Reg. M for two years after the date disclosures are required to be made or action is required to be taken. The records may be maintained in paper form, on microfilm, microfiche, electronically on computer, or in any other way designed to reproduce the records accurately. You must retain only enough information to reconstruct the required disclosures or other records. You do not need to keep records of advertising compliance.

18. What if my state's laws are inconsistent with the CLA and Reg. M?

It does happen. And, when it does, state law requirements that are inconsistent with CLA and Reg. M are preempted by federal law to the extent of the inconsistency. If a lessor cannot comply with a state law without violating the CLA or Reg. M, the state law is inconsistent and is preempted unless it gives greater protection and benefit to the consumer. Simple, huh?

19. Are some states exempt from the CLA and Reg. M?

Yes, a few, but only partly exempt. Odds are your state isn't one of them. The CLA authorizes the Federal Reserve Board to certify that a state's consumer leasing regulations give greater protection and benefit to the consumer, and to give a non-preemption determination as to such state's law. In effect, the FRB says that the state's law will still apply. The FRB, in turn, has granted partial exemptions from portions of the CLA to Oklahoma and Maine. If you're in those states, you'll need to ask your lawyer for a bit more guidance.

20. What is the penalty for violating the CLA and Reg. M?

There are criminal and civil penalties for violating the CLA and Reg. M.

If you "willfully and knowingly" give false information or inaccurate information, or fail to provide information that the CLA or Reg. M require you to give, or if you otherwise don't comply with the CLA or Reg. M requirements, you face a criminal penalty of not more than $5,000 or a year in jail, or both. Ouch!

Criminal actions alleging violations of the CLA and Reg. M are rare. It's the civil action liability, particularly the class action potential, which makes CLA and Reg. M lawsuits so dangerous.

If you violate the CLA or Reg. M and you are sued in an individual (as opposed to a class) action, your potential liability consists of the following:

- The plaintiff's actual damages;

- "Statutory damages" of 25% of the total amount of monthly payments under the lease (but not less than $200* nor greater than $2,000*); and

- The plaintiff's reasonable attorney's fees and court costs.

In a class action, the formula changes a bit. You would be looking at the following potential liability:

- The plaintiff's actual damages;

- "Statutory damages" of "such amount as the court may allow," except that in class actions, there is no minimum recovery and the creditor's maximum liability is capped at the lesser of $1,000,000**, or 1% of the creditor's net worth for any class action or series of class actions arising out of the same failure to comply by the same creditor; and

- The plaintiff's reasonable attorney's fees and court costs.

*The Dodd-Frank Act increased these amounts from $100 and $1,000, respectively, effective July 21, 2011.

**The Dodd-Frank Act increased this amount from $500,000, effective July 21, 2011.

As a practical matter, it is often difficult for a plaintiff to show actual damages in a case alleging CLA and Reg. M violations, so liability is often limited to statutory damages.

21. Are there any defenses to a civil claim for a violation of the CLA or Reg. M?

Yes. There's something called the "bona fide error" defense. A lessor claiming this defense must show by a preponderance of the evidence that the violation was not intentional and resulted from a bona fide error even though the creditor maintained procedures reasonably adapted to avoid such an error. Bona fide errors include clerical and calculation errors, computer malfunctions, programming problems, and printing errors.

There's also a "safe harbor" for a creditor charged with violating the CLA or Reg. M if the lessor relied in good faith on "any interpretation or approval by an official or employee of the Federal Reserve System authorized by the FRB to issue such interpretations or approvals under such procedures as the FRB prescribes." The safe harbor applies even if a court or some other authority later determines that the FRB's interpretation or approval was invalid.

22. If I violate the CLA or Reg. M, is there a way I can remedy the violation and avoid civil liability?

Yes. If, within 60 days of discovering an error and before you are sued for the error, you notify your customer of the error and make those adjustments to the customer's account necessary to assure that the customer will not be required to pay an amount in excess of the charge actually disclosed, you can avoid civil liability.

23. What is the statute of limitations for a CLA and Reg. M violation—how much time must pass after the violation before a consumer is barred from bringing a suit against me?

A consumer has to sue you within one year from the date of the occurrence of the violation (usually the date that you gave the consumer the disclosures). This rule doesn't apply, though, to a claim brought by way of defense, recoupment, or set-off in a collection action, except as otherwise provided by state law.

Chapter 4

The Equal Credit Opportunity Act & Regulation B

By Lisa C. DeLessio and
Anne P. Fortney

Twenty-Three Things a Dealer Should Know
About the ECOA

When a customer walks onto a lot and wants to buy a car, the dealer's job is to help him or her make the right choice and to close the deal. Sometimes, in order to make the sale, the dealer needs to help the shopper with *financing*. When a dealer is actively involved in helping a customer find financing, or the dealer finances the sale, the dealer is also a "creditor," *whether he knows it or not.* All creditors are required to comply with the federal Equal Credit Opportunity Act, or ECOA, and Regulation B, which includes the rules for complying with ECOA.

1. So the ECOA is a federal law? What does it do?

The federal ECOA prohibits discrimination in every aspect of a credit transaction, including car financing. Under the ECOA, creditors may not treat one person less favorably than another because of color, religion, national origin, sex, marital status, or age; because the person receives some type of public assistance; or because a person has asserted rights under a consumer credit protection statute. Incidentally, many states also have equal credit opportunity laws, and in certain states, the list of prohibited reasons is longer.

The ECOA also requires certain notifications. Creditors must tell every applicant whether they (the creditors) approve the application, reject the application, or would approve the application on different terms. When creditors decline to extend credit, they need to send a written notice, called an "Adverse Action Notice."

Dealers who think they aren't creditors because they don't lend money are probably wrong. In fact, in most cases, dealers really are creditors, because they are involved in some way in figuring out what the shopper will pay and when it will be paid. If the dealer is involved at all in making the credit decisions— like setting the downpayment or refusing to do a deal if the dealer can't get a good buy rate—then the dealer is a "participating creditor" and needs to give an Adverse Action Notice. Even if a dealer only refers shoppers to direct lenders (and this is rare), the ECOA's rules against illegal discrimination still apply.

The Federal Reserve Board and the Consumer Financial Protection Bureau share responsibility for Regulation B, which implements the federal ECOA. The ECOA can be found at www.dealerdeskbook.com/resources/ecoa/. Reg. B is at www.dealerdeskbook.com/resources/ecoaregb/.

2. What does Regulation B require?

Regulation B, or "Reg. B," contains the rules implementing the ECOA. Reg. B applies to all creditors. Besides prohibiting discrimination, Reg. B tells creditors what information they can collect in the application, how they can use information collected in the application process, and it dictates how the notification process should work (what notices to send, when to send them, and so on) when creditors take action (or cannot yet take action) on requests for credit. Reg. B also tells creditors what records they need to keep.

3. What is the purpose of Reg. B?

Reg. B is designed to make sure that (i) creditworthy applicants are treated fairly in every aspect of a credit transaction; and (ii) when someone applies for a loan or financing, the credit decision is not influenced by race, color, religion, national origin, sex, marital status, or age (as long as the person is old enough to contract); or the fact that the person receives some type of public assistance or benefits; or the fact that the person has, in good faith, exercised any right under the Consumer Credit Protection Act (which includes TILA, the CLA, and the FCRA, all discussed in this book). Reg. B also requires creditors to tell applicants what action will be taken on their credit requests, including

- extending the credit as requested;

- declining to offer the credit; or

- extending credit if the applicant will agree to different or additional terms.

Creditors' letter packages can include forms advising applicants of action taken on their credit requests. However, when the creditor's action is to deny credit, the notice of this "Adverse Action" must be in writing.

4. What are the important terms to know under Reg. B?

Reg. B defines certain key words that all creditors need to know.

Who is a "creditor"?

A "creditor" is a person who, in the ordinary course of business, regularly participates in a credit decision, including setting the terms of the credit. Dealers who "regularly participate in a credit decision" are "creditors," even if the dealer forwards the shopper's application to a bank or finance company. For example, dealers may be setting the terms of the credit when they

- determine the APR (based on a buy rate);

- set the payment term (such as 48 or 60 months); or

- set other terms (such as the downpayment and amount financed).

The term "creditor" also includes a person who, in the ordinary course of business, regularly refers shoppers to creditors or selects or offers to select creditors to whom requests for credit may be made. Remember the note above—even if a dealer merely refers shoppers to direct lenders (and this is rare), the ECOA's rules against illegal discrimination still apply.

What does "adverse action" mean?

The term "adverse action" means refusing to grant credit in substantially the amount or on substantially the terms requested in an application. "Adverse action" includes a counteroffer to grant credit in a different amount or on other terms, unless (and only unless) the person uses, or expressly accepts, the counteroffer. If the person doesn't use or expressly accept the counteroffer, then there is adverse action.

Does the term "application" have a special meaning? What about a "completed application"?

An application can be an oral or written request for credit that is made according to the procedures used by the creditor for the type of credit requested. In some cases, Reg. B distinguishes between an application and a "completed application." An application might be "complete" under Reg. B even if some information is missing. A "completed application" is one in which the creditor has all the information needed to evaluate applications for the amount and type of credit requested.

What is a "prohibited basis" under Reg. B?

Under Reg. B, any of the following is a "prohibited basis" (for denying credit or offering credit on less favorable terms):

- Race

- Color

- Religion

- National origin

- Sex

- Marital status

- Age (as long as the applicant is old enough to contract)

- The fact that the applicant receives public assistance

- The fact that the applicant has, in good faith, exercised any right under the Consumer Credit Protection Act

5. Reg. B prohibits creditors from taking a consumer's national origin into account in weighing creditworthiness. However, other factors related to an individual's national origin might be taken into account in deciding whether to extend credit. What are they?

Although creditors may not discriminate on the basis of national origin, creditors may ask about and consider the permanent residency and immigration status of an applicant. For example, an applicant's immigration status and ties to the community (like employment and continued residency in the area) could bear on a creditor's ability to obtain repayment. Therefore, creditors may consider immigration status, and they can differentiate between a non-citizen who is a longtime resident with permanent resident status and a non-citizen who is temporarily in this country on a student visa. A creditor must be careful not to arbitrarily deny credit to some aliens, and not others, merely on the grounds that the ones denied are not citizens.

In addition, a creditor may also consider any applicable law, regulation, or executive order if such law, regulation, or order restricts dealings with citizens (or the government) of a particular country or imposes limitations regarding credit extended for the use of those citizens. For example, at the time of this writing, certain federal regulations prohibit U.S. citizens from entering into transactions with citizens of Cuba or North Korea.

6. What are the rules regarding discriminating against or discouraging a credit applicant?

A creditor cannot discriminate in any way in the application process, which includes advertising, application procedures, criteria used to evaluate creditworthiness, administration of accounts, and treatment of delinquent or slow accounts. Any practice that treats applicants differently on a prohibited basis violates the law, even if unintentional. For example, it is illegal for a creditor to provide information only about sub-prime auto finance programs to minority applicants but to provide information on a wider variety of auto finance programs to similarly situated, non-minority applicants. It is also illegal for a creditor to require a minority applicant to provide greater documentation to obtain credit than a similarly situated, non-minority applicant.

A creditor may not make any oral or written statement, in advertising or otherwise, to applicants or prospective applicants that would discourage them from applying. For example, a creditor may not tell an applicant not to bother applying after the applicant states that he or she is retired. A creditor may not use words, symbols, models, or other forms of communication in advertising that express, imply, or suggest a discriminatory preference or a policy of exclusion that would violate the ECOA. A creditor may not use an interview script that would discourage applications on a prohibited basis.

7. If a creditor predominantly trades with consumers who speak a language other than English and provides disclosures in that language, is the creditor required also to provide disclosures in English?

Yes. Disclosures can be made in languages other than English, but the disclosure must be available in English if someone asks for it.

8. What are the rules regarding the information that a creditor can request in connection with a credit transaction?

A creditor may ask for any information needed to make a decision subject, of course, to a list of exclusions in Reg. B (some of which are discussed in Questions 9–12). A creditor may always collect information required by a state statute, regulation, or ordinance without violating the ECOA.

9. What are the rules about whether, and to what extent, a creditor may request information about an applicant's race, color, religion, national origin, or sex?

Generally, a creditor may not ask an applicant (or anyone else) about the race, color, religion, national origin, or sex of an applicant or any other person.

However, a creditor may ask an applicant to list any account on which the applicant is contractually obligated and to provide the name and address of the person in whose name the account is held, even if the creditor may learn from the answer that there is a spouse. A creditor may ask an applicant to list all other names the applicant previously has used to receive credit. A creditor may include an item on the application requesting the applicant to designate a title (such as Ms., Miss, Mr., Mrs.), but only if the application clearly informs the applicant that disclosing the title is optional. An application form must otherwise use only terms that are neutral as to sex.

The Dodd-Frank Act (Title X, Subtitle G (Regulatory Improvement), Sec. 1071) amends the ECOA by adding a new section (§ 704B) that will require financial institutions to collect certain data about women-owned, minority-owned, and small businesses, including the race, sex, and ethnicity of the principal owners of the business. The purpose of the new data collection provision is to facilitate enforcement of fair lending laws and enable communities, governmental entities, and creditors to identify business and community development needs and opportunities of women-owned, minority-owned, and small businesses.

No dealer should collect this data until the Consumer Financial Protection Bureau and the Federal Reserve Board write rules implementing the data collection requirements.

10. What are the rules about whether, and to what extent, a creditor can request information about an applicant's spouse or former spouse?

As a general rule, a creditor cannot ask for information about a spouse or former spouse.

There are some permissible questions that a creditor can ask that might inadvertently disclose the fact that the applicant has a spouse. For example, the creditor can ask:

- If the spouse will have permission to use the account being applied for
- If the spouse will be contractually liable on the account
- If the applicant is relying on the spouse's income to repay the credit requested
- If the applicant resides in a community property state or is relying on property located in a community property state as the basis to repay the credit
- If the applicant is relying on alimony, child support, or separate maintenance payments from a spouse or former spouse as a basis for repayment of the credit requested (but there are special rules on this one)

11. What are the rules about whether, and to what extent, a creditor may request information about an applicant's marital status; income from child support, alimony, or other maintenance; and childbearing or childrearing status?

Marital Status

The rule varies depending upon the type of credit requested. If a person applies for unsecured credit, a creditor may not ask about marital status unless the applicant lives in a community property state or is relying on property located in a community property state to repay the creditor.

If a person applies for credit that will be secured, for example, by a vehicle, then the creditor may ask about the applicant's marital status, but may only use the terms *"married," "unmarried,"* and *"separated."* The creditor may explain that the category "unmarried" includes single, divorced, and widowed persons.

Income from Child Support, Alimony, or Other Maintenance Payments

This one is a little tricky. A creditor may ask whether a person receives income from alimony, child support, or separate maintenance payments, but the applicant does not need to answer the question unless the applicant wants the creditor to consider that income in determining creditworthiness. Thus, before asking whether a person receives income from alimony, child support, or separate maintenance payments, the creditor always needs to tell the applicant very clearly that the applicant *doesn't need to share that income information unless the applicant wants the creditor to consider it in determining creditworthiness.*

Childbearing or Childrearing Status

A creditor cannot ask about birth control practices or whether an applicant is going to have children. But a creditor can ask about the number and ages of an applicant's children or about dependent-related financial obligations or expenditures if the information is requested without regard to sex, marital status, or any other prohibited basis.

12. Is it permissible for a creditor to request information about an applicant's residency or immigration status?

Yes. A creditor can ask about permanent residency and immigration status. An applicant's immigration status and ties to the community (like employment and continued residency in the area) could bear on a creditor's ability to obtain repayment. Therefore, the creditor can consider immigration status and differentiate between a non-citizen who is a longtime resident with permanent resident status and a non-citizen who is temporarily in this country on a student visa. A creditor must be careful not to arbitrarily deny credit to some aliens, and not others, merely on the grounds that the ones denied are not citizens.

13. What is the general rule regarding what is permissible in evaluating credit applications?

A creditor may consider any information it needs to make its decision, so long as the information is not used to discriminate against an applicant on a prohibited basis.

14. How, and to what extent, may a creditor take the following information about an applicant into account when evaluating a credit application?

Age

If an applicant is old enough to enter into a contract, a creditor may not discriminate on the basis of age. In some cases, age may be considered as a factor, but it can't be a negative factor. In other cases, a creditor may treat some applicants—like those who are 62 years or older—more favorably than others. But a creditor should be very careful when using age as a factor at all in its decision, and age can never be a negative factor.

A creditor may not refuse to extend credit and may not terminate an account because credit life, health, accident, disability, or other credit-related insurance is not available on the basis of the applicant's age.

Receipt of Public Assistance

A creditor may consider whether an applicant's income is from a public assistance program, but only for the purpose of determining a pertinent element of creditworthiness, such as likelihood of continuation of that source of income, just as the creditor would scrutinize any other source of income for the probability that it will continue.

Childbearing or Childrearing

In evaluating creditworthiness, a creditor may not make assumptions, or use aggregate statistics, relating to the likelihood that certain categories of persons will have children or will, for that reason, receive less or interrupted income in the future.

Telephone Listing

A creditor may not take into account whether there is a telephone listing in the name of an applicant but may take into account whether there is a telephone in the applicant's residence.

Income

A creditor may not discount or exclude from consideration the income of an applicant or spouse because of a prohibited basis or because the income comes from part-time employment or an annuity, pension, or other retirement benefit. However, a creditor may consider the amount and probable continuance of any income. When an applicant relies on alimony, child support, or separate maintenance payments in applying for credit, the creditor may consider the payments as income to the extent that they are likely to be consistently made.

Credit History

When a creditor uses credit history to evaluate creditworthiness, a creditor must consider all of the following:

- The credit history of accounts that the applicant and spouse are permitted to use or for which both are contractually liable

- On the applicant's request, any information the applicant provides to explain that the credit history does not accurately reflect the applicant's creditworthiness

- On the applicant's request, the credit history of any account reported in the name of the applicant's spouse or former spouse that the applicant can demonstrate accurately reflects the applicant's creditworthiness

Immigration Status

A creditor may consider the applicant's immigration status or status as a permanent resident of the United States and any additional information that might be necessary to determine the creditor's rights and remedies regarding repayment.

Marital Status

A creditor is required to evaluate married and unmarried applicants by the same standards. If the creditor receives a joint application, the creditor cannot treat the applicants differently based on the existence, absence, or likelihood of a marital relationship between the parties.

Race, Color, Religion, National Origin, or Sex

A creditor may not consider race, color, religion, national origin, or sex (or an applicant's or other person's decision not to provide the information) in any aspect of a credit transaction.

State Property Laws

A creditor may consider state property laws directly or indirectly to the extent that they affect creditworthiness or complexity in recovering collateral upon default.

15. In extending credit secured by a vehicle, what are the rules regarding the signature of a spouse or other person?

Qualified Applicants

A creditor may not require the signature of an applicant's spouse or other person, other than a joint applicant, on any credit instrument if the applicant qualifies for the amount and terms of the credit requested. Unless it is clear that an application is "joint," a creditor can't just assume that fact, even if the applicant submits information that includes details about a spouse or other person.

Secured Credit

If an applicant asks for secured credit, a creditor can require the spouse or other person to sign an instrument so that the secured property will be available to satisfy the debt in the event of default. *The instrument cannot be the retail installment sale contract or a similar instrument that would obligate the spouse or other person to repay the debt.*

Additional Parties

A creditor can request a cosigner, guarantor, endorser, or similar party if the applicant does not qualify separately, but the creditor cannot require that the spouse be the additional party. A creditor cannot impose requirements upon an additional party that the creditor is prohibited from imposing upon an applicant.

16. What are the timing requirements for notifying applicants of action taken?

Within 30 days after receiving a "completed application," the creditor must tell the applicant whether the creditor will extend the credit as requested, make a counteroffer, or deny the request for credit.

If the creditor makes a counteroffer within the 30 days, and the applicant actually tells the creditor that the applicant will use it, or the applicant does, in fact, use it, then the creditor doesn't need to send any written notice. However, if the applicant refuses the counteroffer or doesn't use it, then the creditor needs to send a written Adverse Action Notice within 90 days of making the counteroffer. These two notices (of a counteroffer and of adverse action) can be combined, if the combined notice includes all of the information required. In that case, the reasons for declining the credit request should be expressed in terms that leave open the possibility that the counteroffer would be accepted.

If the creditor declines credit, then the creditor must send a written Adverse Action Notice within 30 days after receiving the application.

There are special rules about what needs to be included in Adverse Action Notices.

17. What information needs to be included in an Adverse Action Notice?

An Adverse Action Notice, given by whoever is required to give one, needs to include the following:

- A statement that adverse action has been taken (although the creditor is not required to use the term "adverse action").

- The name and address of the creditor.

- An ECOA anti-discrimination notice, with substantially the following language: The federal Equal Credit Opportunity Act prohibits creditors from discriminating against credit applicants on the basis of race, color, religion, national origin, sex, marital status, or age (provided the applicant has the capacity to enter into a binding contract); or because all or part of the applicant's income derives from any public assistance program; or because the applicant has in good faith exercised any right under the Consumer Credit Protection Act. The federal agency that administers compliance with this law concerning this creditor is the Federal Trade Commission [include regional address or Equal Credit Opportunity, Washington, DC 20580].

- A statement of the specific reasons for the action taken or a disclosure of the applicant's right to a specific statement within 30 days, if the statement is requested within 60 days of your Adverse Action Notice. This disclosure must also include the name, address, and telephone number of the person or office where the applicant can obtain the statement of reasons. If you, as the creditor, choose to provide the reasons orally, you must also tell the applicant that he or she has the right to have the reasons confirmed in writing within 30 days after you receive a written request for confirmation from the applicant.

There are model disclosures in Reg. B that you can use to help create your own notices that contain all the required information. Please note that there are additional notice requirements under the Fair Credit Reporting Act when adverse action is based on information in a credit report or information bearing on credit obtained from a third party. The Dodd-Frank Act also amended the FCRA to require disclosure of credit scores in Adverse Action Notices. A creditor sending an Adverse Action Notice must then comply with both the ECOA and the FCRA. See Chapter 5 for more details.

18. Do notification rules ever vary? For example, what are the notification rules regarding the following?

Incomplete Applications

If the credit application is incomplete, you have a choice of sending a written "Notice of Incompleteness" or an Adverse Action Notice denying the application within 30 days of receiving the application.

If you opt to send a "Notice of Incompleteness," the notice must include (i) the additional information needed, (ii) the time within which the applicant must supply the additional information (this must be a reasonable time), and (iii) a statement telling the applicant that the application will not be further considered unless the applicant provides the requested information within that time. If the applicant does not respond to the notice of incompleteness, then you are not required to send an Adverse Action Notice.

Withdrawal of Approved Application

Sometimes an applicant submits an application, and the parties contemplate that the applicant will inquire about its status. If the creditor approves the application and the applicant has not inquired within 30 days after applying, the creditor may treat the application as withdrawn and does not need to send any further notice. Be sure, however, that the requirement for the applicant to ask about the application's status is clear to all parties concerned. If unsure, send a written notice approving the application.

Multiple Applicants

When an application involves more than one applicant, you, as the creditor, need to give notice only to the primary applicant. Please note that this notice requirement differs from that under the Fair Credit Reporting Act (FCRA), described in this chapter at Question 17. Adverse Action Notices required under the FCRA must be sent to all applicants, not only the primary applicant. If you're not sure that you can manage this difference in Notice Requirements (as required by Reg. B versus FCRA), consider sending all Adverse Action Notices to the co-applicant's address, too, when the addresses for applicant and co-applicant are different.

Applications Submitted Through a Third Party

When an application is made on behalf of an applicant to multiple creditors, and the applicant expressly accepts or uses credit offered by any one of them, then the other creditors do not need to send an Adverse Action Notice. If no credit is offered by any of them, or if the applicant does not expressly accept or use the credit offered, each creditor taking adverse action must send an Adverse Action Notice, directly or through a third party, to the applicant. A notice given by a third party must disclose the identity of each creditor on whose behalf the notice is given.

19. What rules apply when state law differs from the requirements of Reg. B?

Reg. B alters, affects, or preempts only those state laws that are inconsistent with the ECOA and Reg. B—and only to the extent of the inconsistency. A state law is not inconsistent with Reg. B, and will be enforced, if it offers more protection to an applicant than Reg. B. A state law is inconsistent with Reg. B if it is less protective of the applicant, permits a practice prohibited by the ECOA or Reg. B, or prohibits a practice permitted or required by the ECOA or Reg. B.

The ECOA and Reg. B do not alter or annul any provision of state property laws, any laws relating to the disposition of decedents' estates, or any federal or state banking regulations directed only toward ensuring the solvency of financial institutions.

20. What are the rules regarding the retention of information and preservation of records in the collection and evaluation of credit?

The general rule is that a creditor must keep certain records for at least 25 months. (There are different rules that apply to records concerning business credit.) The following documents must be preserved for 25 months after notifying the applicant about the action taken on an application:

- The application itself

- Any written record of information used in evaluating the application that is not returned to the applicant (including a credit report obtained to evaluate the application)

- Any documents that show notice given to the applicant, including notes or computer records showing that oral notice was given

- The statement of specific reasons for adverse action

- Any written statement submitted by the applicant alleging a violation of ECOA

If you have actual notice that you are under investigation, or subject to an enforcement proceeding for an alleged violation of the ECOA or Reg. B, then you must retain the records listed above until the matter is finally resolved; that is, unless the agency or court enters an order stating that you may dispose of the records at an earlier time.

If an applicant withdraws an application, never uses the credit offered, or if the application is submitted to multiple creditors and one offers credit, the creditor still needs to keep the application and related information for 25 months from the date of the application, even though the creditor was not required to send an Adverse Action Notice.

While in most situations general rules apply, in special circumstances they may vary. These are detailed as follows.

Records Concerning Business Credit

If the business credit applicant is a small business (less than $1 million in gross revenues), the creditor must keep records related to the credit application for one year after telling the business of the credit decision. If the business grosses more than $1 million, the creditor must keep the records on file for only 60 days after denying credit. However, if the business asks the creditor to keep the records for a longer time, or if the business requests a written statement of the reasons for denial, the creditor must keep the records for one year. If the business does not ask about the reasons for denial within 60 days, the creditor is not required to keep the records.

In addition, the Dodd-Frank Act requires that data collected about women-owned, minority-owned, and small businesses (as discussed above in Question 9) must be retained for at least three years after the date of preparation.

Records of "Self-Testing"

If a creditor completes a "Self-Test" (described in Question 21), the creditor must retain all written or recorded information about the self-test for 25 months. A creditor must retain information beyond 25 months if it has actual notice that it is under investigation, if it is subject to an enforcement proceeding for an alleged violation, or if it has been served with notice of a civil action. In such cases, the creditor must retain the information until final disposition of the matter, unless an earlier time is allowed by the appropriate agency or court order.

Records of "Prescreening"

A creditor who sends out a prescreened solicitation (typically done through direct mail marketing, and also known as "firm offers of credit") must keep, for 25 months after the date on which an offer of credit is made to potential customers (12 months for business credit), the original or copy of (i) the text of any prescreened solicitation, (ii) the list of criteria the creditor used to select potential recipients of the solicitation, and (iii) any correspondence related to complaints (formal or informal) about the solicitation.

21. What is the purpose of a "self-test" as defined in Reg. B?

A self-test is any program, practice, or study that meets two standards:

- It is designed and used specifically to determine the extent or effectiveness of a creditor's compliance with the ECOA and Reg. B.

- It creates data or factual information that is not available and cannot be derived from loan or application files or other records related to credit transactions.

Certain information obtained in connection with a self-test may be privileged. However, loan and application files or other business records related to credit transactions, and information derived from such files and records, are not privileged even if the information has been aggregated, summarized, or reorganized to facilitate analysis in the self-test.

22. What are the rules for complying with Reg. B when business is conducted via electronic communication?

A creditor may electronically provide any disclosure required by Reg. B to be in writing, in accordance with the provisions of "ESIGN," which is the Electronic Signatures in Global and National Commerce Act (see www. dealerdeskbook.com/resources/esign/). Disclosures provided electronically must be provided in a clear and conspicuous manner and in a form the applicant may retain.

When disclosures are required to be in writing, a creditor usually obtains an applicant's affirmative consent to receive electronic disclosures in accordance with ESIGN, unless the applicant accesses the application electronically, in which case certain disclosures can be given without the consumer's consent.

If the applicant accesses the application electronically, such as online at a home computer, certain disclosures that accompany the application may be given in electronic form on or with the application form, without regard to the consumer consent or other provisions of ESIGN. These include (i) self-testing disclosures, (ii) the disclosure that titles, such as Ms., Miss, Mr., or Mrs., are optional, (iii) an explanation that the use of "unmarried" includes single, divorced, and widowed persons when there is an application for joint credit or in a community property state, and (iv) the disclosure that income from alimony and child support need not be revealed.

If, however, an applicant is physically present in the creditor's office and accesses a credit application electronically (such as through a terminal or kiosk of the creditor located at the office of an affiliate or a third party that has arranged with the creditor to provide applications to consumers), the creditor may provide the disclosures in either electronic or paper form, as long as the creditor complies with the timing, delivery, and retainability requirements.

For guidance on complying with ESIGN procedures for consent, technology, and delivery requirements, consult www.dealerdeskbook.com/resources/esignhelp/.

23. What are the penalties and liabilities for non-compliance with Reg. B?

Any creditor failing to comply with a requirement imposed by the ECOA or Reg. B is subject to civil liability for actual and punitive damages in individual or class actions.

Liability for punitive damages can apply only to non-governmental entities and is limited to $10,000 in individual actions and to $500,000, or one percent of the creditor's net worth in class actions, whichever amount is less. A successful applicant may recover costs and reasonable attorney's fees.

The Dodd-Frank Act extended the statute of limitations for violations of the ECOA. Section 1085(7) amends ECOA § 706(f) to extend the statute of limitations for civil liability from two years to five years.

Chapter 5

The Fair Credit Reporting Act

By Michael A. Benoit and
A. James Chareq

Sixteen Things a Car Dealer Needs to Know About the Fair Credit Reporting Act

The federal Fair Credit Reporting Act (FCRA) is one of the country's primary consumer protection/privacy laws. It has protected the accuracy and privacy of information in the files of the nation's consumer-reporting agencies for the past 40 years. In that time, it has been amended several times to add additional consumer protections and to impose new compliance obligations upon users of consumer reports, such as car dealers. The most recent revision—one that nearly *doubled* its length— occurred in 2003 with the passage of the Fair and Accurate Credit Transactions Act (FACTA). An understanding of the FCRA—as amended by FACTA—is crucial for car dealers who want to avoid penalties of as much as $3,500 per violation.

We believe there are 16 key aspects of the FCRA that you should know. If you'd like to take a walk through the FCRA for yourself, go to www.dealerdeskbook.com/resources/fcra/.

1. What is the purpose of the Fair Credit Reporting Act?

The FCRA's stated purpose is to require that consumer-reporting agencies adopt reasonable procedures for meeting the needs of commerce for consumer credit, personnel, insurance, and other information in a manner that is fair and equitable to the consumer with regard to the confidentiality, accuracy, relevancy, and proper use of the information. Some of these protections include requiring the consumer-reporting agencies to have a permissible purpose to furnish a consumer report to a user and requiring users to certify their permissible purposes to the consumer-reporting agencies from which they obtain consumer reports. Other protections include requirements for proper disposal of consumer information, limitations on using consumer reports for marketing purposes, truncation of credit card numbers and expiration dates on electronically printed credit card receipts, and new rules guidelines to help prevent identity theft or mitigate its effects once it occurs.

The FCRA affects creditors, consumers, and consumer-reporting agencies in many different ways. For purposes of this chapter, we will only discuss certain aspects of the FCRA that are relevant to the credit transactions car dealers engage in on a daily basis.

2. What are some of the important defined terms in the FCRA?

The FCRA provides special definitions for some of the words it uses. Of course, it would be nice if words meant what you thought they did, but the FCRA is a product of the federal government, so it's a good thing there are lawyers like us around to tell you what the words really mean!

Adverse Action

Adverse action under the FCRA occurs when a consumer report is obtained and used by a dealer or creditor with a result that is adverse to the consumer. When applied to a credit transaction, the FCRA's definition of adverse action is the same as that found in the Equal Credit Opportunity Act (ECOA) and its implementing rule, Reg. B (see Chapter 4). The ECOA defines "adverse action" to mean a denial or revocation of credit, a change in the terms of an existing credit arrangement, or a refusal to grant credit in substantially the amount or on substantially the terms requested.

Consumer

A consumer is pretty much who you think—a human being (and not a corporation, partnership, association, or other entity).

Consumer Report

Whether or not something is a consumer report depends on (i) the nature of the information in the report, (ii) the nature of the person or entity providing the information, and (iii) the reason for which the information was collected or will be used. So, not all reports about a human being amount to a consumer report. However, it is important to realize that you could become a "consumer-reporting agency" without even knowing it by transmitting information that is deemed to be a "consumer report."

For FCRA purposes, a "consumer report" is information:

- Conveyed by a "consumer-reporting agency;"

- Bearing on the consumer's creditworthiness, credit standing, credit capacity, character, general reputation, personal characteristics, or mode of living; and

- Used, expected to be used, or collected, in whole or in part, to serve as a factor in establishing the consumer's eligibility for either credit or insurance to be used primarily for personal, family, or household purposes; for employment purposes; or for any other "permissible purpose" authorized under the FCRA.

In English, this means (i) information about a consumer received from a consumer-reporting agency (ii) that contains one or more of the seven characteristics described above (iii) collected or used to determine the consumer's eligibility for credit is a consumer report for purposes of the FCRA.

With this in mind, it is clear that the information you receive from the big three agencies (Experian, Equifax, and Trans Union), including credit scores, are "consumer reports." But reports from other persons can also be consumer reports. An everyday example is a financing source's communication of its credit decision to a dealer who requested the extension of credit to a consumer. While you wouldn't think so, this "report" meets the definition of a "consumer report" because it is (i) information about a consumer from a consumer-reporting agency (we'll discuss below why the financing source could be a consumer-reporting agency) (ii) that bears on the one or more of the seven characteristics described above (iii) that was collected or used to determine the consumer's eligibility for credit. However, the FCRA excludes these reports from the definition of "consumer report" if the financing source complies with its FCRA notice obligations (for example, the Adverse Action Notice requirements) and the dealer provides the names and addresses of the finance sources it works with to the consumer. This statutory exclusion from the definition of "consumer report" is the reason why the dealer agreements you have with your financing sources typically require that you disclose their name and address to your customers.

Consumer-Reporting Agency

A "consumer-reporting agency" is "any person which, for monetary fees, dues, or on a cooperative non-profit basis, regularly engages in whole or in part in the practice of assembling and evaluating consumer credit information (or other information on consumers) for the purpose of furnishing consumer reports to third parties, and which uses any means or facility of interstate commerce for the purpose of preparing or furnishing consumer reports."

Well, this is another mouthful. In essence, what this means is that any person (including entities) who regularly assembles or evaluates consumer credit information and delivers those reports to third parties via fax, phone, mail, Internet, etc., is a consumer-reporting agency. They don't even have to get paid for the reports for this to be true! So, back to our previous finance source example, the finance source could be a consumer-reporting agency because it regularly evaluates consumer credit information and reports it to a third party (you, the dealer).

An important thing to note here is that you could be a consumer-reporting agency yourself if you're not careful. For example, if you took information from a consumer's credit application about his or her bank accounts, employment, or salary and transmitted that information to a third party (other than a financing source), you would be a consumer-reporting agency for FCRA purposes. That status comes with a lot of obligations that you'd rather not think about, so this is more reason to be careful about how you handle and protect your customer's information.

File

For FCRA purposes, the term "file" means all of the information regarding a consumer recorded and retained by a consumer-reporting agency, regardless of how the information is stored.

Active-Duty Military Consumer

An "active-duty military consumer" is a consumer who is in military service and who is on active duty or a reservist who has been called to active duty and assigned to service away from his or her usual duty station.

Firm Offer of Credit

Many dealers work with vendors to send out direct mail solicitations offering credit to customers who respond to the solicitation. If the mailing list used is derived from consumer reports, then these direct mail solicitations must be "firm offers of credit."

For a dealer, such credit is typically offered to permit a consumer to finance some, or all, of the purchase price of a vehicle at the dealership. The name and address of the consumer who receives the firm offer of credit is obtained from a consumer-reporting agency based on selection criteria provided by the dealer or creditor. These criteria often include such factors as the consumer's credit score, the number of delinquent credit accounts held by the consumer, and the number of open accounts held by the consumer.

Under the FCRA, "firm offer of credit" means "any offer of credit" that will be honored if, based on information in the consumer report on the consumer, the consumer is determined to meet the specific criteria used to select the consumer for the offer. The offer may be conditioned on one or more of the following: (i) the consumer being determined, based on *application information,* to meet specific creditworthiness criteria that were established before the consumer's selection for the offer (the "prescreen"); (ii) verification, based on *consumer report information,* that the consumer continues to meet the criteria used to select the consumer for the offer (the "postscreen"); and (iii) the consumer furnishing any required collateral if that requirement was established before the consumer's selection for the offer and the requirement was disclosed to the consumer in the firm offer solicitation. The dealer must retain its selection criteria, creditworthiness criteria, and any collateral requirement associated with the offer for three years from the date of the offer.

Sounds easy, right? Not so much. This is one of the most complicated (and convoluted) areas of the FCRA. It has also been the subject of literally hundreds of lawsuits—particularly prior to 2008, when the federal court that began all the trouble clarified its earlier decision.

The trouble began in 2004 when the Seventh Circuit Court of Appeals issued a decision in a case called *Cole v. U.S. Capital*. In the decision, the court interpreted "firm offer of credit" to include concepts of "validity" and "value." Under this interpretation, a firm offer of credit was "valid" only if it contained sufficient terms to permit the consumer to determine whether the offer had "value" and therefore was worth accepting. Where the court came up with this concept is a mystery. The plain language of the FCRA defines a "firm offer of credit" as "any offer of credit that will be honored." It doesn't say "any *valuable* offer of credit." But according to the court, the offer must be sufficiently valuable to the consumer to justify the invasion of the consumer's privacy in obtaining the consumer's credit report information for prescreening purposes. To determine whether an offer had "value," the "entire offer" must be examined as well as "the effect of all the material conditions that comprise the credit product."

In making the value assessment, the court indicated that one important term was the amount of credit offered. In addition, it indicated that both consumer and creditor must know other terms to determine whether it is advantageous to extend or accept the offer. Among these terms were (i) the rate of interest, (ii) the method of computing interest, and (iii) the length of the repayment period. Other courts held that these terms had to be disclosed to the consumer *in the written offer.*

Literally hundreds of lawsuits were filed contending that written firm offers of credit were invalid because they either didn't contain supposedly required terms or failed to make a sufficiently valuable firm offer of credit. The cases were most often filed as class actions, meaning that a plaintiffs' attorney found an individual who would lend his or her name to a complaint so that the attorney could represent every person who might have received a copy of the same written offer of credit. When the cases were certified as class actions by the court—that is, when the court decided that the case could proceed with potentially thousands of plaintiffs—the defendants most often settled the cases rather than risk a judgment that could bankrupt the company.

Thankfully, the federal courts got tired of dealing with cases that should have never been brought in the first place. More and more judges read the FCRA and couldn't find a "value" concept or any requirement that certain terms of credit be included in the written firm offer of credit. The courts began dismissing the lawsuits and granting judgment to the defendants before the cases got to trial (something lawyers call "summary judgment").

The Seventh Circuit had another chance to revisit the issue of "value" in 2008. In three cases, *Murray v. New Cingular, Bruce v. KeyBank,* and *Price v. Capital One,* the court rejected the idea that certain "material" terms had to be included in the offer for it to be valid. Relying upon the FCRA's definition of "firm offer of credit," the court explained that the central question is whether the offer will be honored (if the verification checks out), not whether all terms appear in the initial letter sent to a prospective vehicle buyer. Although the 2008 decisions seem to have put a damper on the class action lawsuits, dealers are well advised to ensure that any offer made to a consumer is one that can be honored at the dealership; that is, those consumers selected to receive the offers should have consumer report characteristics that are similar to the consumers the dealer typically finances.

As part of any firm offer of credit, the dealership or other creditor also must notify the consumer of the right to opt-out of future offers. The required content of the notice, as well as its form and location in the firm offer of credit, are set forth in great detail in the FCRA and its associated rules. In addition, consumers may contact the consumer-reporting agencies directly and request that they be excluded from prescreening lists for five years.

Fraud Alert and Active Duty Alert

A "fraud alert" is a statement in the consumer's file at a consumer-reporting agency that notifies all users of a report generated from that file that the consumer might be a victim of fraud, including identity theft. An "active duty" alert is a similar statement that indicates to the user of the consumer report that the consumer is a military service member on active duty.

Identity Theft

"Identity theft" is fraud committed by using the identifying information of another person.

Identifying Information

"Identifying information" is any name or number that may be used, alone or in conjunction with any other information, to identify a specific person. These include any name, Social Security Number, date of birth, government-issued driver's license number, government-issued identification number, passport number, taxpayer identification number, alien registration card, unique electronic identification number, address or routing number, fingerprint, voice print, retina or iris image, or other unique physical characteristic.

Identity Theft Report

The term "identity theft report" generally means a report that (i) alleges identity theft with as much specificity as the consumer can provide; and (ii) is a copy of an official, valid report filed by the consumer with a federal, state, or local law enforcement agency.

3. What are the permissible purposes (uses) of consumer reports?

Under the FCRA, a consumer-reporting agency may furnish a consumer report to a user of consumer reports, such as a dealer, only for "permissible purposes." The user must certify its permissible purpose to the consumer-reporting agency. This certification is usually contained in the user's subscriber agreement with the consumer-reporting agency.

There is a very specific and detailed list of "permissible purposes" in the FCRA. In the credit context, three are relevant:

- In accordance with the written instructions of the consumer to whom the report relates;

- To a person who intends to use the information in connection with a credit transaction involving the consumer and involving the extension of credit to, or review or collection of an account of, the consumer; and

- To a person who otherwise has a legitimate business need for the information in connection with a transaction initiated by the consumer, or to review an account to determine whether the consumer continues to meet the terms of the account.

As a general rule and best practice, a dealership should not attempt to obtain a consumer report without the consumer's written authorization, as indicated in the first instance above. Even though a permissible purpose would exist without such authorization if the consumer has submitted a complete credit application to the dealership (the second instance above), it is helpful to have written authorization as evidence if there is a dispute at some later date.

The third permissible purpose applies in the context of a lease financing. If you are a dealer who only leases vehicles, you would want to be sure your certification in your subscriber agreement with the credit bureaus includes this permissible purpose. That is because a lease transaction is generally not considered to be a "credit" transaction; that is, in all parts of the country except the 9th Circuit (Montana, Idaho, Nevada, Arizona, and all states west, including Alaska, Hawaii, Guam, and the Mariana Islands). Yes, it's odd that the whole country can't be on the same page about this, but that's what makes a book like this necessary.

A consumer-reporting agency may also furnish selected consumer report information in connection with a credit or insurance transaction that is not initiated by a consumer, if the transaction consists of a *firm offer of credit* as we discussed previously. Unless the consumer has requested that the consumer-reporting agency exclude him or her from prescreening lists (in which case, no information will be provided), the only consumer report information that can be provided is the consumer's name, address, a non-unique identifier that is used solely to identify the consumer, and other information pertaining to the consumer that does not identify the particular creditor or other entity. Consumer-reporting agencies record this type of inquiry in the consumer's file as a "soft" inquiry (disclosed only to the consumer). The inquiry is not disclosed to other consumer report users and, therefore, does not impact a consumer's credit score.

Consumer reports are used for a variety of purposes other than credit. Therefore, the FCRA provides for additional permissible purposes for which a consumer-reporting agency can furnish a consumer report. These include:

- In response to a court order or a federal grand jury subpoena;

- To a person who intends to use the information for employment purposes;

- To a person who intends to use the information for the underwriting of insurance involving the consumer; and

- To a person who intends to use the information in connection with a determination of the consumer's eligibility for a license or other benefit granted by a governmental instrumentality.

As a practical matter, it is unlikely that F&I personnel will use a consumer report exclusively for one of these purposes. Therefore, it is unusual for a dealer's subscriber agreement to include certifications for these purposes.

4. What must the dealers who furnish information to consumer-reporting agencies do?

If you are a dealer who retains your own retail installment sales contracts, or works through an affiliated finance company to obtain financing for consumer vehicle purchases, then you may have specific and direct FCRA obligations if you furnish account-related information to the consumer-reporting agencies.

First and foremost, no furnisher of information to a consumer-reporting agency may furnish information that it knows, or has reasonable cause to believe, is inaccurate. To meet your obligations, the FTC requires dealers and others subject to its jurisdiction to have written policies and procedures regarding the accuracy and integrity of the information furnished to consumer-reporting agencies. The requirements for the policies and procedures are complex, and dealers should consider consulting with counsel in developing such policies and procedures.

The FTC has explained that "accuracy" means that the information reflects the terms of and liability for the account or other relationship, the consumer's performance and other conduct with respect to the account, and identifies the appropriate consumer. "Integrity" means that the information is substantiated by the furnisher's records at the time it is furnished, is furnished in a form and manner that is designed to minimize the likelihood that the information may be incorrectly reflected in a consumer report, and includes the information in the furnisher's possession about the account that the FTC has determined is necessary to ensure that the information is not materially misleading. To meet the integrity requirement, the information furnished should include the credit limit, if available.

If a consumer has informed you that the information you provided to a consumer-reporting agency is inaccurate, and your investigation reveals that it is inaccurate, you may not report the information. If your investigation reveals that the information is accurate, then you may not furnish the information to a consumer-reporting agency without also providing notice that the consumer disputes the information. If, after you furnish information to a consumer-reporting agency, you determine that the information is inaccurate, you must correct the information with the consumer-reporting agency. Regardless of the outcome of the investigation, you must report the results to the consumer within the required period, typically 30 days.

If the information you furnish to a consumer-reporting agency is negative, you must notify the consumer that negative information is being furnished. The notice must be provided either before the negative information is furnished to the consumer-reporting agency, or within 30 days of the furnishing of the information. Once the notice is provided, you need not provide another notice in order to furnish the same or additional negative information regarding the same consumer and account.

If a consumer disputes the information you've furnished to a consumer-reporting agency directly to you, you must conduct an investigation that includes reviewing the materials provided by the consumer. If the investigation reveals that the information is inaccurate, you must notify each consumer-reporting agency to which you provided the inaccurate information and provide the corrected information. Your obligation to conduct the investigation is not triggered until the consumer specifically identifies the information being disputed, explains the basis of the dispute, and provides any supporting documentation you've reasonably required.

If the consumer disputes the information you've furnished through the consumer-reporting agency that received the information from you, you will receive a notice of the dispute from the consumer-reporting agency. Upon receipt of that notice, you must conduct an investigation, review the materials provided by the consumer-reporting agency, and report the results of the investigation to the consumer-reporting agency, which will notify the consumer of the results. If the investigation reveals that the information furnished is incomplete or inaccurate, you must correct the information with the consumer-reporting agency that provided the notice of the dispute and notify any other consumer-reporting agency to which you furnished the same information.

5. What information must consumer-reporting agencies exclude from a credit report?

Depending upon the age and nature of the information in its files, consumer-reporting agencies must exclude certain information about consumers. Except in very limited circumstances, the following information may not be reported by any consumer-reporting agency:

Bankruptcies

A consumer-reporting agency may not report bankruptcy cases where the discharge order was entered more than 10 years prior to the date of the consumer report.

Medical Information

A consumer-reporting agency may report the name, address, and telephone number of any medical information furnisher *only if* the name, address, and telephone number are reported in a way that does not identify, or permit the inference of, the name of the provider or the nature of the services, products, or devices provided.

Lawsuits, Judgments, and Arrests

A consumer-reporting agency may not report civil suits, judgments, and arrest records that predate the issuance of the consumer report by more than seven years. If the governing statute of limitations has not expired at the end of the seven-year period, the consumer-reporting agency may continue to report such suits, judgments, or arrests until it does.

Tax Liens

A consumer-reporting agency may not report paid tax liens that predate the issuance of the consumer report by more than seven years.

Bad Debts

A consumer-reporting agency may not report accounts placed for collection or charged off that predate the issuance of the consumer report by more than seven years. Certain information about government-insured or issued student loans may be reported for a longer period.

Other

A consumer-reporting agency may not report any other adverse information, other than records of convictions for crimes, which predate the issuance of the consumer report by more than seven years.

The seven-year period for accounts placed for collection or charged off (referred to previously) begins to run 180 days after the date of the most recent delinquency that precedes the placement for collection or charge off. For example, John Brown buys a car and misses several car payments. His last missed payment occurs on March 1, 2006, and the finance company charges the debt off on April 15, 2006. In this example, the seven-year period will begin to run on August 27, 2006, 180 days after March 1, 2006.

The prohibitions (also discussed previously) on the reporting of certain information do not apply to a consumer report that is to be used in connection with

- a credit transaction involving a principal amount of $150,000 or more;

- the underwriting of life insurance involving a face value of $150,000 or more; or

- the employment of an individual at an annual salary of $75,000 or more.

6. What information must consumer-reporting agencies disclose?

If a consumer-reporting agency furnishes a consumer report that contains any information regarding a consumer's bankruptcy, the report must include the identification of the chapter of the Bankruptcy Code under which the bankruptcy petition was filed. Further, if the consumer withdrew the petition before a final judgment was entered, the consumer-reporting agency must include that fact in the report upon receipt of documentation certifying the withdrawal.

If a creditor notifies a consumer-reporting agency that the consumer voluntarily closed his account, the agency must indicate that fact in any communication related to the account. If a consumer notifies a reporting agency that he or she disputes information in his or her file, the consumer-reporting agency must indicate that fact in any subsequent report that includes the disputed information. The consumer may include a brief statement describing the nature of the dispute in the file.

7. Under what conditions may a creditor extend credit to a consumer whose consumer report contains an Initial Fraud Alert, an Active Duty Alert, or an Extended Fraud Alert?

If a consumer's credit report contains an "Initial Fraud Alert" or an "Active Duty Alert," the dealership or other creditor *may not* extend credit to a consumer *unless* the dealership uses reasonable procedures to form a reasonable belief that it knows the identity of the person making the credit request. If the consumer specified a telephone number when requesting the Initial Fraud Alert or Active Duty Alert, the dealership must contact the consumer using that telephone number *or* take other reasonable steps to verify the consumer's identity and confirm that the credit application is *bona fide,* and not the result of identity theft.

If a consumer's credit report contains an "*Extended* Fraud Alert," the FCRA requirements are less flexible—the dealership *may not* extend credit to a consumer *unless* it verifies the consumer's identity by contacting the consumer in person or by contacting the consumer using the telephone number or other contact method specified by the consumer when the Extended Fraud Alert was requested.

8. How should the dealership respond to an identity theft victim's request for information if, in error, the dealership extended credit to the individual who stole the victim's identity?

In these unfortunate instances, the identity theft victim has a right to the dealership's records if he or she makes a proper written request to the dealership. If the dealer provided credit, products, goods, or services for payment, or accepted payment from, or otherwise entered into a consumer transaction for payment with a person alleged to have committed identity theft, the dealership must provide the victim a free copy of the application and business transaction records that it controls.

In order to get the dealership's records, the identity theft victim must mail a written request to the dealership at the address specified by the dealership. If requested by the dealership, the victim's request must include relevant information about the allegedly fraudulent transaction sufficient for the dealership to comply with its disclosure obligations. For instance, the dealership may ask the victim to provide a date range for the credit application or the transaction and any identifying information relating to the transaction that the victim may have, such as an account or transaction number.

The dealership must confirm the identity theft victim is who she says she is (and not another identity theft perpetrator). This means that before the dealership may provide the victim with any application information or business transaction records, the dealership must (i) verify the identity of the person requesting the information and (ii) verify that the person has made a claim of identity theft.

To establish the victim's identity, the victim must provide one or more of the following to the dealership: (i) a government-issued identification card, (ii) personally identifying information of the same type that was provided to the dealership by the unauthorized person, or (iii) personally identifying information that the dealership typically requests from new credit applicants or for new transactions. The regulations implementing the FCRA make clear that "identifying information" includes any name or number that may be used, alone or in conjunction with any other information, to identify a specific person (for example, Social Security Number, date of birth, government-issued driver's license number, government-issued identification number, passport number, taxpayer identification number, alien registration card, etc.).

To establish that he or she has made a claim of identity theft, the victim must provide the dealership with a copy of an identity theft report.

The dealership may, in good faith, decline to provide the requested information if the dealership (i) does not have a high degree of confidence that it knows the identity of the person requesting the information, or (ii) believes that the request is based on a misrepresentation of fact.

9. How often, and under what circumstances, is a consumer entitled to receive a free credit report?

The FCRA provides several opportunities for consumers to obtain a free copy of their credit report.

All nationwide consumer-reporting agencies, such as Experian, Equifax, and Trans Union, upon the consumer's request, provide a free disclosure of the consumer's file information once during any 12-month period. Similarly, all nationwide *specialty* consumer-reporting agencies must also provide a free annual disclosure to consumers. *Specialty* consumer-reporting agencies prepare reports on consumers' histories for specific purposes (for example, employment, insurance claims, residential rentals, check writing, and medical records).

The nationwide consumer-reporting agencies are required to provide the free annual disclosure only if the consumer requests the disclosure using the "centralized source" the consumer-reporting agencies have established for that purpose. For the nationwide consumer-reporting agencies, a free annual report may be obtained through the www.annualcreditreport.com website, by calling 877.322.8228, or by completing the Annual Credit Report Request Form, available at www.dealerdeskbook.com/resources/requestforcreditreport/, and mailing it to:

Annual Credit Report Request Service
P.O. Box 105281
Atlanta, Georgia 30348-5281

The nationwide *specialty* consumer-reporting agencies will provide a free annual file disclosure if the consumer requests the disclosure through the toll-free number established by each of the agencies for that purpose. Here is information about some specialty agencies that might be of interest to a dealership's consumers:

Comprehensive Loss Underwriting Exchange (CLUE)
Personal Property and/or Auto Report
Phone: 866.312.8076

Automated Property Loss Underwriting System (A-Plus)
Loss History Report
Phone: 800.627.3487

Workplace Solutions, Inc.
Employment History Report
Phone: 866.312.8075

In addition, if a consumer has been the subject of "adverse action," the consumer may request and obtain a credit report without charge by requesting the report from the consumer-reporting agency identified in the Adverse Action Notice within 60 days of receiving the dealership or creditor's Adverse Action Notice.

A consumer may also obtain a free file disclosure from a consumer-reporting agency if the consumer certifies in writing that he or she has reason to believe that the file contains inaccurate information due to fraud.

Finally, a consumer who has requested an Initial Fraud Alert may request one free file disclosure, which the consumer-reporting agency must provide within three business days after receiving the consumer's request. A consumer who has requested an Extended Fraud Alert may request two free file disclosures during the 12-month period following the date on which the Extended Fraud Alert was included in the file. The consumer-reporting agency must provide the file disclosure within three business days after receiving the consumer's request.

10. If a dealership denies credit, or refuses to grant credit in substantially the amount or the terms requested by the consumer, what notices must the dealership give to the consumer?

If a dealership denies credit to a consumer, or refuses to grant credit in the amount requested or on the terms requested, and the denial or refusal is based in whole or in part on information contained in a consumer report, the dealership must provide notice of the adverse action to the consumer. The notice must:

- Provide the name, address, and telephone number of the consumer-reporting agency that furnished the consumer report used by the dealership;

- If a credit score was used, even in part, to take adverse action against the consumer, provide written or electronic disclosure of the credit score and: (i) the range of possible credit scores under the model used; (ii) all of the key factors that adversely affected the credit score—the provider of the credit score will give you this; (iii) the date on which the score was created; and (iv) the name of the provider of the credit score;

- Include a statement that the consumer-reporting agency did not make the decision to take the adverse action and is unable to provide the consumer with the reasons why the adverse action was taken;

- Inform the consumer of the right to obtain a free copy of a consumer report from the agency that provided the report to the dealership, but only if the consumer requests the report within 60 days; and

- Inform the consumer of the right to dispute the accuracy or completeness of any information in the consumer report furnished by the consumer-reporting agency.

While, under the FCRA, notice may be oral, written, or electronic, as a practical matter (given the details required to be included) and for purposes of proving compliance, most creditors use written means.

To minimize the compliance burden, most creditors combine this FCRA Adverse Action Notice with the Adverse Action Notice required under the ECOA (see Chapter 4).

11. What obligations does the FCRA impose with respect to disposing of consumer information?

The "Disposal Rule" was created as a result of FACTA. It applies to consumer reports or information derived from consumer reports and requires dealers to employ disposal practices that are reasonable and appropriate to prevent the unauthorized access to—or use of—information in a consumer report. The Federal Trade Commission (FTC) wrote the Disposal Rule, and provides some examples, for illustrative purposes only, and which are neither exclusive nor exhaustive, of reasonable methods of disposing of consumer information at www.ftc.gov/bcp/edu/pubx/business/alerts/alt152.shtm:

- Burn, pulverize, or shred papers containing consumer report information so that the information cannot be read or reconstructed;

- Destroy or erase electronic files or media containing consumer report information so that the information cannot be read or reconstructed; or

- Conduct due diligence when you hire a document destruction contractor to dispose of material specifically identified as consumer report information consistent with the Rule. Due diligence could include:

  - Reviewing an independent audit of a disposal company's operations and/or its compliance with the Rule;

  - Obtaining information about the disposal company from several references;

– Requiring that the disposal company be certified by a recognized trade association; and

– Reviewing and evaluating the disposal company's information security policies or procedures.

Because dealers are also subject to the Gramm-Leach-Bliley Safeguards Rule (see Chapter 11), you should incorporate practices dealing with the proper disposal of consumer information into your Information Security Program required by the Safeguards Rule.

12. How does the FCRA regulate information sharing?

As you'll see in Chapter 11, the Gramm-Leach-Bliley Act's Privacy Rule regulates how car dealers may share "non-public personal information" with non-affiliated third parties. It is the FCRA that governs how dealers may share certain information with their affiliated companies and how all consumer report information is shared, regardless of with whom.

The FCRA excludes certain communications for certain purposes from its definition of "consumer report," effectively deregulating the sharing of what would otherwise be a consumer report. Four of the exclusions are of interest to car dealers.

The first one is the example we used earlier in this chapter— a credit decision communicated to a dealer from a finance source to which the dealer forwarded a customer's credit application. As we discussed in the definition of consumer-reporting agency previously, the financing source could be a consumer-reporting agency because it regularly evaluates credit and communicates a credit decision to a third party (you, the dealer). In this communication, the credit decision is definitionally a consumer report. However, the FCRA excludes this kind of communication from the definition of "consumer report" when the dealer advises the customer of the name and address of the financing source, and the financing source advises the customer of the action it took on the application (for example, an approval, denial, counteroffer, notice of incompleteness, etc.).

The other three are a bit more complicated, and require some mental gymnastics if you actually try to use them. So, we lead off with the caveat that you should work with counsel who is well versed in FCRA compliance if you plan to share any customer information.

Exclusion A: Transaction and Experience Information Shared with a Third Party. A communication containing information solely as to "transactions or experiences" between the consumer and the dealer, which could be used as a factor to determine the consumer's eligibility for credit, is excluded from the definition of "consumer report." A good example of this type of communication would be a communication from you to an insurance company containing information about a consumer's payment history with you.

Exclusion B: Transaction and Experience Information Shared Among Affiliates. A communication of transaction and experience information among persons related by common ownership or affiliated by corporate control is excluded from the definition of "consumer report." An example of a dealership affiliate would be a finance company owned or controlled by the dealership or the dealer principals.

Exclusion C: Other Information Shared Among Affiliates. A communication of information other than transaction and experience information among affiliates is also excluded from the definition of "consumer report" if the party seeking to share such information clearly and conspicuously discloses to the consumer that the information may be communicated among the affiliates and the consumer is given the opportunity to "opt-out" of such sharing before it occurs.

If the information will be used for marketing purposes, the affiliate that receives the information is prohibited from using it to solicit consumers unless the consumer is given the opportunity to opt-out of such use. This "marketing opt-out notice" requires the following elements:

- The notice must be in writing, or if the consumer agrees, electronic;
- The notice must be clear and conspicuous; in other words, reasonably understandable and designed to call attention to the nature and significance of the information in the notice;
- The notice must be concise; in other words, reasonably brief;
- The notice must provide for a reasonable opportunity for the consumer to opt-out of the sharing;
- The opt-out method must be simple; and
- The notice must be sent by the party (for example, you or your affiliate) who has the actual business relationship with the consumer.

If you've been reading closely, you'll note that the exclusion for information that is not transaction and experience information already requires an opt-out before information can be shared. However, that opt-out applies only to sharing for non-marketing purposes. The marketing opt-out notice is different, and somewhat more onerous. So, if you share information with affiliates for both marketing and non-marketing purposes, you will need to provide two separate opt-out opportunities.

The marketing opt-out notice must disclose the following:

- The name of the affiliate(s) providing the notice (for example, your dealership);

- The identity of the affiliates whose information is covered by the notice (including companies that become affiliates after the notice is provided);

- The information that may be used for marketing purposes;

- That the consumer may elect to limit the use of information for marketing purposes;

- The effective period of the opt-out (at least five years) and, if applicable, that the opt-out may be renewed after expiration;

- That if the notice is provided to consumers who may have previously opted-out (such as when an annual notice is furnished under GLBA), no action is required until the consumer receives a renewal notice; and

- A reasonable and simple method to opt-out.

If a consumer exercises his or her right to opt-out of marketing solicitations, it must be effective for a minimum of five years. Once the effective period expires, you must send another marketing opt-out notice that gives the consumer the right to continue the opt-out from marketing solicitations for at least another five years before any information covered by the exclusion is used by an affiliate for marketing purposes.

There are several exceptions to the marketing opt-out requirement. The requirement does not apply when:

- You make solicitations to a consumer with whom you have a pre-existing business relationship; in other words, someone (i) with whom you are a party to a financial contract that is continuous and ongoing, (ii) who has purchased or leased goods or services from you in the last 18 months, or (iii) who has inquired about goods or services in the last three months;

- You facilitate communications on behalf of a person related to the provision of employee benefit or other services;

- You perform services for another affiliate not related to making a solicitation;

- You respond to a communication initiated by the consumer about your products or services; or

- You make a solicitation that has been authorized or requested by the consumer.

Suffice it to say that the FCRA micromanages information sharing and mandates that you observe some fairly stringent procedures when engaging in this activity. Some dealers will think this is too much to handle and simply choose not to share information covered by the FCRA for any purpose. Others will reach out to a third-party vendor to manage this for them—be careful here, because using a third party has no effect on your liability for a violation. Still others will try to navigate this compliance minefield on their own (at their own peril).

Whatever you do, make no mistake about it. This stuff is just plain hard and is worth a visit with your FCRA counsel.

13. FACTA added the Red Flag Rule and Guidelines to the FCRA. What obligations does this impose on car dealers?

The Red Flag Rules and Guidelines (the "Rule") are mandated by FACTA as a means of combating identity theft. Effective January 1, 2008, it was issued with a mandatory compliance date of November 1, 2008. While the FTC has delayed its enforcement of the Rule several times, make no mistake that the Rule is in effect and compliance is mandatory.

The Rule requires auto dealers who engage in financing activities to establish an Identity Theft Prevention Program that is designed to detect, prevent, and mitigate identity theft. For most dealers, this means creating a written program with respect to new credit accounts. For those of you in the buy-here, pay-here community, your program will need to address your existing accounts as well. All consumer accounts are covered by the Rule, as well as business accounts to the extent you determine that there is a reasonably foreseeable risk to the business customer or yourself from identity theft.

Your program must be composed of four distinct elements containing reasonable policies and procedures to:

- Identify relevant red flags (patterns, practices, or activities that indicate the possibility of identity theft) relevant to the credit origination process;

- Detect and evaluate these red flags in connection with individual customer transactions;

- Respond to red flags you detect in an appropriate way to prevent identity theft; and

• Ensure your program is updated periodically to reflect changes in risks to customers from your experiences and new identity theft activity.

The term "red flag" refers to a pattern, practice, or specific activity that indicates the possible existence of identity theft. You have to include red flags that are relevant given the nature and scope of your activities in your program. Most car dealers engage in significant financial activities with their customers, so you should pay attention to the red flags that impact those activities. You won't have to justify why you didn't use a particular red flag as part of your program, but you will be held responsible for the overall effectiveness of your program—effectively, this means that if you choose not to use a particular red flag in your program, you won't get dinged, but if your program suffers as a result of that choice, you may find yourself liable anyway.

The Rule identifies a number of examples of red flags you should consider for your program. Some of the more pertinent red flags for car dealers include:

• A Fraud or Active Duty Alert in a consumer report.

• A consumer-reporting agency provides a notice of credit freeze in response to a request for a consumer report.

• A consumer-reporting agency provides a notice of address discrepancy.

• A consumer report indicates a pattern of activity that is inconsistent with the history and usual pattern of activity of an applicant or customer, such as:

  – A recent and significant increase in the volume of inquiries;

- An unusual number of recently established credit relationships; or

- A material change in the use of credit, especially with respect to recently established credit relationships.

• Documents provided for identification appear to have been altered or forged.

• The photograph or physical description on the identification is not consistent with the appearance of the applicant or customer presenting the identification.

• Other information on the identification is not consistent with information provided by the person opening a new covered account or customer presenting the identification.

• Other information on the identification is not consistent with readily accessible information that you have on file, such as a signature card or a recent check.

• An application appears to have been altered or forged, or gives the appearance of having been destroyed and reassembled.

• Personal identifying information provided is inconsistent when compared against external information sources you use. For example:

- The address does not match any address in the consumer report; or

- The Social Security Number (SSN) has not been issued or is listed on the Social Security Administration's Death Master File.

• Personal identifying information provided by the customer is not consistent with other personal identifying information provided by the customer. For example, there is a lack of correlation between the SSN range and date of birth.

- Personal identifying information provided is associated with known fraudulent activity as indicated by internal or third-party sources you use for fraud prevention. For example:

  – The address on an application is the same as the address provided on a fraudulent application or the phone number on an application is the same as the number provided on a fraudulent application;

  – A material increase in the use of available credit;

  – A material change in purchasing or spending patterns;

  – A material change in electronic fund transfer patterns in connection with a deposit account; or

  – A material change in telephone call patterns in connection with a cellular phone account.

- Personal identifying information provided is of a type commonly associated with fraudulent activity as indicated by internal or third-party sources you use. For example:

  – The address on an application is fictitious, a mail drop, or prison; or

  – The phone number is invalid or is associated with a pager or answering service.

- The SSN provided is the same as that submitted by other customers.

- The address or telephone number provided is the same as or similar to the account number or telephone number submitted by an unusually large number of customers.

- The customer fails to provide all required personal identifying information on an application or in response to notification that the application is incomplete.

- Personal identifying information provided is not consistent with personal identifying information that you have on file.

- If you use challenge questions, the customer cannot provide authenticating information beyond that which generally would be available from a wallet or consumer report.

- You are notified by a customer, a victim of identity theft, a law enforcement authority, or any other person that it has opened a fraudulent account for a person engaged in identity theft.

The Rule also provides that you should include your own experience in your program. For example, if you entered into a credit transaction with someone engaged in identity theft, the circumstances surrounding that transaction should be considered red flags.

In addition to red flag guidelines, the Rule also provides final guidance regarding actions a user of consumer reports must take when a consumer-reporting agency sends the user a notice of address discrepancy (note that receipt of such a notice is a red flag under the Rule). When you receive such a notice, you must use policies and procedures you have designed to enable you to form a reasonable belief that the consumer report relates to the actual person standing in the dealership or otherwise applying for credit. To the extent you furnish information to consumer-reporting agencies, you must also furnish a corrected address for the consumer.

14. FACTA added the Risk-Based Pricing Rule to the FCRA. What obligations does this impose on car dealers?

As you may recall, FACTA added a number of new rules to the Fair Credit Reporting Act. The last of these rules to be published (no less than six years after Congress mandated it!) is the Risk-Based Pricing Rule (RBP Rule). The 2003 FACT Act amendments to the FCRA required two federal agencies, the Federal Trade Commission (FTC) and the Federal Reserve Board (FRB), to issue a risk-based pricing rule. Congress wanted higher risk consumers to be aware of the fact that a creditor's "risk-based pricing" decision could result in the consumer receiving less favorable terms than those offered to other customers, and from that the agencies developed a "risk-based pricing" notice (RBP Notice) and a Credit Score Disclosure Exception Notice (Exception Notice). To read about these notices and the Rule in more detail, pick up a copy of **CARLAW®** **Dealer Compliance Guide: Risk-Based Pricing** at www. counselorlibrary.com.

For background, an RBP Notice is directed at only those consumers who apply for credit and receive an offer of credit from you and who are offered credit terms (in this case, an APR) that are less favorable than the credit terms you've given to a substantial proportion of your customers (it is not given to applicants who are denied credit; they get an Adverse Action Notice as usual). Figuring out who got less favorable terms is the challenge, and all but the biggest and most sophisticated creditors are sure to get it wrong. Getting it wrong comes with the potential for penalties, so we wonder why *any* creditor would go there.

On the other hand, the Exception Notice contains a consumer credit applicant's credit score (the one you used to decide which finance source to send the application to) and other required information. This one is hard to get wrong, and the FTC and FRB both expect most creditors to use the Exception Notice to fulfill their RBP Rule obligations.

What is risk-based pricing anyway? In today's credit world, it is common for creditors to set the price and other terms of credit offered to a particular consumer to reflect the risk that he will not pay. The creditor calculates his relative risk based on consumer report information (including credit scores) and slots him in a certain risk tier. If he has a good credit history, he'll be placed in lower risk tier with more favorable buy rates than consumers with poor credit histories.

You get to help Congress achieve its goal of letting folks know when their credit scores and credit histories are keeping them from getting the most favorable credit terms. To that end, you must provide a RBP Notice to a customer who applies for retail installment sale financing if, based on a credit report, the contract APR for that customer is less favorable than the APR a "substantial proportion" of your customers receive, unless you choose to give all consumer credit applicants an Exception Notice.

As we've said, it is far easier operationally to comply with the RBP Rule using the Exception Notice instead of the actual RBP Notice. Most dealers simply don't have the systems or sophistication needed to figure out which of their customers should get an RBP Notice. With the Exception Notice, it's simple—just give it to every consumer who applies for credit. From a compliance perspective, why risk a violation for not giving some who should have gotten it an RBP Notice, when you can simply give every consumer credit applicant the Exception Notice? Chances are, the credit bureaus and other of your vendors will be providing the Exception Notice to you to deliver to your consumer credit applicants, and so it should be easy.

The RBP Rule requires that whichever notice you use, it must conform to specific format and content requirements. An RBP Notice must be given to the consumer *before* he or she executes a retail installment sale contract, but *after* the risk-based pricing decision is actually made and communicated to him or her. As you can see, the timing requirement for an RBP Notice is much different from the timing for an Adverse Action Notice. Creditors generally have 30 days after taking an adverse action to send an Adverse Action Notice; the RBP Notice must be given *before* the consumer is obligated on the credit transaction. Apparently, the FTC and FRB wanted consumers who receive RBP Notices to be able to consider the information they contain before agreeing to be bound by less favorable credit terms.

We're sure you're asking by now why you, and not the financing source that buys the paper from you, need to give a notice. Well, here it is. A dealer is a "creditor" in a retail installment sale transaction when the retail installment sale contract is initially payable to the dealer. This is true in probably 99.9% of the auto finance transactions that take place in a dealership. The RBP Rule say that if you offer financing to a customer with an APR that is "materially less favorable" than that offered to a substantial proportion of your customers, and the APR decision is based in any way on consumer report information, you must give a RBP Notice, unless you provide an Exception Notice.

It may seem odd to require a dealer to give an RBP Notice when the APR in a retail installment sale contract may not be based on the consumer's creditworthiness, but on the combination of the buy rate (which is determined by the third-party creditor's underwriting standards) and the mark-up that the dealer negotiates with the consumer. When the FTC and the FRB were considering the scope of the RBP Rule, dealer industry representatives argued that it should not apply to dealers because they do not engage in risk-based pricing. They explained that it is only the third-party creditor, and not the dealer, that uses the consumer report information to assess the consumer's creditworthiness. Neither agency bought this argument, choosing instead to require that dealers give the RBP Notice. The agencies observed that dealers use consumer report information to determine which third-party financing source will be offered a retail installment sale contract, and on what material terms, i.e., the APR. The agencies concluded that dealers engage in risk-based pricing when they use a consumer report to determine which third-party financing source is likely to purchase the retail installment sale contract and at what buy rate, and to set the APR based in part on the buy rate. It is also likely that the RBP Rule's provisions for the time when the RBP Notice must be given drove this conclusion. Ergo, a dealer who is the original creditor in a three-party financing transaction must provide either a RBP Notice or Exception Notice to consumers.

15. Most car dealers accept credit cards for payment for services and products. What obligations does the FCRA impose with respect to the credit card receipts that are printed electronically?

The FCRA provides that no person who accepts credit or debit cards may print more than the last five digits of the card number or the expiration date on any receipt provided to the cardholder at the point of the sale or transaction. This applies only to those receipts that are electronically generated—it does not apply to receipts that are handwritten or imprinted.

Take a look at the receipts coming out of your terminals and make sure they do not include a credit or debit card expiration date or more than the last five digits of the credit or debit card number.

16. What are the civil penalties for non-compliance with the Fair Credit Reporting Act?

A dealership's liability under the FCRA can be divided into two categories: (i) civil liability to a consumer for non-compliance with the FCRA, and (ii) exposure to civil penalties in enforcement actions brought by federal or state authorities. A dealership can be civilly liable to a consumer for either willful or negligent non-compliance with the FCRA.

A dealership found to have willfully violated the FCRA is liable to affected consumers for (i) any actual damages sustained by the consumer as a result of the violation or statutory damages of not less than $100, nor more than $1,000, per violation; plus (ii) any punitive damages as the court may allow; plus (iii) in a successful action by the consumer, the costs of the action together with reasonable attorney's fees as determined by the court.

A dealership found to have negligently violated the FCRA is liable to affected consumers for (i) any actual damages sustained by the consumer as a result of the violation, plus (ii) in a successful action by the consumer, the costs of the action together with reasonable attorney's fees as determined by the court.

The dealership may also be liable for civil penalties in a civil enforcement action brought by the Federal Trade Commission or the relevant state Attorney General. Further, consumers may be able to obtain additional recoveries under state law.

Chapter 6

Federal Trade Commission: The Used Car Rule

By Daniel J. Laudicina

Nineteen Things a Dealer Should Know About the Federal Used Car Rule

The Federal Trade Commission's Trade Regulation Rule Concerning the Sale of Used Motor Vehicles, commonly referred to as the "Used Car Rule," became effective on May 9, 1985.

The Used Car Rule is intended to ensure that buyers receive all material facts in connection with the sale of used cars, and to prevent dealers from verbally misrepresenting the terms of warranty coverage prior to, or during, the sale. The Rule accomplishes these goals by requiring dealers to provide various written disclosures to prospective buyers, including placing a window sticker on the vehicle prior to offering it for sale and adding a specific disclosure to the sales contract.

The FTC enforces the Used Car Rule and does so with a rather large stick (perhaps more appropriately referred to as a billy club). The FTC is authorized to impose civil penalties of up to $16,000 per violation of the Rule—quite an incentive to get it right.

With that background, this chapter covers what we believe dealers should know about the Used Car Rule.

1. What is the Used Car Rule?

The Used Car Rule is a federal regulation. The Rule was issued by the Federal Trade Commission, which by federal law (the Federal Trade Commission Act) is charged to protect consumers from unfair and deceptive acts and practices. The Used Car Rule is intended to protect consumers from deceptive acts and practices in connection with the sale of used vehicles. Apparently, the FTC viewed these transactions as being particularly susceptible to such bad acts.

Under the Used Car Rule, when a dealer sells or offers a used car for sale, it is a deceptive act or practice for any used car dealer to (i) misrepresent the mechanical condition of a used car, (ii) misrepresent the terms of any warranty offered in connection with the sale of a used car, or (iii) represent that a used car is sold with a warranty when the vehicle is sold without any warranty.

It also is an unfair act or practice under the Used Car Rule for any used car dealer to (i) fail to disclose, prior to sale, that a used car is sold without any warranty; and (ii) fail to make available, prior to sale, the terms of any written warranty offered in connection with the sale of a used car.

2. Who is subject to the Used Car Rule?

Any dealer who offers to sell more than five used cars in a 12-month period is subject to the Used Car Rule. Note that the trigger for coverage is not the actual sale of vehicles, but rather only the offering for sale. The Used Car Rule doesn't give special favor to dealers who are poor closers.

According to the FTC, a car is offered for sale when it is displayed for sale or when a dealer permits a customer to inspect the car for the purpose of buying it, even if the car is not fully prepared for delivery.

Banks and other depository financial institutions are exempt from the Used Car Rule (though non-bank affiliates and subsidiaries are not). Lessors are subject to the Used Car Rule in connection with the offer to sell leased cars "off lease," except where the offer is made to the lessee, an employee of the lessee, or a buyer referred by the lessee. Businesses that sell cars to their employees are not subject to the Used Car Rule, nor are dealers who sell vehicles to other dealers.

Auction dealers who conduct auctions open to the public (as opposed to those open only to dealers) are subject to the Used Car Rule.

The Used Car Rule applies in all states except Maine and Wisconsin. These states have enacted laws that provide the same (or greater) protection to their citizens. (If you are a Maineiac or a Cheesehead, check your state law to determine what you need to do—we don't cover that in this book.) The Used Car Rule also applies in Territories of the United States, including Puerto Rico, Guam, the U.S. Virgin Islands, and American Samoa.

3. Does the Used Car Rule apply to the sale of cars to businesses?

Yes. The Used Car Rule applies to the sale of cars to any person who is not a used car dealer.

4. Does the Used Car Rule apply even to "sleds," pieces of metal sitting on wheels and good only for sliding downhill, although nominally powered by an engine?

No. The Used Car Rule applies only to vehicles with a gross weight rating of less than 8,500 pounds, a curb weight of less than 6,000 pounds, and a frontal area of less than 46 square feet (get out those tape measures). Therefore, demonstrator vehicles are subject to the Used Car Rule. Cars sold for scrap and motorcycles are specifically excluded from the coverage of the Used Car Rule, and depending on their dimensions, many large trucks and RVs are also excluded.

5. When is a car "used" for purposes of the Used Car Rule?

Calling a car "pre-owned" instead of "used" doesn't help (apologies to the marketing folks). A car is "used" if it has been driven more than is necessary to move or road test it prior to delivery to a consumer.

6. What does the Used Car Rule generally require?

The Used Car Rule imposes the following broad requirements on car dealers:

Buyers Guide

Dealers often refer to the Buyers Guide as the "window sticker," which is exactly what the Buyers Guide typically is. The Used Car Rule requires dealers to affix a disclosure form to a car before offering the car for sale. The form must include such things as a statement of whether the car is sold with a warranty, the terms of any warranty, and a list of defects that can occur in cars. The Buyers Guide requirements are discussed in more detail below.

Sales Contract Disclosures

The Used Car Rule requires dealers to conspicuously disclose the following statement within the contract for sale:

> The information you see on the window form for this vehicle is part of this contract. Information on the window form overrides any contrary provisions in the contract of sale.

Further, the Used Car Rule prohibits dealers from making any statements, oral or written, or taking other actions that alter or contradict the disclosures required under the Used Car Rule. It is a common practice for dealers to have car buyers sign a "buyers order" or "purchase agreement," and in credit transactions, a retail installment sale contract.

Because plaintiffs will argue that both documents are a "contract of sale," we recommend that the notice appear in all of these documents.

7. Tell me more about the content of the Buyers Guide.

The Buyers Guide informs consumers of the following:

- Whether the car is sold with a warranty

- The repair costs, if any, a dealer will pay

- That verbal promises made by the dealer are hard to enforce and that consumers should get all promises in writing

- The typical problems that can occur with respect to certain mechanical systems in the car

- That the consumer should keep the window sticker after buying the car

- To ask to have the car inspected by a mechanic before purchasing the car

The Buyers Guide includes a description of the car and the dealer's name and address. Dealers are permitted to include a signature line for the buyer to acknowledge receipt of the Buyers Guide. If such an acknowledgment is requested, the form must also include a disclosure near the acknowledgment that states:

> I hereby acknowledge receipt of the Buyers Guide at the closing of this sale.

8. What warranty information must I provide on the Buyers Guide?

Dealers must disclose one of three things with respect to warranties: (i) that the car is being sold "as is" without any warranties, (ii) that only implied warranties apply, or (iii) the terms of any express warranty the dealer provides. This can be tricky, so be sure to consult your legal counsel to make sure you are doing this right in your state.

The dealer indicates a car is sold "as is" when no warranty, express or implied by law, is given. Some states, however, prohibit or restrict a dealer's ability to sell cars "as is." In these states, certain warranties are implied by law (even if the dealer does not expressly give them). If state law requires a car to be sold with implied warranties, or the dealer voluntarily chooses not to sell a car "as is" (in states that permit such sales), but the dealer does not provide an express written warranty, then the dealer must indicate the car is sold with implied warranties only. Finally, dealers who give an express warranty must indicate that a warranty is given and provide the terms of the warranty.

If the dealer provides a written warranty, it must include whether the warranty is a full warranty or a limited warranty.

9. What is the distinction between a full warranty and a limited warranty?

A warranty is "full" if all of the following apply:

- The dealer agrees to provide service to any owner of the car during the warranty period, and all services will be performed free of charge;

- The buyer does not need to take any action to receive service (other than to request service);

- The dealer does not limit the term of any implied warranties; and

- The buyer has the option to either replace the car or obtain a refund if the dealer is unable to repair the car after a reasonable number of tries.

If any one of these conditions *does not* apply, the warranty is "limited."

If only a certain number of the car's systems are covered by a full warranty, and others are subject to a limited warranty, the dealer should indicate on the Buyers Guide that the warranty is limited if most of the systems are covered by a limited warranty.

10. Do I have to disclose the terms of any warranty on the Buyers Guide?

Yes. Dealers that give warranties must disclose the general terms of the warranty. In addition to indicating whether the warranty is full or limited, the dealer must indicate the percentage of the repair cost that the dealer will pay, the specific systems covered by any warranty, and the duration of the warranty. In disclosing the systems covered by the warranty, the dealer must be specific—it may not use general terms like "drive train" or "power train."

11. What if the manufacturer's warranty still applies?

At the dealer's option, the dealer may include a disclosure on the Buyers Guide that an unexpired manufacturer's warranty applies. The FTC offers suggestions on how to provide this disclosure. If the dealer does not give an express warranty, the dealer should, nonetheless, check the warranty box on the Buyers Guide and include the following statement:

MANUFACTURER'S WARRANTY STILL APPLIES. The manufacturer's original warranty has not expired on the vehicle. Consult the manufacturer's warranty booklet for details as to warranty coverage, service location, etc.

In addition, if state law permits a dealer to sell a car "as is," the dealer may add the following statement below this disclosure: The dealership itself assumes no responsibility for any repairs, regardless of any oral statements about the vehicle. All warranty coverage comes from the unexpired manufacturer's warranty.

If the dealer also offers its own express warranty, the dealer should mark the box on the Buyers Guide indicating that a warranty is offered and complete the rest of the Buyers Guide warranty section, indicating whether the dealer's warranty is full or limited, the percentage of parts and labor covered, the systems covered, and the duration of coverage. The dealer may then place the "MANUFACTURER'S WARRANTY STILL APPLIES" statement below the dealer's warranty disclosure.

12. Are service contracts the same as warranties?

No. However, if a "service contract" is offered on a car, the Used Car Rule also requires dealers to disclose that on the Buyers Guide.

A service contract is an agreement by the dealer to provide certain services to the buyer *at an extra charge beyond the price of the vehicle.* Warranties are distinguishable from service contracts because the buyer does not have to pay an extra charge beyond the cost of the car for warranty coverage.

If a service contract is offered, the dealer must mark a box below the warranty disclosure information on the Buyers Guide stating:

SERVICE CONTRACT. A service contract is available at an extra charge on this vehicle. If you buy a service contract within 90 days of the time of sale, state law "implied warranties" may give you additional rights.

Note that if a dealer sells a service contract to the buyer within 90 days after the date of the vehicle sale, the dealer cannot disclaim implied warranties on the systems covered by that service contract.

13. Where do I place the Buyers Guide on the car?

The Buyers Guide does not have to be affixed to the car's window. It may be displayed "prominently and conspicuously" in any location on a vehicle and in such a fashion that both sides are readily readable. Dealers may remove the form temporarily from the vehicle during any test drive, but must return it as soon as the test drive is over.

14. Can I prepare the Buyers Guide using colored paper and crayons? (Just kidding.)

No. The Used Car Rule requires the window sticker to be in a particular format and wording. Window stickers must be on white stock paper that is at least 11 inches high and 7-1/4 inches wide. The sticker must be printed using 100% black ink only. The capitalization, punctuation, and wording of all items, headings, and text on the form must be exactly as required by the Used Car Rule, including type styles and sizes. You cannot add advertising or other material to the Buyers Guide. If you conduct your used car sale transactions in Spanish, then you must post a Spanish language Buyers Guide on the car before you display or offer it for sale. See Questions 17 and 18 below.

15. I have only colored paper and crayons on the premises. Does the FTC maintain model Buyers Guide forms, so I do not mess this up?

Yes. The front and back side window sticker forms are available at www.dealerdeskbook.com/resources/frontofwindow sticker/ (front), and www.dealerdeskbook.com/resources/back ofwindowsticker/ (back).

If you go to these sites and print the forms, make sure that the printing program you are using reproduces—*accurately and precisely*—the font, type size, and paper size requirements mentioned above. If you have any doubt about your ability to reproduce the forms accurately, consider buying the forms from a reputable forms supply company.

Important

If your state's law limits or prohibits "as is" sales of vehicles, the heading "As Is—No Warranty" on the front of the sticker and the paragraph immediately accompanying that phrase must be deleted from the form, and the following heading and paragraph must be substituted:

> Implied Warranties Only. This means that the dealer does not make any specific promises to fix things that need repair when you buy the vehicle or after the time of sale. But, state law "implied warranties" may give you some rights to have the dealer take care of serious problems that were not apparent when you bought the vehicle.

If you sell vehicles in states that permit "as is" sales, but you choose to offer implied warranties only, you must also use the "Implied Warranties Only" disclosure instead of "As Is—No Warranty" disclosure.

16. Does the Used Car Rule impose any requirements in connection with the actual sale of a car (as opposed to the requirements that apply to the offer of sale)?

Yes. The Used Car Rule requires dealers to provide the Buyers Guide to the buyer to take with him or her. At the dealer's option, the dealer may provide the buyer with a copy of the original, so long as that copy accurately reflects all of the disclosures required by the Used Car Rule and the warranty coverage agreed upon.

In addition, the Used Car Rule provides that the information on the final version of the window form is incorporated into the contract of sale for each used car. Further, information on the window form overrides any contrary provisions in the contract of sale. To inform the consumer of these facts, dealers must include the following language conspicuously in each consumer contract of sale:

> The information you see on the window form for this vehicle is part of this contract. Information on the window form overrides any contrary provisions in the contract of sale.

If a financing document also serves as the contract of sale, this disclosure should be given in the financing document (for example, the retail installment sale contract). See the discussion above at Question 6.

17. If I negotiate a sale in Spanish, do I have to give the buyer a Spanish language version of any disclosures?

Yes. Recognizing that an English version Buyers Guide is of little use to consumers who speak only Spanish, the Used Car Rule requires Spanish language window forms and contract disclosures if the sale is conducted in Spanish.

It is important to note that the Spanish translation requirement does not alter the timing of the required window disclosure from that of the English version. Dealers are required to post a Spanish language Buyers Guide on the vehicle *before it is offered for sale* when the dealer conducts a used car transaction in Spanish. A dealer who merely keeps the Spanish window form on hand to give to a Spanish-speaking customer after offering a vehicle for sale is not complying with the Used Car Rule.

In order to satisfy the timing requirements for providing the Spanish language translation of the Buyers Guide, the Rule allows dealers to display on the vehicle both an English language window form and a Spanish language translation of that form. A dealer who displays both versions of the window form is complying with the Used Car Rule.

18. Does the FTC provide Spanish language versions of the model Buyers Guide?

Yes. The Spanish language versions of the front and back of the model Buyers Guide provided by the FTC are available at www.dealerdeskbook.com/resources/spanishfrontofwindow sticker/ (front of sticker), and www.dealerdeskbook.com/ resources/spanishbackofwindowsticker/ (back of sticker).

As discussed above, if your state's law limits or prohibits "as is" sales of vehicles, the following should be used as a translation of the "Implied Warranties Only" disclosure:

> Garantías implícitas solamente. Este término significa que el vendedor no hace promesas específicas de arreglar lo que requiera reparación cuando usted compra el vehículo o después del momento de la venta. Pero, las "garantías implícitas" de la ley estatal pueden darle a usted algunos

derechos y hacer que el vendedor resuelva problemas graves que no fueron evidentes cuando usted compró el vehículo.

19. Where can I obtain additional information about the Used Car Rule?

The FTC's website includes helpful information about the Rule. The Rule itself is available at www.dealerdeskbook.com/resources/ucr/.

Additional information is available online from the FTC at:

- www.dealerdeskbook.com/resources/ucrdealersguide/ (A Dealer's Guide to the Used Car Rule)

- www.dealerdeskbook.com/resources/ucrcomplianceguide/ (Used Car Rule Compliance Guide)

- www.dealerdeskbook.com/resources/ucrconsumerguide/ (Consumer Guide to Used Car Rule)

Federal Trade Commission Credit Rules: The "Holder" Rule & The Credit Practices Rule

By Michael A. Benoit and
Catharine S. Andricos

CHAPTER 7

Twenty-Three Things a Car Dealer Should Know About the Federal Trade Commission Credit Rules: The "Holder" Rule and the Credit Practices Rule

Over the years the Federal Trade Commission (FTC) has come out with two major rules that affect the financing of motor vehicle sales. These are the "Holder Rule" and the "Credit Practices Rule."

Now, before you nod off, you should know that these two rules affect pretty much every aspect of your finance operation; that is, who can sue whom if there's a breach of the contract; what happens to everyone's rights when you assign the contract; what you can and cannot put in your contracts; what you have to tell cosigners on the deal; and when you can charge late fees. And this is in addition to all those other laws and regulations that affect your rights and obligations! So wake up, grab some coffee, and let's get going.

The Holder Rule, formally called "Preservation of Consumers' Claims and Defenses," went into effect in 1976. It provides consumers with certain protections in the event that their financing agreements are sold to another creditor. The Holder Rule doesn't impose any limitations as to who can buy or sell the financing agreements; it's simply a disclosure law. It requires that the credit agreement contain language to notify the consumer of certain rights, in the event of a sale, or assignment of the agreement.

So, why, exactly, should *you* care about the Holder Rule? Because unless you never sell your paper, your dealership arranges financing subject to the Holder Rule.

The Credit Practices Rule, formally called "The Credit Practices Trade Regulation Rule," went into effect in 1985. It has to do with what kinds of provisions creditors are prohibited from including in a credit agreement with a consumer and what kinds of disclosures must be given to cosigners.

Given that background, here are the 23 things you need to know about the Holder Rule and the Credit Practices Rule.

1. What is the Holder Rule?

The FTC's Holder Rule is designed to keep the consumer from losing his or her rights under the credit agreement and under state law if the creditor assigns the contract to another creditor. It does so by (i) creating broad, substantive rights in the consumer to bring claims against subsequent holders of the consumer's credit obligations for the acts and omissions of prior holders, and (ii) it deems it an unfair and deceptive practice for a seller or lessor of goods and services to (a) enter into a retail installment sale contract or lease unless it provides notice to consumers of these rights in the contract or lease or (b) accept the proceeds of a loan from a lender to whom he refers consumers, or with whom he is affiliated by common control, contract, or business arrangement, unless the loan agreement contains a notice of these rights.

Here's how it works. You originate a retail installment sale of a vehicle. As the seller in the transaction, you are the "holder" of the retail installment sale contract. If you sell a retail installment sale contract to Ally Financial, Ally becomes the holder. The retail installment sale contract must contain the language mandated by the Holder Rule that informs the buyer and Ally that Ally is subject to the same claims that the buyer could bring against you and that the buyer can assert the same defenses against Ally that the buyer could assert against you.

Essentially, The Holder Rule applies in two situations: (i) whenever you enter into a retail installment sale, or (ii) whenever your buyer pays you with proceeds from a purchase money loan from a lender to whom you referred the buyer or with whom you are affiliated by common control, contract, or business arrangement (in other words, not a loan that the buyer gets from his own bank or credit union with whom you have no particular business relationship, but a loan from a direct lender that you have some sort of relationship with regarding your customers).

Why does the FTC care about preserving all these rights and remedies?

The FTC spent more than five years developing the Holder Rule, mainly because it thought, after extensive review, that retailers and lenders were "victimizing" consumers by selling defective products, selling the contract or note, and then not being held responsible for the product defects.

The Holder Rule was adopted specifically to prevent the seller from making the consumer's obligation to pay independent of the seller's obligation to perform on the contract or note.

Back in the day, private actions by consumers against retailers were pointless; many retailers that preyed on consumers were frequently on the move and, therefore, judgment proof. Also, many consumer claims were so small in value that even the plaintiff's attorneys wouldn't waste their time pursuing them.

The FTC figured that if the seller was out of business, or sold defective merchandise, the current holder of the credit agreement, rather than the consumer, was in the best position to protect itself against dealer misconduct. So, the FTC figured that a rule allowing a consumer to maintain his claims and defenses against whoever owned the credit agreement would internalize the costs of failed seller performance. Also, if the holder was open to claims and defenses by the consumer, then buying credit agreements from a "bad" seller, or making loans to consumers to purchase items from bad sellers, would be a bad economic decision for lenders and assignees, and they'd stop doing business with those sellers.

2. Where can I find the text of the Holder Rule?

The Holder Rule is part of Chapter 16 of the Code of Federal Regulations at 16 C.F.R. Part 433, which can be accessed electronically at www.dealerdeskbook.com/resources/holder rule/.

3. Who has to comply with the Holder Rule?

The Act applies to "sellers," which means a person who, in the ordinary course of business, sells or leases goods or services to consumers (in other words, you). In this instance, a "lease" is something other than the typical lease you do in your dealership —the "lease" we're talking about is one where the lessee effectively pays the full price of the car (for example, the depreciation, the lease charge, and the residual value) over the term of the lease. A "consumer" is a natural person—someone with a pulse, as opposed to a corporation, partnership, or some other entity—who seeks or acquires goods or services for personal, family, or household use. Keep in mind, though, that the definition of "consumer" excludes business entities and people who are buying these goods and services for other purposes, such as a business or agricultural purpose.

4. What kinds of transactions trigger the Holder Rule?

The Holder Rule is triggered when there is a sale of goods or services to consumers, in or affecting commerce, coupled with the extension of credit in connection with that sale.

5. Does the Holder Rule require disclosures?

The FTC must have been feeling "friendly" the day it came up with the Holder Rule, because it gives you the exact language and format for the notice. That said, the language of this "Holder Notice" is the sort of legalese that leaves most folks scratching their heads and wondering what it all means.

The Holder Notice varies slightly, depending on whether the financing transaction is a retail installment sale (the typical transaction that occurs in the dealership) or a loan from a lender to whom you referred the buyer, or with whom you have an affiliation as a result of common control, a contract, or another business relationship.

In a retail installment sale transaction, where you sell goods or services to a consumer, the Holder Notice must appear in the retail installment sale contract in at least 10 point font, in bold face type as follows:

NOTICE: ANY HOLDER OF THIS CONSUMER CREDIT CONTRACT IS SUBJECT TO ALL CLAIMS AND DEFENSES WHICH THE DEBTOR COULD ASSERT AGAINST THE SELLER OF GOODS OR SERVICES OBTAINED PURSUANT HERETO OR WITH THE PROCEEDS HEREOF. RECOVERY HEREUNDER BY THE DEBTOR SHALL NOT EXCEED AMOUNTS PAID BY THE DEBTOR HEREUNDER.

When your customer pays you with the proceeds of a loan from a lender to whom you referred the customer, or with whom you are affiliated by common control, contract, or through a business relationship, you are actually prohibited from accepting the proceeds of that loan as payment if the loan document does not contain the following version of the Holder Notice in at least

10 point font, in bold face type:

NOTICE: ANY HOLDER OF THIS CONSUMER CREDIT CONTRACT IS SUBJECT TO ALL CLAIMS AND DEFENSES WHICH THE DEBTOR COULD ASSERT AGAINST THE SELLER OF GOODS OR SERVICES OBTAINED WITH THE PROCEEDS HEREOF. RECOVERY HEREUNDER BY THE DEBTOR SHALL NOT EXCEED AMOUNTS PAID BY THE DEBTOR HEREUNDER.

6. What is the Credit Practices Rule?

The Credit Practices Rule places certain restrictions on what a creditor can and can't put into a contract. It requires that certain disclosures be given to certain parties to a transaction. It also places limitations on how late charges are imposed.

Why did the FTC find the need to implement a rule like this? It was because of the notion of "fairness." Certain things, the FTC figured, are just "unfair," such as the following:

- Making a consumer sign away his wages in order to get credit

- Taking a consumer's wedding ring in lieu of payment

- Forcing a consumer to agree they are responsible for anything that goes wrong before it ever happens

- Contracting in a way that makes consumers who buy defective goods or services on credit unable to assert any claims or defenses against the retailer

- Forcing consumers to pay late charges on top of late charges when only the first payment was late (called "pyramiding" late charges)

• Convincing someone to cosign a loan or retail installment sale contract for another person, without explaining to the cosigner that he *just might* have to pony up one day

7. Where can I find the text of the Credit Practices Rule?

The Credit Practices Rule is codified in the Code of Federal Regulations at 16 C.F.R. Part 444 and can be found electronically at www.dealerdeskbook.com/resources/creditpracticesrule/.

8. Who has to comply with the Credit Practices Rule?

The Credit Practices Rule applies to all "creditors" subject to the jurisdiction of the Federal Trade Commission. In other words, any creditor who is not regulated by one of the federal banking regulators. "Creditor" includes retail installment sellers, and unless you're also a national bank, that means you, Mr. Dealer!

9. What kinds of transactions trigger the Credit Practices Rule?

The Credit Practices Rule covers all consumer credit transactions (except those involving purchases of real estate). It covers loans made to consumers who use the proceeds to purchase goods or services for personal, family, or household uses, even though those loans may be secured by real estate owned by the consumers. A "consumer" is a natural person— again, someone with a pulse, not a business entity. The Credit Practices Rule also applies to the sale of goods or services under lease-purchase plans. In other words, it applies to most of your customers who are natural persons, who buy a vehicle or services for personal use, and who finance the purchase.

10. What are the main components of the Credit Practices Rule?

The Credit Practices Rule has three main components. First, it prohibits you from using certain contract provisions that the FTC has found to be "unfair" to consumers. These are: (i) confessions of judgment, (ii) waivers of exemption, (iii) wage assignments, and (iv) security interests in household goods. We explain all this legalese below. Second, it requires you to advise consumers who cosign obligations about their potential liability if the other person doesn't pay up. Third, it prohibits you from assessing late charges in certain circumstances.

11. No more confessions of judgment?

Once upon a time, consumer credit contracts regularly contained language taking away certain rights consumers being sued ordinarily would have had. These included the right to receive notice of the suit, the right to appear in court, and the right to raise any defenses that they may have had. By including a "confession of judgment" in the consumer credit agreement, the creditor could appear *ex parte* (legalese that means that only one party—the creditor—is required to show up in court) in a lawsuit against the debtor, and ensure that the creditor would win the lawsuit, assuming that the debtor didn't find out about the suit in time to defend himself. Most folks agree that it's not fair to sue someone without giving them the opportunity to defend themselves, even if they might have agreed to it in a contract. The Credit Practices Rule prohibits this practice.

The Credit Practices Rule isn't intended to interfere with whatever rights you have to repossess property securing the debt. It does not prohibit power-of-attorney provisions that allow you to repossess and sell collateral, as long as these provisions don't impede the consumer's right to his day in court.

The Credit Practices Rule also doesn't prohibit a consumer from acknowledging liability after a suit has been filed and the consumer has been duly notified.

12. No more waivers of exemption?

A long time ago, in a dealership far, far away, some consumer credit agreements contained "waiver of exemption" provisions. These provisions allowed creditors to seize (or threaten to seize) a specific possession, or possessions, of a specified value, even if state law treated them as exempt from the seizure. These days, every state has a law that defines certain property (generally, property considered necessities) that a debtor is allowed to keep, even if a creditor sues and obtains a judgment. Back then, by signing a waiver of exemption, a debtor made that property available to a creditor who obtained a judgment to satisfy a debt. Take the following example:

> Each of us hereby both individually and severally waives any or all benefit or relief from the homestead exemption and all other exemptions or moratoriums to which the signers or any of them may be entitled under laws of this or any other State, now in force or hereafter to be passed, as against this debt or any renewal thereof.

In this beautifully legalistic example, the consumer signs away his right to the homestead exemption (this refers to that dollar amount or percentage of the value of his house he can keep, under state law, even if a creditor gets a lien). Under the Credit Practices Rule, this Exemption Waiver no longer is permitted, even if your customer is willing to sign up in order to get into that new car.

13. Does that mean I can't use household items as collateral?

No. The Rule's prohibition on waiver of exemption provisions doesn't prevent you from using particular kinds of collateral, such as, in the above example, a house. However, if state law provides an exemption for certain kinds or amounts of property (like the homestead exemption does), the contract can't contain a provision causing the consumer to give up that protection. If certain collateral is important to you, take and perfect a security interest in it. (See Questions 16 and 17, below.)

14. No more wage assignments either?

If you have a good memory, you'll recall the days when, if you didn't pay as agreed, some big thug with huge biceps and a fondness for breaking noses or legs would show up on your doorstep to give you a little encouragement to pony up. (That practice was never legal, but not because of the Credit Practices Rule.) You may also remember that if you did not pay as agreed, some consumer credit contracts permitted creditors to go directly to your employer to have your wages, or some part of them, paid directly to the creditors. This is known as "wage assignment."

The Credit Practices Rule prohibits wage assignments. It prohibits consumers from assigning their wages (or any monies that may be due them) to you in the consumer credit agreement in the event they do not pay as agreed.

15. Is the prohibition on wage assignments absolute?

No. The Credit Practices Rule lets you use payroll deduction plans, in which consumers choose to pay by regular deductions from paychecks. You can even structure those plans such that, if a borrower changes employers, his final paychecks will be assigned to you to be credited toward balances due on obligations, without notice to debtors, and without allegations of default or delinquency. Your contracts also may provide for wage assignments that can be revoked at will by consumers and for wage assignments already earned at the time of the assignment. In addition, you may require that the revocation of a voluntary wage assignment be in writing.

The Credit Practices Rule's prohibition against wage assignments also does not prohibit garnishment in those states in which garnishment is permitted. If a creditor obtains a court judgment against a debtor, the creditor may continue to use wage garnishment to collect that judgment, subject to the consumer protections provided by federal (and sometimes state) law.

16. What about security interests in household goods?

In the past, some consumer credit contracts contained security clauses that allowed a creditor to repossess a consumer's existing household goods if the consumer did not pay for the new goods as agreed. Under the Credit Practices Rule, you can no longer take a security interest in or repossess certain "household goods" that are not the subject of the credit transaction. "Household goods" include household necessities, such as clothing, appliances, and linens, and some items of little economic value to others, but of unique, personal value to the consumer. Think photos of grandpa's birthday party, steamy love letters, the "souvenirs" from your spring break in Cancun, and pets. "Household goods" do not include works of art, electronic entertainment equipment (except one television set and one radio), items acquired as antiques (more than 100 years old), and jewelry (except wedding rings).

17. What household goods can I take a security interest in?

The Credit Practices Rule permits consumers to offer as security the valuable possessions described above (that original Van Gogh hanging in the living room, that antique lamp, and the other items listed above) as well as pianos or other musical instruments, boats, snowmobiles, bicycles, cameras, and similar items.

18. What notices are required under the Credit Practices Rule?

If you use cosigners on your deals, pay attention to this one. The Credit Practices Rule requires you to inform each cosigner of his or her potential liability before the cosigner becomes obligated for the debt. It's considered deceptive for a retail installment seller or lender to misrepresent the nature or extent of the cosigner's liability (for example, telling someone that cosigning is "just a formality" or that "no cosigner ever actually has to pay up"). It's also considered deceptive to obligate a cosigner unless the cosigner is informed of the nature of her liability before she becomes obligated (for example, telling a cosigner to sign the papers now, because you've got other buyers lined up for the car, and you'll mail her the information later).

If the proper notice is given to cosigners, you don't have to worry about any of this. The Credit Practices Rule requires you to use this "Cosigner Notice":

> Notice to Cosigner: You are being asked to guarantee this debt. Think carefully before you do. If the borrower doesn't pay the debt, you will have to. Be sure you can afford to pay should you have to, and that you want to accept this responsibility.
>
> You may have to pay up to the full amount of the debt, if the borrower does not pay. You may also have to pay late

fees or collection costs, which increase this amount.

The creditor can collect this debt from you without first trying to collect from the borrower. The creditor can use the same collection methods against you that he can use against the borrower, such as suing you, garnishing your wages, etc. If this debt is ever in default, that fact may become a part of your credit record.

This notice is not the contract that makes you liable for debt.

19. Do I have to use that exact language?

Usually yes. However, if a state statute or regulation requires a different notice to cosigners, you may include that notice on the document if it is not inconsistent with the notice required by the Credit Practices Rule. If a statement in the federal notice (such as one that says you can collect from the cosigner without first trying to collect from the primary debtor or the one that says wage garnishment may be used) is inaccurate under state law, you may omit it from the notice used in that state.

20. Do I have to give that notice to every cosigner?

No. You don't have to give it to someone who merely signs a security agreement and has no personal liability for the debt.

Also, remember that a cosigner is different from a co-buyer. A cosigner doesn't get any tangible benefit from the agreement; he undertakes liability as a favor to the main debtor who would not otherwise qualify for credit. On the other hand, a co-buyer does receive benefits as one who shares in the purchased goods—think a husband and wife, boyfriend and girlfriend, Laurel and Hardy, or any two people who are buying the vehicle together. Therefore, co-buyers aren't considered cosigners under the Credit Practices Rule, and you're not required to provide the notice to them.

21. What should the cosigner notice look like?

There's no need to order special forms or to create anything fancy. You can print the cosigner notice on your letterhead and include identifying information, such as the credit account number, the name of the cosigner, the amount of the debt, and the date. You also may provide a signature line for the cosigner to acknowledge that he received the notice. However, you can't include any additional statement in the notice that would distract the cosigner's attention from the message in the notice. Nor can you attach the notice form to other documents, unless it appears before any other document in the package. In other words, make sure it's clear and at the top of the pile.

22. What language should the cosigner notice be in?

The cosigner notice should be in the same language as the agreement to which it applies. For example, if the agreement is in Spanish, the cosigner notice also should be in Spanish.

23. Can I charge late charges under the Credit Practices Rule?

Yes, but be careful how and when you charge them.

Before adoption of the Credit Practices Rule, some creditors calculated late fees for delinquent payments using a practice called "pyramiding." After receiving a first late payment and assessing a late fee that goes unpaid, assume the creditor receives a second payment of just the contract amount, paid on time. The creditor applies the payment first to satisfy the unpaid late fee, leaving the payment amount insufficient to cover the payment due, and (here begins the pyramid) assesses another late fee. When the third, fourth, and fifth contract payments arrive, each on time, the creditor repeats the practice, assessing successive late fees that claim that first portion of each successive payment.

Unless either the borrower or the creditor changes his behavior, the string of late fees will continue, monthly, until the end of the term of the contract. Assuming a 36-month term, despite having made only one payment late, the borrower would pay 35 late fees (good for revenue, but bad for business) for missing that first payment due date.

To paraphrase our friend, Ronald Reagan, the Credit Practices Rule says, "Mr. Dealer, tear down that pyramid."

The Credit Practices Rule prohibits this "pyramiding" of multiple late fees for a single instance of delinquency. It prohibits you from charging the fee if the payment made is otherwise a full payment for the applicable period and is paid on its due date, or within the grace period, and when the only delinquency is attributable to a late fee assessed on an earlier installment.

Chapter 8

Federal Advertising Rules

By L. Jean Noonan and
Michael A. Goodman

Seventeen Things a Car Dealer Needs to Know About Federal Advertising Rules

For better or for worse, federal regulators basically look at deceptive advertising in the same way the U.S. Supreme Court once approached obscenity: They know it when they see it. Deciding whether an advertisement is deceptive, or not, necessarily involves some subjective analysis. The key regulator —the Federal Trade Commission—has issued formal and informal guidance on how it approaches this issue. Its enforcement history also indicates how it assesses advertising.

This chapter will cover key sources of this information: statutory law, formal FTC statements, and informal business education.

With that background, here are 17 things that we think dealers need to know about federal advertising rules.

1. I have enough to worry about without also worrying about being sued by the federal government. How do I keep the feds from banging down my door about my advertising?

Let's take it one step at a time. Federal advertising rules begin with the Federal Trade Commission Act ("FTC Act" or "the Act"). The wording of the key provision is fairly straightforward, but it has spawned a great deal of interpretation.

The FTC Act prohibits *unfair* or *deceptive* acts or practices in or affecting commerce. About 25 years ago, the FTC issued formal statements on what's considered "unfair" and "deceptive." Note that practices are illegal if they are unfair OR deceptive. A practice does NOT need to run afoul of both the unfairness standard and the deception standard before it violates the law. Once one of these standards is triggered, the practice is unlawful.

Section 5 of the FTC Act, where this standard is introduced, is available at www.dealerdeskbook.com/resources/udapstandards/.

2. OK, so what's an "unfair" practice?

In 1980, Congress asked the FTC to explain "unfairness." In response, the FTC established the following standard: An act or practice is "unfair" if it "causes, or is likely to cause, substantial injury to consumers, which is not reasonably avoidable by consumers themselves, and not outweighed by countervailing benefits to consumers or to competition."

That definition may seem a little vague. Some examples of unfair practices may help. The FTC has argued successfully that credit card "cramming"—placing unauthorized charges on a consumer's credit card—is unfair. This practice causes substantial injury, because consumers may pay charges that they don't legally owe. It is not reasonably avoidable because any merchant with a consumer's credit card information can place an unauthorized charge on the consumer's account. It is not outweighed by countervailing benefits, because there are no legitimate benefits associated with credit card cramming.

The FTC also has used its unfairness authority to target unreasonably sloppy data security procedures and nefarious Internet-based practices that disable the usual operation of a consumer's computer.

Notably, the *unfairness* standard rarely applies to advertising. Rather, the FTC's *deception* standard is typically at stake with respect to advertising.

3. What's a "deceptive" practice?

In 1983, the FTC wrote a similar letter to Congress, this time discussing the "deception" standard. According to the

FTC's letter, an act or practice is "deceptive" if it is likely to mislead a consumer acting reasonably under the circumstances about a material fact.

The act or practice may be either a representation (*something said* in an advertisement) or an omission (*failure to say* something in an advertisement). A representation may be expressed (something actually stated), or implied (something not actually stated but suggested by the ad). Of course, advertisers won't always realize when they make an implied representation. The FTC's letter says "extrinsic evidence" may be used to establish whether an implied representation has been made. In this setting, "extrinsic evidence" usually means a consumer survey, for example, stopping people at a shopping mall, showing them sample advertising, and asking them to describe what they think the ad is saying.

The FTC's letter also explains who the "reasonable consumer" is, or, rather, who the reasonable consumer is *not*: "Perhaps a few misguided souls believe, for example, that all 'Danish pastry' is made in Denmark. Is it therefore an actionable deception to advertise 'Danish pastry' when it is made in this country? Of course not."

This example tells us that the reasonable consumer knows that not all Danish pastries are made in Denmark. The bigger picture is that the reasonable consumer is not the smartest person in the room, but not the dumbest, either.

One of the best measures of the reasonable consumer is the point of view of the actual consumer. If you start receiving comments from consumers that they were confused by something in your ad, that's a sign that a reasonable consumer is likely to be deceived by the ad.

An act or practice concerns a material fact if it is likely to affect a consumer's choice of, or conduct regarding, a product or service. In other words, material information is information that is important to consumers. You don't want to use this third element of the deception standard to get you out of trouble. If your representation is likely to mislead reasonable consumers, you don't want to be left arguing that, while your ad misled consumers, it was only about something unimportant.

4. Is that all there is to it?

Not exactly. Because the deception standard is somewhat subjective, the devil is in the details. The FTC or the court will focus on the details in determining whether an act or practice is deceptive.

One important detail is that the FTC says you must look at an ad in its entirety to decide what representations are being made and whether any of those representations is deceptive. This is called the "net impression" doctrine: Looking at the ad as a whole, what impressions are established? This doctrine comes into play when a misleading claim is made in huge letters at the top of an ad, and fine print at the bottom of the ad indicates that the prominent claim is not all it appears to be. For example, if an ad included a headline that says: "This truck gets 75 miles per gallon!" and fine print at the bottom says: "On the moon," the FTC would say that the net impression of the ad was misleading.

In plenty of situations, disclosure in a footnote will be fine. The keys are to avoid tiny print and big, dense blocks of text. Overall, the FTC will look to see if all material disclosures are made clearly and conspicuously.

5. Are there specific kinds of deception that dealerships should be especially concerned about?

Yes. One typical type of deception is "bait-and-switch." The FTC says a bait-and-switch marketing technique is deceptive, because the offer to sell a product or service is not a bona fide offer. This situation could arise when a dealer's ad offers unbelievably low prices, but no, or only a small number of, vehicles are actually available at the price promoted by the dealer. In the latter case, it is problematic to make that offer without explaining that the offer is only good for a limited number of vehicles (or, as another example, only for a limited amount of time).

6. Do these advertising rules apply to all forms of advertising, or are there different standards for direct mailers, telemarketing, Internet banner ads, and so on?

The FTC's advertising rules apply equally to all forms of advertising, no matter what medium is at issue. However, additional specific rules apply to telemarketing, marketing via fax, and email marketing. These rules are discussed elsewhere in this book (see Chapters 14, 15, and 16). In addition, the FTC has published special guidance for online advertising. *The Dot.Com Disclosure Guide* is a very useful resource for advertising on the Internet. It is available at www.dealerdeskbook.com/resources/dotcomdisclosureguide/.

The Dot.Com Disclosure Guide is so useful that you may find yourself employing it for other forms of advertising as well. Most importantly, it provides helpful tips on how to make sure a disclosure is "clear and conspicuous" as required by the FTC. This is a topic that some find difficult or obscure without additional guidance from the FTC.

7. I've seen FTC cases against weight-loss products that talk about the advertiser's obligation to have data supporting their advertising claims. Does that affect me and my advertising?

It might. The FTC has issued a policy statement on advertising "substantiation." According to this statement, advertisers *must have* this substantiation in hand before making an advertising claim. According to the FTC:

> "Objective claims for products or services represent explicitly or by implication that the advertiser has a reasonable basis supporting these claims [and]... are material to consumers. [C]onsumers would be less likely to rely on claims for products or services if they knew the advertiser did not have a reasonable basis for believing them to be true. Therefore, a firm's failure to possess and rely upon a reasonable basis for objective claims constitutes an unfair and deceptive act or practice in violation of Section 5 of the Federal Trade Commission Act."

While it's true that the issue of substantiation most often arises in health-related claims, the principle applies to all types of advertising. If your ads promote a sealant that will prevent rust for 10 years, you better *have* data to back that up.

8. Are there any other federal advertising rules I should know about besides the FTC Act and statements made by the FTC?

Depending on what kind of advertising you are doing, there may be additional FTC rules or formal guides and policy statements that apply. For example, the FTC has specific rules on Telemarketing, the Sale of Used Cars, and Motor Vehicle Leasing. These are discussed elsewhere in this book (see Chapters 14, 6, and 3, respectively).

In addition, the FTC has issued guides and statements on comparative advertising, the use of endorsements and testimonials, pricing, and use of the Internet. You may find it is wise to add the FTC's website, at www.ftc.gov, to your list of resources when addressing advertising issues.

Also, if you use sweepstakes to promote your dealership, you should be aware of the Deceptive Mail Prevention and Enforcement Act. It is discussed at the end of this chapter at Question 15. Finally, there are extensive rules governing credit advertising for loans (Regulation Z) and leases (Regulation M) (see Chapters 2 and 3).

9. Do the federal advertising rules impose any recordkeeping requirements?

The FTC does not impose specific recordkeeping requirements. However, if you are investigated or sued by the FTC, you will want thorough records of your efforts to comply with the law.

10. Are there any available defenses if I get sued?

Your only defense may be that you didn't do what the FTC says you did. There are no defenses based on a violation being a technicality or that you didn't intend for your advertising to be deceptive. Over time, a daunting series of court opinions has given ammunition to the FTC and little comfort to defendants. For example, relying on the advice of your attorney is not a recognized defense if you get sued by the FTC.

The best strategy is to avoid being sued in the first place. That includes responding quickly to consumer complaints, training personnel on compliance, and monitoring personnel for compliance.

FEDERAL ADVERTISING RULES

11. Let's say I hire a third-party marketer and that person violates the law while working on my behalf. Can I be in trouble in that situation?

This is a point that bears repeating in each chapter involving the FTC: The FTC has clearly indicated that both the business promoted in an advertisement and any third party responsible for promoting that business face liability for violations of federal advertising rules. In announcing a $5.3 million penalty against DirecTV, the FTC chairman stated, "Sellers are on the hook for calls placed on their behalf." The FTC's suit against DirecTV targeted both the business being promoted and the callers hired by the business.

If you use a third party to develop advertising for you, you must monitor its activities and respond promptly to consumer complaints. Addressing responsibility for legal compliance in your contract with a third-party marketer may be a good idea for other reasons, but will not provide you with a defense in a federal enforcement action.

12. But I'm not some notorious criminal. Is anyone really going to come after me if I break these laws?

Maybe. There's no doubt that the FTC focuses its enforcement efforts on the people causing the most harm. And there is also no doubt that the FTC does not have a track record of suing people for putting one toe over the line of what is allowed.

On the other hand, the FTC takes compliance with its laws very seriously. The FTC considers itself the nation's consumer protection agency. That's why the Commission likes to say that "FTC" stands for "For The Consumer." As a result, it responds aggressively to consumer complaints, and it is always on the lookout for practices that harm consumers, even those consumers may not complain about to the FTC (for example, the harmful effects of spyware).

That is why the best policy is one of robust compliance and vigilant response to consumer complaints. If consumers don't complain to the FTC about you, then the FTC is unlikely to investigate you.

13. If I get sued, what penalties can I face?

If the FTC sues you, it can ask a court to impose a wide variety of penalties. The court can order you to pay back all the money you improperly received from consumers. It can order you to pay back all the money you made from an illegal advertising campaign. For the worst violations, the court can appoint a receiver to take over your business.

The point here is to make you just a little nervous. If you make a good-faith effort to stay on the right side of the law concerning federal advertising rules, you will not be subjected to the biggest weapons in the FTC's arsenal. The FTC simply wants to make sure that consumers are treated fairly in the marketplace. For minor infractions, that means a warning or a light penalty; for major infractions, that means a harsh penalty.

14. What about state advertising laws? Do I have to comply with them, too? Or do the federal laws preempt state laws?

Federal advertising laws do NOT preempt state laws in this area. The federal and state laws are complementary in many ways; typically, they both prohibit fraudulent, misleading, deceptive, and abusive business practices. Many states go further than the federal government. States may require registration with a state regulatory authority, the posting of a bond before doing business, the review of advertising material by the state before it is used, and so on.

Clearly, this is a complex issue, and you should involve your lawyer when it comes to complying with state advertising laws. The message here is that the federal advertising rules are in addition to—not in place of—the state laws.

15. I like to use sweepstakes to generate interest in my dealership. Are sweepstakes regulated by federal law?

Yes. In 2000, the Deceptive Mail Prevention and Enforcement Act took effect, and it is very specific about what a marketer can and cannot do. It is enforced by the U.S. Postal Service, which means that it applies to sweepstakes sent through the U.S. mail. However, you and your lawyer should also be aware of state laws regulating sweepstakes; those state laws are NOT preempted.

According to the federal law, a sweepstakes is a game of chance that a person plays voluntarily and for which the person is not required to pay anything to enter to win a prize. Sweepstakes mailings must disclose (i) that no purchase is necessary and purchase will not increase chances of winning, (ii) the sponsor's name and address (Note: The sponsor is you), (iii) the estimated odds of winning, (iv) a description of every prize, and (v) a clear statement of the payment schedule of any prize.

Sweepstakes mailings may not (i) suggest that the sweepstakes is offered by or endorsed by the government, (ii) suggest that failure to make a purchase may exclude people from future sweepstakes, (iii) require an entry to be accompanied by an order or payment, (iv) say that someone has won when that is not true, or (v) say anything to contradict or limit the rules or required disclosures.

This law also gives consumers the right to stop receiving sweepstakes mailings. Specifically, marketers must give consumers a reasonable way to request removal from sweepstakes mailing lists, maintain a record of all such requests, and honor such requests within 60 days and for five years. Marketers may not disclose, transfer, sell, or rent a list of consumers who have opted-out.

Note that this law also regulates mailings involving skill contests and facsimile checks, as well as mailings made to resemble government documents.

16. There is a lot of concern that the Consumer Financial Protection Bureau is very aggressive in enforcing advertising and other consumer protection laws. Do dealers need to worry about the CFPB?

It depends on the type of dealer. Congress excluded dealers from the CFPB's authorities if they are predominantly engaged in the sale and servicing of motor vehicles or the sale and leasing of motor vehicles. To be excluded from the CFPB's reach, the dealer must service cars as well as sell them. Also, a dealer is under the CFPB's jurisdiction if it provides financing but does not routinely assign the contracts to an unaffiliated third-party finance or leasing source.

17. What's an "abusive" practice, and is this another thing to worry about?

The Dodd-Frank Wall Street Reform and Consumer Protection Act, which created the Consumer Financial Protection Bureau, gave the CFPB the power to protect consumers from abusive acts and practices. If you are the type of dealer over which the CFPB has authority, such as a dealer that does not service cars or a dealer that does not sell its financing contracts or leases, you must pay attention to the CFPB's power regarding abusive practices.

The Dodd-Frank law defines an abusive practice, but we don't know much yet about how the CFPB will use this power. The law describes several types of abusive practices. You can be in trouble if consumers cannot understand a term or condition of your credit extension or lease; it is an abusive practice to "materially interfere with the ability of a consumer to understand" the financial product you are offering. The law also says a covered dealer may not "take unreasonable advantage" of a consumer in certain ways. For example, it is abusive to take advantage of the fact the consumer doesn't understand the material risks, costs, or conditions of the financing. If a consumer reasonably relies on you to act in her best interest, it is abusive to take unreasonable advantage of that trust.

Even if you are not a dealer subject to the CFPB's powers, it's useful to think about the abusive standard. The line between an abusive practice and an unfair or deceptive practice is not bright. If the CFPB decides a certain dealer practice is abusive, there's a good chance that the Federal Trade Commission could view the same practice as unfair or deceptive.

CHAPTER 8

The Magnuson-Moss Warranty Act

By Patricia E.M. Covington

Eighteen Things a Car Dealer Needs to Know About the Federal Magnuson-Moss Warranty Act

The Magnuson-Moss Warranty Act (MMWA) applies to warranties given in connection with consumer products. It doesn't *require* manufacturers or sellers of consumer products to give warranties. But if a warranty *is* given, the MMWA requires that the warranty comply with certain requirements. It was enacted to protect consumers from deceptive warranties and to make warranties more readily understandable and enforceable against the manufacturer or seller.

1. What is the Magnuson-Moss Warranty Act?

The Magnuson-Moss Warranty Act is a federal law regarding consumer product warranties. Congress passed the MMWA to require manufacturers and sellers that offer written warranties with their consumer products (such as motor vehicle dealers) to provide consumers with complete information about the warranties being given. The MMWA defines the rights of the consumer regarding written warranties and sets out the requirements for folks who offer them. Because the MMWA is a law passed by Congress (as opposed to a regulation issued by a government agency), only Congress may change it.

2. Why was it enacted?

Prior to its enactment, there were a number of studies done by the Federal Trade Commission (FTC) regarding warranties on consumer products. What the FTC discovered was:

- Consumers did not understand the warranties given;

- Warranties were sometimes written deceptively so that they promised more than they actually covered;

- Many warrantors were not honoring their warranties;

- Consumers had no practical way of compelling warrantors to be responsible for performing; and

- "Good" warrantors had no encouragement to continue doing "good," because the "bad" warrantors were misbehaving and making lots of money.

Consequently, Congress enacted the MMWA. Its goal was to increase customer satisfaction, ensure warrantors did what they said, and encourage the development of additional warranties giving consumers more and better choices. Congress also wanted to make it possible for consumers to comparison shop products and warranties; that way, consumers could find the best combination of price, features, and coverage for their situation. Finally, Congress wanted to ensure that there would be timely and complete resolution of disputes of warranty claims.

3. Does the MMWA have an accompanying regulation?

Yes. Congress directed the FTC to draft regulations to fill in the gaps left open by the MMWA. The regulation can be found at 16 C.F.R. Part 700 (see Question 4 for a website address). Because the FTC (a government agency) issued the regulation, the FTC can amend and revise it. The FTC has also issued "Interpretations of MMWA" (Interpretations) that provide more detail and guidance regarding how the FTC interprets the MMWA and its regulations. These can be found with the regulations.

4. Where can I find the MMWA and its regulation and Interpretations?

The full text of the MMWA is available at www.dealerdeskbook.com/resources/mmwa/. Its implementing regulation and Interpretations (mentioned in Question 3) are available at www.dealerdeskbook.com/resources/mmwaregsand interpretations/.

5. What is a warranty, anyway?

When enacting the MMWA, Congress described a warranty as an *"express or implied"* statement or representation made by a seller of goods with reference to the character or quality of the goods being sold. A warranty can also be described as an assurance that the goods sold are as represented or promised.

Express Warranties

Express warranties result from some type of overt action on the part of the person giving the warranty. They can be created three ways: (i) either through a promise or affirmation of fact that relates to the goods, (ii) a description of the goods, or (iii) on the basis of a sample or model of the goods.

A salesperson's statement that, "This car will never break down," is an express warranty, because it is a statement presented as a fact or promise. A statement that, "This car has six cylinders" also creates an express warranty because it describes the goods. You'll note here that you create the opportunity for express warranties all day long because you (most likely) have a practice of describing vehicle features to customers. Finally, an express warranty also can be created by a sample or model, if the customer assumes that the goods purchased will conform to the sample or model.

In addition to the expression (be it the promise, description, or sample), there is one other element that must be present for an express warranty to be created; that is, the expression must be "part of the basis of the bargain." In other words, the buyer must rely on the expression, and he or she must expect that the goods he or she is purchasing will conform to the expression. It is very likely any expression made to the buyer before you close the sale will be assumed to be "part of the basis of the bargain." Sometimes, even expressions made to the buyer after the sale might also become "part of the basis of the bargain."

To complicate matters further, express warranties can be either written or oral. Verbal statements can be express warranties, as can advertisements in newspapers and other media.

The MMWA only applies to express warranties if they are in writing. However, there is plenty of state law out there that gives effect to express oral warranties, so always be careful what you say.

Implied Warranties

Implied warranties are entirely different animals. They are creatures of laws passed by your "friendly" state legislatures. The seller/warrantor doesn't need to do anything for these warranties to apply. The warranties do not need to be written or appear in any type of documentation. The law automatically attaches them to goods when they are sold. Examples of implied warranties are the implied "warranty of merchantability" and the implied "warranty of fitness for a particular purpose."

Example #1: An "implied warranty of merchantability" is a promise that the goods sold will do what they are supposed to do, without any major problems. For example, vehicles are supposed to drive—so unless the seller disclaims it, vehicles are sold with an implied warranty of merchantability that promises the purchaser that it will drive. Thus, if the vehicle breaks down within some reasonable period of time after the sale, the implied warranty that it will drive without major problems is probably breached.

Example #2: The "implied warranty of fitness for a particular purpose" is a promise that the goods are suited for a particular purpose or task. The particular purpose must be one that the consumer has identified to the seller, and the seller has assured the buyer that the goods will fulfill. For example, if a consumer has said that he needs a truck to haul a full ton of weight, and the salesperson has assured the consumer that the truck could handle such weight (or even if the salesperson stayed quiet purposely on the issue, knowing that the consumer had this specific need), the truck had better do so, or the implied warranty of fitness for a particular purpose will have been breached.

Implied warranties can generally be disclaimed and waived, so long as specific language is used to do so. But, as explained later in this chapter, if the seller or manufacturer gives a written warranty, the MMWA prohibits the disclaimer of the implied warranties.

6. What's covered under the MMWA and its regulation?
The MMWA applies only to written warranties and implied warranties on "consumer goods." It does not apply to oral warranties. It also does not apply to warranties on services. Thus, if a written warranty is not offered and there are no implied warranties (for example, where you disclaimed them

effectively), the MMWA does not apply. If the product is not a consumer good, the MMWA does not apply. However, if the written warranty covers both goods and services, the MMWA will apply to the whole—both the goods and services. A note of caution here—state laws may give effect to warranties not covered by the MMWA.

7. What do the MMWA and its regulation and Interpretations generally require?

Let's start with the MMWA. There are three basic requirements under the MMWA on which all other requirements are based.

- First, if a seller or manufacturer gives a written warranty, the MMWA requires that it be clearly and conspicuously labeled as "full" or "limited." This requirement applies to all consumer products valued over $10.

- Second, the warranty coverage information must be contained in a single, clear, and easy-to-read document. This requirement applies to all consumer products valued over $5.

- Third, warrantors and sellers must ensure that written warranties are available where the consumer goods are sold, so that consumers have an opportunity to read the warranties before making the purchase. This requirement applies to all consumer products valued over $15.

Under the MMWA, Congress directed the FTC to specify the rules regarding how these basic requirements would work. Many times Congress gave the FTC specific guidance as to what they wanted covered; other times it did not. Thus, the FTC in its regulation and Interpretations put "the meat on the bones." The regulation and Interpretations will be covered in the remainder of this chapter, including the content of what must be included in "full" and "limited" warranties, how warrantors are to make written warranties accessible to consumers before the sale, and how disputes are to be resolved.

8. What is a "consumer good" anyway?

A "consumer good" is tangible personal property normally used for personal, family, or household purposes. How the buyer will ultimately use the product is irrelevant. Rather, what is important is how the product typically is utilized. If it is used typically for personal, family, or household purposes, it is a "consumer good" under the MMWA. If it can also be used for commercial purposes, but generally is used for personal, family, or household purposes, it will be deemed a "consumer good" under the MMWA. (A consumer good sometimes will be referred to as a "consumer product" in this chapter.)

9. Are all consumer goods covered by the MMWA and its regulations?

Practically speaking, yes—but officially, no. Certain provisions in the MMWA and its regulations apply only to warranties covering consumer goods costing more than a specified amount. The provisions in the MMWA that relate to the *content* of warranties (that is, what the warranty *must say*), apply to all warranties covering consumer goods costing more than $5.

Provisions in the MMWA and the FTC's warranty regulations regarding disclosure and the pre-sale availability of warranties apply to consumer goods costing more than $15. Some of the provisions dealing with the designation of warranties apply only to those warranties for products costing the consumer more than $10.

10. What are some other basic terms used in the MMWA and its regulation and Interpretations, and what do they mean?

Here is a list of the key definitions contained and used in the MMWA and its regulation and Interpretations.

Consumer

A buyer of any consumer product (not including someone who buys consumer products for resale, or with the intention of resale, no matter whether the product is actually resold), or any person the product is transferred to during the duration of the implied or written warranty or service contract, and any other person who can enforce the warranty or service contract obligations against the warrantor or service contractor.

Consumer Product

Any tangible personal property that is distributed in commerce, which is normally used for personal, family, or household purposes. Remember, it is what the product is normally used for that matters. Thus, a product that is normally considered a consumer product, even if used for commercial purposes, is still a consumer product subject to the MMWA. For example, most automobiles are consumer products, even though they may be purchased for a commercial fleet. On the other hand, a dump truck is probably not a consumer product, even though, if you're a bit odd, you might buy one for recreational purposes.

Warrantor

Any supplier or other person, who gives, or offers to give, a written warranty or who is obligated under an implied warranty.

Supplier

Any person engaged in the business of making a consumer product directly or indirectly available to consumers.

Commerce

Trade, traffic, commerce, or transportation (i) that is between a place in one state and any place outside such state or (ii) that affects trade, traffic, commerce, or transportation in between states. This is a broad definition that covers almost everything you can think of.

Service Contract

A contract in writing to perform, over a definite period of time, maintenance and/or repair services on a consumer product.

Distributed in Commerce

Sold in commerce, introduced or delivered for introduction into commerce, or held for sale or distribution after introduction into commerce. "Distributed in commerce" does not include consumer products exported to foreign jurisdictions, unless distributed to a military post in a foreign jurisdiction.

Written Warranty

Any written promise or factual statement that promises or states that workmanship and/or material provided is defect free or will perform at a particular level over a definite period of time, and which is made in connection with the sale of a consumer product by a supplier to a buyer. A key requirement is that the written promise or factual statement is included in the cost of the consumer product—the consumer does not have to pay any extra for the benefit of this promise; or

Any writing under which the supplier promises to refund, repair, replace, or take other corrective action with respect to a consumer product sold in the event that the consumer product fails to meet the specifications set forth in the writing. Again, the key component is that this promise to meet the specifications set forth in the writing is included in the cost of the consumer product and the consumer doesn't have to pay any extra for it. Note that the MMWA's definition of written warranty covers more than just the express warranties discussed previously.

An example of a promise that is not a "written warranty" is a "free trial period." This occurs when a dealership gives the consumer the right to return the vehicle within X days after purchase in the event the consumer decides he or she just doesn't want it. In this case, the consumer could return the vehicle, regardless of whether it had any problems or defects.

Reasonable and Necessary Maintenance

Maintenance that the consumer can be reasonably expected to perform and that is necessary to keep the consumer product performing as intended and operating at a reasonable level of performance (for example, keeping the tires inflated to the appropriate level and changing the oil when needed).

Remedy

The measures that the MMWA (and its regulation and Interpretations) require the warrantor to take to "fix" the situation when a written warranty has been breached. The MMWA provides for three measures—repair, replacement, and refund. The warrantor may choose which measure(s) it wishes to offer the consumer as his or her remedy under the written warranty. There is one limitation, however. The warrantor can't choose a refund unless (i) the consumer is willing to accept a refund or (ii) the warrantor cannot repair or replace the consumer product (because it is not commercially reasonable or cannot be completed in a timely manner).

Replacement

Providing a new consumer product that is identical or reasonably equivalent to the warranted consumer product.

Refund

Refunding the actual purchase price, less reasonable depreciation based on actual use.

On the Face of the Warranty

Text placement either on (i) the side of the page where the warranty text begins, if the warranty is on a single page with the text appearing on both sides; or (ii) the page where the warranty text begins, if the warranty is a multi-page document; or (iii) the page where the warranty text begins, when the warranty is included in a document that contains other things, such as a use and care manual.

Mechanism

An informal dispute settlement procedure that is incorporated into the written warranty terms.

Members

The person(s) actually deciding the dispute within the mechanism.

11. So what are the differences between "full" and "limited" warranties anyway?

Remember that the MMWA requires all written warranties on consumer products worth more than $10 to have a clear and conspicuous label as either "full" or "limited." A "full" warranty is one that meets the minimum federal standards for warranties, requiring that *all* of the following are true:

- The duration of implied warranties is not limited.

- The warranty coverage is not limited to the original purchaser (in other words, the warranty extends to anyone who owns the covered goods).

- The warranty service is provided without charge, including costs related to returning the product or removing and reinstalling the product. (Incidental expenses the consumer incurs are not considered a charge that the warrantor must reimburse, unless the remedy is not completed within a reasonable time or the warrantor imposes an unreasonable duty on the consumer to get the remedy).

- If, after a reasonable number of tries, the consumer product cannot be repaired, the consumer receives, at the consumer's discretion, either a replacement product or full refund.

- Customers do not have to perform any unreasonable duties as a prerequisite for receiving service, beyond notification that service is needed. Note that requiring customers to return a warranty registration card or similar notice, or else the "full" warranty is void, is considered an unreasonable duty. However, the warrantor may suggest that the customer fill out and return a card as proof of the date of purchase, but this suggestion must be accompanied by a notice informing the customer that failure to return the card does not affect the customer's rights under the warranty.

If any one of the above statements is not true, the warranty cannot be labeled as "full." Rather, it must be labeled as a "limited" warranty. A warranty also may be part "full" and part "limited." For example, a motor vehicle may be warranted for defects for two years and satisfy all of the above requirements (a "full" warranty), then for years three through five, the consumer may have a warranty on parts, but not on labor (a "limited" warranty). Written warranties that are both "full" and "limited" must clearly differentiate between the two, labeling one part as "full" and the other as "limited."

12. Are there any disclosures that apply to all written warranties, both "full" and "limited"?

Yes, there are general disclosures that apply to all types of written warranties.

Written warranties for consumer products worth more than $15 must contain the following items of information in language that is clear and easily understood:

- The identity of the parties whom the written warranty covers, and if the written warranty coverage is limited to the original consumer purchaser, a statement to that effect.

- What is covered under the warranty and what is excluded, including clear descriptions and identifications of parts, characteristics, components, or properties.

- The point in time or event upon which the warranty term begins and its expiration.

- What remedies exist when a problem occurs. This must include a statement of what the warrantor will do if a defect, malfunction, or failure to conform with the written warranty occurs, including what items or services the warrantor will, or will not, pay or provide for and the length of time it will take to remedy the problem. In addition, the warrantor must provide a step-by-step explanation of the procedure the consumer should follow to get performance of the warranty. The explanation should include the name of the warrantor, the warrantor's mailing address, and its toll-free telephone number. Furthermore, the consumer must understand what expenses are not covered (for example, time lost from work, gas expenses). Finally, the warrantor must alert the consumer to any informal dispute mechanism included in the written warranty.

- A statement regarding the state law impact on the consumer's rights. Every written warranty *must* contain the following language, adopted by the FTC: "This warranty gives you specific legal rights, and you may also have other rights which vary from state to state."

These disclosures must be provided in a *single document,* which must be labeled as either a "full" or "limited" warranty, as applicable.

13. Are there any other disclosures that must be provided?

Well, that depends on the terms of the written warranty. If the warranty contains a provision that restricts the duration of an implied warranty (remember, this can occur only with a "limited" warranty), the following statement approved by the FTC must be included:

> Some states do not allow limitations on how long an implied warranty lasts, so the above limitation may not apply to you.

If the warranty contains a provision that restricts or eliminates potential liability for consequential or incidental damages, the following statement approved by the FTC must be included:

> Some states do not allow the exclusion or limitation of incidental or consequential damages, so the above limitation or exclusion may not apply to you.

If the warranty restricts *who* has rights under the warranty *(remember, this can only occur with a "limited" warranty)*, the warranty document has to explain what kind of consumer has rights under the warranty (for example, only the original purchaser and not any future owners). Also, don't forget the necessary disclosures about the mechanism for alternative resolution of disputes discussed later in Question 17.

14. Do copies of written warranties need to be available before the sale?

Yes. Written warranties covering products that cost the consumer more than $15 must be made available to the consumer *before* he or she makes the purchase. The MMWA requires that sellers of consumer products with a written warranty make the text of the written warranty readily available by displaying the text of the warranty in close proximity to the warranted product. Alternatively, the seller can provide the text of the warranty prior to the sale upon request by the consumer. This is only allowed if the seller has placed signs in prominent locations advising consumers of the availability of the written warranty and when the signs are reasonably likely to make the consumer ask for the warranty.

If the consumer product is purchased through the mail, by telephone, or over the Internet (in other words, the consumer can order the product without actually making a personal visit to the dealership), the seller must clearly and conspicuously disclose either the full text of the written warranty or that the written warranty can be obtained by the consumer upon request at a specified address free of charge. In written media (for example, catalogs and websites), this disclosure must appear on the page describing the warranted product or on the page facing the page describing the warranted product.

To enable the seller to comply with the pre-sale availability obligation, the warrantor (as distinguished from the seller) must provide the seller with:

- A copy of the written warranty with every warranted product; *and/or*

- A tag, sign, sticker, label, decal, or other attachment to the product that contains the full text of the warranty; *and/or*

- A display package, carton, or other container to which the text of the warranty is attached or printed on (a copy of the warranty would also have to accompany each warranted product); *and/or*

- A notice, sign, or poster disclosing the text of the warranty (a copy of the warranty would also have to accompany each warranted product).

15. Do the MMWA and its regulation and Interpretations place any restrictions or requirements regarding written warranties in advertisements?

Technically no, but practically yes. The pre-sale availability requirements discussed in Question 14 will apply to advertisements of consumer goods costing more than $15 with written warranties. The advertisement should indicate that a copy of the warranty is available for review prior to the sale in the location where the product is sold. If the advertisement discusses buying the item by mail, telephone, or Internet, it should inform consumers how to get a copy of the warranty before a purchase.

16. Are there certain things that are prohibited acts under the MMWA?

Yes. The MMWA puts certain restrictions on implied warranties, "tie-in sales" provisions, and deceptive or misleading warranty terms.

Implied Warranties

The MMWA regulation provides that if a written warranty is given, or if the seller offers its own service contract (this would not include offering for sale a service contract that is provided by a third party like the manufacturer), and sells it to the consumer, the warrantor may not disclaim or exclude the implied warranties. For service contracts, this restriction applies when it is sold the same day as the consumer good to which it applies or within 90 days after that sale. Even though the implied warranties cannot be disclaimed, the "duration" or time period during which a consumer may raise a breach of an implied warranty may be limited. The duration may be limited to the same period of time that applies to the written warranty or service contract. One notable exception is a "full" warranty. The implied warranties cannot be limited in any way when a "full" warranty is given. It's important to understand that these rules apply no matter what the actual written warranty says.

As mentioned previously, the duration of implied warranties can be limited in some circumstances. To be effective, the limitation must be prominently displayed *on the face of the warranty,* and it has to be stated in clear and unmistakable language. For example, if the supplier offers a one-year "limited" warranty, the supplier can also state that implied warranties are limited to one year as well. The differences between "full" and "limited" warranties are discussed in greater detail in Question 11.

"Tie-in Sales" Provisions

A "tie-in sales" provision is one in which the purchaser is required to buy an item or service from a particular company to keep the warranty in effect. These types of provisions are generally prohibited. The only time they are allowed is when (i) the item or service required is necessary to make the product work properly, (ii) the FTC has given its prior approval to such a provision, or (iii) the item or service required is free of charge. An example of an impermissible "tie-in sales" provision is: "In order to keep your *Premium Brand* motor vehicle warranty in effect, you must only use *Premium Brand* replacement products and have your motor vehicle serviced at *The Best Service Station, Inc.*" Though this type of requirement is prohibited, the following is permissible: "While we recommend that service of the motor vehicle be performed at *The Best Service Station, Inc.,* you may have your motor vehicle serviced by any company. However, improper or incorrect service voids the warranty."

Deceptive Warranty Terms

Deceptive warranties are prohibited. A deceptive warranty is one that contains false or deceptive statements or is missing necessary information—the absence of which would mislead a reasonable and careful consumer. For example, a consumer product that comes with both "full" and "limited" warranties, but fails to distinguish between the two in a clear and conspicuous manner, will be found to contain deceptive warranty terms. This is because the consumer could reasonably conclude that the "full" warranty applies to areas in which only the "limited" warranty applies. The warranty is missing crucial information; therefore, it is misleading.

17. How are warranty disputes decided?

Although consumers may sue for a breach of warranty and recover court costs and attorney's fees, the MMWA and its regulation and Interpretations encourage that warranty disputes be settled through informal dispute resolution "mechanisms" (as defined in Question 10). Accordingly, the MMWA provides that written warranties may include provisions requiring consumers to use a dispute resolution mechanism before going to court. If such a requirement is included in the warranty, it must include the following—clearly and conspicuously—*on the face of the warranty:*

- A statement of the availability of the informal dispute resolution mechanism

- The name and address of the mechanism (for example, the National Arbitration Forum) or the name and telephone number of the mechanism that consumers may use without charge

- A statement that explains if the consumer must use the mechanism before pursuing litigation, and if the consumer seeks remedies not covered by the MMWA, he or she is not required to use the mechanism

- A statement explaining where further information on the mechanism can be found (for example, a website)

The following information also must be provided either in the written warranty or in a separate section of materials accompanying the product:

- An appropriate method of contact. That is, one either addressed to the mechanism with spaces indicating the type of information the mechanism may require to quickly resolve the warranty dispute, *or* a telephone number of the mechanism that the consumers may use without charge

- The name and address of the mechanism

- A brief description of the mechanism

- The time limits the mechanism requires

- The types of information the mechanism may require to quickly resolve the warranty dispute

When a dispute arises, the warrantor must attempt to make the consumer reasonably aware of the mechanism's existence. Note that there are extensive provisions describing (i) the process once a dispute is submitted for resolution; (ii) who may qualify as a "member" (as defined in Question 10) to resolve the dispute; and (iii) other characteristics of the mechanism's organization, such as recordkeeping requirements (for example, a requirement that the mechanism maintain complete records of all disputes), operational procedures (for example, the dispute resolution process), and audits (for example, a requirement that the mechanism perform annual audits to ensure compliance with the MMWA and its regulation).

18. How does the MMWA treat service contracts?

Service contracts, unlike warranties, are bought separately from the product. They are optional, and they provide additional protection beyond what the warranty provides. While warranties are free and part of the "basis of the bargain," service contracts must be purchased for an additional amount. They can be purchased when the product is bought or later. The MMWA requires that service contracts contain conspicuous terms and conditions and that they be written in simple and easily understood language. Service contracts, unlike written warranties, are not required to be labeled as "full" or "limited," and there are no specific disclosure requirements. However, recall that the MMWA and its regulation and Interpretations prohibit disclaiming or limiting implied warranties on a consumer product when the seller's own service contract is sold.

Chapter 10

The Federal Odometer Act

By Patricia E.M. Covington

Twenty-Five Things a Car Dealer Needs to Know About the Federal Odometer Act

The Federal Odometer Act (FOA) requires sellers of motor vehicles to disclose to buyers the odometer reading of the vehicle being sold. Also, it prohibits tampering with odometer devices. The FOA identifies specific rules for odometer disclosures and contains other related requirements and prohibitions. It was enacted to ensure that the mileage readings on odometer devices are accurate, so that buyers will have a reliable reference when determining the condition and value of a vehicle they are considering for purchase. It not only requires sellers of motor vehicles to disclose the odometer reading to a purchaser, but it also prohibits a seller from tampering with odometer devices.

1. What is the Federal Odometer Act?

The FOA is a federal law. It was passed by Congress to prevent the manipulation of odometer devices and the mileage readings on them so that purchasers could rely on an accurate reading of the vehicle's mileage. It requires a person transferring ownership of a vehicle ("transferor") to give to the person to whom the vehicle is being transferred ("transferee") a written disclosure of the odometer's mileage reading. If the transferor knows that the odometer reading is incorrect or inaccurate, he or she must state in the disclosure that the actual mileage is unknown. Because the FOA is a law passed by Congress (as opposed to a regulation, issued by a government agency), only Congress may change it.

2. Does FOA have an accompanying regulation?

Yes. Congress directed the Department of Transportation (DOT) to make regulations to implement the requirements of the FOA. Because the DOT (a government agency) issued the regulations, it can amend and revise them.

3. Where can I find the FOA and the implementing regulations?

The FOA is located in Title 49 of the United States Code, beginning at section 32701, and can be found at www.dealer deskbook.com/resources/foa/. The regulation implementing the FOA is at 49 C.F.R. Part 580, and can be found at www.dealerdesk book.com/resources/foaregulations/.

4. What do the FOA and its regulation generally require?

The most well-known requirement under the FOA is that a seller or other transferor of a motor vehicle must give the transferee (the person receiving the vehicle) a written, accurate disclosure of the odometer's mileage reading. If the transferor knows that the odometer is incorrect or inaccurate, then the statement must indicate that the actual mileage is "unknown."

The odometer disclosure must be made on the vehicle's title unless the title does not have space available for making the transfer and the odometer disclosure. Then, and only then, may the disclosure be made on an official state reassignment form that also provides for the odometer disclosure. The FOA and its regulation provide that "[i]n the case of a transferor in whose name the vehicle is titled, the transferor shall disclose the mileage on the title, and not on a reassignment document." This does not mean that the FOA applies only to a transferor whose name is listed on the title. Any title owner of the vehicle so named—by being on the title, by the title being reassigned on the title itself, or by the title being reassigned through use of an official state reassignment form—must make the FOA disclosure on the title. This ensures that transferees have the opportunity to inspect the prior odometer disclosures appearing on the title. A person cannot make the odometer disclosure on an official state reassignment form, unless there are no spaces available on the title for the disclosure.

The FOA also prohibits persons from tampering with the odometer. This means that a person cannot sell, use, install, or have installed a device that makes the odometer register mileage different from the actual miles driven. Further, a person cannot disconnect, reset, alter, or otherwise have these things done to change the mileage registered by the odometer. Also, if someone knows that the odometer is disconnected or not working, he or she is prohibited from operating the vehicle with the intent to defraud. To say that another way, if you intentionally drive a car with an inoperable odometer, with the intention not to reveal the miles driven to a subsequent buyer, that's fraud.

5. What is a transfer under the FOA?

A transfer is a change in ownership, whether by sale, gift, or any other means.

6. What if all the spaces on the title have been used; how can the odometer disclosure statement be completed on the title?

As mentioned in Question 4, if all of the spaces for the odometer disclosure have been filled in, a transferor is permitted to complete the odometer disclosure on the state's official reassignment form.

7. What happens if the title is lost or with the lienholder?

If the transferor's title is not available because it is either lost or still in possession of the lienholder, he or she can empower another person to give the disclosure on his or her behalf. The FOA requires the use of a special written power of attorney printed by the state on secure paper ("secure power of attorney"). This is not an ordinary power of attorney—here, the authority conveyed is issued by the state and must be printed through a secure process.

How does the "secure power of attorney" work? The transferor makes his or her disclosure of the odometer reading on the secure power of attorney. The transferor also names an attorney-in-fact to complete the odometer disclosure on his or her behalf (often, this is the dealer who accepts a trade subject to a lien). The person named in the secure power of attorney can then make the odometer disclosure on the title when it is received.

How is the procedure described and implemented? The secure power of attorney is divided into three parts—Part A, Part B, and Part C.

- Part A is the *power of attorney to disclose mileage* and is completed when someone transferring a vehicle doesn't have possession of the title, because it is either lost or in the possession of the lienholder (for example, a trade-in scenario). When completed, this part authorizes a third-party (usually the dealer) to make the mileage disclosure on the title with the information provided by the transferor in Part A. It also appoints this person's attorney-in-fact to sign the transferor's name on the title.

- Part B is the *power of attorney to review title documents* and is completed when the transferee from the transfer done under Part A intends to re-transfer the vehicle to yet

195

another person prior to receiving possession of the title (for example, a dealer who receives a trade-in then sells it before having received the title from the lienholder). It is completed by the new transferee and authorizes the original transferee (and now the transferor—usually the dealer) to make the odometer disclosure on the title when received. It also authorizes the original transferee to sign on the new transferee's behalf. Note that Part B is also used by a dealer when the title is issued in the dealer's name; it is held by the lienholder, *and* the lienholder's name and security interest are identified on the title

- Part C is the *power of attorney certification* and must be completed if both Parts A and B are completed. It is a certification that the title (and any reassignment documents) have been received and reviewed, and that no mileage discrepancies exist between the title (and any reassignment documents) and the secure power of attorney (in other words, the mileage disclosed on the title was not more than that disclosed in Parts A and B). Part C must only be completed when both Parts A and B are used.

8. What if there are two or more owners of a vehicle? Must all owners complete the odometer disclosure?

If there are two or more people listed on the title as owners, only one is required to complete and sign the odometer disclosure.

9. Must the odometer disclosure statement be written?

Yes. The FOA and its implementing regulations require a written odometer disclosure statement. That means, at least for now, it cannot be in an electronic format; nor, of course, can it be done verbally.

10. What exactly is on the odometer disclosure statement?

The statement must contain the odometer reading at the time of transfer (in whole miles), the date of the transfer, and a description of the vehicle (year, make, model, body type, and VIN). It must also contain the transferor's name and current address and the transferee's name and current address. The transferor must certify with his or her signature that—to the best of his or her knowledge—at least *one* of the following is true:

- The odometer reading reflects the actual mileage;

- The vehicle's mileage is actually more than that recorded on the odometer reading; or

- The odometer reading differs from the actual mileage and that the difference is more than would be caused by a calibration error. (A statement must be included that the odometer reading does not reflect the actual mileage and, therefore, should not be relied upon.)

The transferee must sign the disclosure statement. Keep in mind that no person can sign an odometer disclosure as both a transferor and transferee, except when a secure power of attorney form names the same person to sign as both transferor and transferee. This is only permitted when the title is in the possession of a lienholder or the title has been lost.

11. Can a dealer accept a vehicle if the odometer disclosure statement is incomplete?

No. No person acquiring a vehicle for resale may accept the odometer disclosure statement unless it is complete.

12. *Are leases handled in the same manner as a regular sale?*

Well, yes and no. Yes, in that an odometer disclosure statement must be completed for a leased vehicle subsequently sold to the lessee or another party. (Note that this is different from a vehicle leased to the customer. For those transactions, the vehicle is still being sold first—albeit, to the leasing company.) The disclosure process differs when the vehicle is in the possession of the lessee. Under the FOA, the lessor can require the lessee to complete the disclosure requirements on its behalf. The lessor gives the lessee a written notice telling him or her of the lessee's requirement to complete the odometer disclosure, that it is required by the FOA, and that there are penalties for failing to do so ("Lessor-Lessee Odometer Disclosure"). This disclosure often appears in the lease agreement. In addition to the notice provided above, the Lessor-Lessee Odometer Disclosure contains the following information, which must be completed by the appropriate party:

- The current odometer reading;
- The lessee's printed name;
- The lessee's signature;
- The date of the lessee's disclosure statement;
- The lessee's name and current address;
- The lessor's name and current address;
- The vehicle information (year, make, model, body type, and VIN);
- The date the lessor notified the lessee of her/his disclosure requirements;
- The date of the lessee's disclosure;

- The date the lessor received the completed disclosure statement; and

- The lessor's signature.

The lessee completes and signs this form and it is delivered to the lessor. With form in hand, the lessor is entitled to rely on the lessee's written disclosure unless the lessor has reason to believe that the mileage disclosed by the lessee does not reflect the actual mileage of the vehicle.

13. What if the odometer device is not working or otherwise needs repair?

Don't worry; odometer devices may be serviced and repaired. However, the mileage registered must remain the same after the service or repair. If the mileage cannot remain the same, it must be adjusted to zero and the owner must attach a written notice to the left door frame identifying the mileage before the service and the date of the service, repair, or replacement ("After Repair Notice"). No one may remove or alter, with the intent to defraud, the After Repair Notice. Also note that the transferor must tell the transferee of the After Repair Notice, and he or she cannot give a false statement in this notice.

14. Are there any other requirements?

Yes, in particular where there are multiple transfers of a vehicle. Remember that each transfer (assuming each transferee takes title to the vehicle) requires a separate FOA disclosure signed by the applicable transferee and transferor.

Think about a three-party transaction with a seller (Larry), a buyer (Moe), and a subsequent buyer (Curly). Moe buys the vehicle from Larry and takes title to it. Larry gives Moe a secure power of attorney to make the FOA disclosure on his behalf because Larry's title is currently at the bank, which has a lien on the vehicle to be paid off. Sometime later, Moe sells the vehicle to Curly. If Curly asks, Moe must show him a copy of both Larry's title and the secure power of attorney that authorized Moe to complete the FOA disclosure for Larry.

Let's assume for a moment that when Curly buys the vehicle from Moe, Moe is still waiting for his title to arrive. Let's also assume that, for whatever reason, Curly doesn't want to give Moe a power of attorney to sign Moe's title on Curly's behalf (thus transferring ownership from Moe to Curly). Instead Curly elects to return to Moe's dealership to sign the title after Moe receives it. If Curly asks, Moe must show Curly a copy of the secure power of attorney Moe received from Larry.

15. Are certain transactions exempted from the FOA?

Yes. An odometer disclosure statement is not required for a vehicle not previously titled (for example, a new vehicle that is being transferred for resale). Also, the FOA does not apply to the sale or transfer of new vehicles from a vehicle manufacturer to a dealer. Nor does it apply to a person engaged in the business of renting or leasing vehicles for a period of 30 days or less. A new vehicle, for purposes of this exemption, is one with no more mileage than necessary to move, transport, or road test prior to delivery from the manufacturer to the dealer; that is, no more than 300 miles.

16. Are any vehicles exempted from the FOA's requirements?

Yes. Under the FOA, the DOT is empowered to exempt vehicles. Thus far, it has elected to exempt the following:

- Vehicles over 16,000 pounds,

- Vehicles that are not self-propelled, or
- Vehicles manufactured in a model year beginning at least 10 years before January 1 of the calendar year in which the transfer occurs.

17. Will the state reject an application for a new title if the odometer disclosure is not properly completed?

Probably. The FOA and its regulation prohibit state vehicle titling agencies (for example, Department of Motor Vehicles, Motor Vehicle Division, etc.) from titling a vehicle, unless the transferee submits with his or her application for title the transferor's title with the odometer disclosure on it, assuming there is sufficient space for the mileage to be disclosed. If there is not sufficient space, then a properly completed official state reassignment form can be submitted.

18. Are there recordkeeping requirements?

Yes. Dealers are required to retain written odometer disclosures for five years. Dealers may retain a photocopy, carbon, or other facsimile copy. These records must be retained at a dealer's primary place of business, and they have to be retained in some manner that provides for a systematic retrieval of these disclosures. In other words, you must be able to put your hands on the statements pretty quickly when called on to do so. Saving the forms by date is always a good idea.

Lessors are also required to retain the disclosures for five years with the same requirements. Lessors must retain the odometer disclosures made by the lessee (see Lessor-Lessee Odometer Disclosure described in Question 12) for four years following the date the leased vehicle is transferred. Secure powers of attorney forms (issued by the state on secure paper) must be retained for five years. If the vehicle is sold at auction, the auction company must maintain the following for four years:

- The name of the most recent owner (except for the auction company),

- The name of the buyer,

- The VIN, and

- The odometer reading on the date the auction company took possession of the vehicle.

19. Can anyone "willy-nilly" come in and look at the odometer readings on vehicles and the statements collected?

Well, yeah—sort of. Under the FOA, the DOT has authority to inspect the documents related to odometer disclosures (for example, disclosure statements, secure powers of attorney, the After Repair Notice, the Lessor-Lessee Odometer Disclosure, etc.). The DOT also may institute an investigation to enforce the FOA and its regulations and to ensure compliance. The DOT may enter and inspect commercial and non-commercial premises and inspect vehicles, and it can impound these vehicles for up to 72 hours.

20. Are there penalties or other consequences for non-compliance or a violation?

Absolutely. The DOT may impose a penalty of up to $2,000 per violation. Note that each vehicle involved is a separate violation. A person can find a little comfort in the fact that the maximum amount, which can be collected for a series of violations, is $100,000—still, quite painful.

Also, there are criminal consequences. A person who knowingly and willfully violates a requirement or prohibition can be fined, or imprisoned for up to three years, or both. If the person is a corporation (in other words, a business), these criminal penalties may be imposed on a director, an officer, or an individual agent of the corporation involved. This means if a person of the business knowingly and willfully authorizes, orders, or performs the violation, he or she can go to jail or prison for the violation and pay a hefty fine. (Think twice if you know such shady business is occurring and you simply are ignoring it or acting as if you don't know about it.)

Furthermore, your local state Attorney General can sue. He or she may bring a civil action to enforce the FOA, either to enjoin further violations and/or to recover the civil penalties allowed for those injured. Finally, as most of us already know, any person hurt by non-compliance or violation may sue to enforce the requirements and prohibitions. He or she can collect three times the actual damages, or $1,500, whichever is greater, if the violator acted with intent to defraud.

Finally, persons granted a secure power of attorney (to complete the odometer disclosure on behalf of the transferor) also are subject to these penalties and consequences. And, if a private individual brings a civil action, he or she may collect reasonable attorney's fees if judgment is entered in his or her favor.

21. What is the statute of limitations for a claim based on a FOA violation? In other words, how much time must pass after the violation before a consumer is barred from suing me?

The statute of limitations is two years from the date the claim accrues—that means two years from the date the violation occurred.

22. Are there any defenses to a civil claim for a violation of the FOA and its regulations?

Very few to none. (See Questions 24 and 25).

23. Can the states regulate the area of odometers?

Yes. The FOA permits states to regulate the tampering with, disconnecting, and altering of odometers, so long as their laws are not inconsistent with the FOA. Any part of a state's law that is inconsistent with the FOA and its regulation cannot be enforced.

24. When exactly can a private individual sue a dealer and collect money damages based on a violation of the FOA?

This one is tough. It really depends on your geography. Some courts have held that to collect damages under the FOA (three times the actual damages, or $1,500, whichever is greater) the claim brought must be based on a violation where the violator had intent to defraud with respect to the *vehicle's mileage*. One of the more notable decisions is *Ioffe v. Skokie Motor Sales*, 414 F.3rd 708 (7th Circuit 2005). In *Ioffe*, the Court of Appeals held that a claim fails as a matter of law unless the plaintiff can prove that the defendant had intent to defraud the purchaser specifically as to the mileage. If the defendant has intent to defraud as to anything else, he is not liable. The intent to defraud is specific to odometer reading.

Other courts have held that whenever there is "intent to defraud" involved and *any* violation *of the FOA occurs*, a violator can be held liable for damages. A notable decision holding this way is *Owens v. Samkle Automotive, Inc.*, 2005 WL 2318643 (11th Circuit 2005). Under this interpretation, the violation of the FOA does not have to relate to the vehicle's mileage or an inaccurate odometer disclosure. It can be based on any violation of the FOA, so long as there is intent to defraud. For example, an FOA violation may occur if a disclosure is made on an official state reassignment form, instead of the actual title, because the seller does not wish the buyer to know certain information appearing on the title (for example, that the vehicle previously was a rental vehicle.)

Thus, under the more general "any violation" interpretation, if a person violates the FOA, and does so with the intent to defraud, he or she can be held liable.

By the way, the *Ioffe* holding reflects the majority view of most courts that have considered the issue. The *Owens* decision is the minority view, and it is not uncommon for a minority view to win the day as the issue climbs up the judicial ladder. Bottom line—consult with your attorney if you have questions about this one.

Not to beat a dead horse, but remember the one important element that must always be present—that is, the *intent* to defraud. If there is no intent to defraud, there can be no liability for damages to a private individual. The DOT or your state Attorney General could come chasing, though.

25. Must a dealer have actual knowledge that the odometer reading is incorrect for "intent to defraud" to be found?

While there must be intent to defraud, a court can find that intent exists when the dealer has actual knowledge of the inaccuracy or "shoulda" known about it. Courts have held that a dealer need not have "actual knowledge" that the odometer reading is inaccurate before liability can be imposed, and that "reckless disregard" is sufficient. This issue is litigated frequently in the courts. Most courts take the position that if there are any indicators that the mileage is inaccurate, the dealer must appropriately investigate. By doing nothing (failing to investigate), courts have held that the dealer acted with "reckless disregard" or had "constructive knowledge" sufficient to establish an intent to defraud. Indicators would include that the vehicle isn't in the condition one would expect for a vehicle with the mileage disclosed. Therefore, the failure to verify the odometer disclosure, especially in light of clues or red flags that the reading is inaccurate, can be sufficient to establish "intent to defraud."

The Gramm-Leach-Bliley Act & Privacy Regulations: Privacy Notices & Safeguards Rule

By Alicia H. Tortarolo

CHAPTER 11

Five, Fifteen, and Sixteen Things a Dealer Should Know About the Gramm-Leach-Bliley Act & the FTC Privacy Rule and Safeguards Rule

Think about the types of "Customer Information" that flow through your dealership each day. Then, consider your dealership's responsibility for that information, and what would happen if that information fell into the wrong hands, or was used in a way that was harmful, unfair, or deceptive to a customer.

The Gramm-Leach-Bliley Act (GLB Act) was intended to raise consumers' awareness about how their personal information is shared and to protect consumers from threats of identity theft and other harm by requiring financial institutions (yes, this means *you*, Mr. Dealer!) to take steps to protect this information. Question 5 explains why a dealership must worry about identity theft and other harm. Understanding your obligations under the GLB Act is key to understanding your dealership's responsibilities.

Part One: Five Things to Know for Starters

1. What is the Gramm-Leach-Bliley Act?
The GLB Act is the main federal law that sets forth your dealership's obligations regarding sensitive information that flows in and out of your dealership. GLB has two main parts—the Privacy Rule and the Safeguards Rule.

The **Privacy Rule** is concerned with how your dealership shares information about customers who obtain, or apply for, credit or lease products from your dealership. It deals primarily with disclosures you make to non-affiliated third parties. Disclosures you make to your affiliates are governed by the Fair Credit Reporting Act (see Chapter 5).

The *Safeguards Rule* addresses how your dealership protects information about its finance and lease customers.

2. Where can I find the Gramm-Leach-Bliley Act, the Privacy Rule, and the Safeguards Rule?

The GLB Act, the FTC Privacy Rule, and the FTC Safeguards Rule are available on the FTC's website at www.ftc.gov. Regulation P is the Consumer Financial Protection Bureau (CFPB) Privacy Rule and is available on the CFPB's website at www.cfpb.gov. For your convenience, we've made access available through a link at www.dealerdeskbook.com/resources/privacyinitiatives/. In addition to the GLB Act, the FTC Privacy Rule, and the FTC Safeguards Rule, the FTC also provides educational information and business guidance on this site.

3. Who enforces the Privacy and Safeguards Rules against car dealers?

It depends. The FTC is the federal agency that enforces the Privacy Rule against all dealers that enjoy the dealer exemption under the Dodd-Frank Wall Street Reform and Consumer Protection Act (Dodd-Frank Act; see Chapter 19). The Consumer Financial Protection Bureau (CFPB) is the federal agency that enforces the Privacy Rule against non-exempt dealers. The FTC is the federal agency that enforces the Safeguards Rules against all dealers. When the FTC hits, it hits hard.

Consider a true story: In 2003, the FTC wrote to a dealer and announced that the FTC staff "is conducting a non-public inquiry" into the dealership's compliance with the security standards contained in the Gramm-Leach-Bliley Act and the dealership's implementation of the FTC's Safeguards Rule.

If this was your dealership, and you were opening the mail,

how would your day be going so far?

Wait, it gets worse. The letter outlined the requirements and purpose of the Safeguards Rule, and then turned deadly, asking for enough documents to fill the bed of a Ford F-150.

What did the FTC ask for? Check this list:

- The dealership's complete legal name, its principal place of business, date and state of incorporation, and any d/b/a names;

- A description of the dealership's corporate structure, and the names of all parents, subsidiaries (whether wholly or partly owned), divisions, affiliates, joint ventures, operations under assumed names, websites, and entities over which it exercises supervision or control, and the nature of the relationship of each to the dealership;

- A description of each type of information obtained from or about customers (such as customer name, street and email addresses, telephone number, Social Security Number, bank and credit card numbers, income, and credit history) that is collected or maintained by or for the dealership, or its affiliates, along with a copy of each form used to collect the information;

- A copy of the dealership's written information security program, and a statement of when it was written and implemented;

- A copy of each policy, manual, or other written document that relates to the dealership's procedures and practices respecting the security of information, including, but not limited to, access to and the maintenance of, retention, and transmission of the information within the dealership and between the dealership and its affiliates and other entities;

- A description of, or documents describing, the security risks to the confidentiality and integrity of the dealership's Customer Information that the dealership identified in developing its security plan, and a description of how the plan does, and does not, address each of these risks; and

- The name and title of the employee responsible for coordinating the dealership's information security program and all documents that record, concern, or reflect policies, practices, procedures, instructions, and directions followed by that employee, or that the employee is required to follow, in coordinating the program.

In addition to elevating your heart rate, this letter tells a little about the FTC's approach. The FTC's relatively small staff can't monitor every dealer, so it must hit hard and make an example of those who fall short of regulatory requirements.

But, we return to the 2003 correspondence as an example: How would you respond to one of these letters?

4. What are the penalties for failing to comply with the Privacy and Safeguards Rules?

If your dealership is exempt from the Dodd-Frank Act and fails to comply with Privacy Rule, the FTC can initiate an enforcement action. Otherwise, the CFPB can initiate an enforcement action for a dealership that is subject to the Dodd-Frank Act. The FTC can initiate an action against any dealership for failure to comply with the Safeguards Rules. While neither Rule permits an individual to bring a claim against your dealership, your dealership could be subject to "piggyback" claims under the "unfair and deceptive acts and practices" laws of the various states (by consumers or a state Attorney General) for failure to comply. These laws often count a violation of a federal law or rule as a violation of state law as well.

5. But, I am a car dealer! The Privacy and Safeguards Rules apply to financial institutions. Must dealers comply with the Privacy and Safeguards Rules?

Traditional car dealers must comply with both Rules. Both Rules apply to all dealers who are "financial institutions" under the GLB. A dealer will be acting as a "financial institution" if it is significantly engaged in financial activities, such as entering into finance or lease transactions with consumers. While most dealers who finance or lease vehicles are subject to both Rules, there are some instances where the Rules do not apply or vary in their application.

Transactions for Business Purposes

The Privacy and Safeguards Rules will not apply to transactions with companies or individuals, like sole proprietors, that obtain products or services for business purposes; rather, they apply only to those transactions involving natural persons who obtain financial products for family, personal, or household purposes. So, if your dealership does not engage in commercial transactions, these Rules may not apply to you.

Cash Transactions

The Privacy and Safeguards Rules also do not apply to every customer transaction. The Rules do not apply in connection with *cash* sales of motor vehicles, or *cash services* performed by your vehicle service center. However, as you develop appropriate privacy and safeguarding procedures, consider including cash customers; that way, you maintain courtesy and simplicity in your transactions.

Financing

The Rules do apply to "financial activities," such as extending credit to a customer to purchase a vehicle or arranging vehicle leasing or financing. Also, the Rules apply when an individual applies for credit, regardless of whether credit is extended. But, the Rules *do not* apply if the buyer arranges financing on his or her own through an outside lender.

Part Two: Fifteen Things You Should Know About the Privacy Rule

1. What are the three purposes of the Privacy Rule?

As one of the primary means of regulating the treatment of non-public personal information about consumers by financial institutions, the Privacy Rule's three purposes are as follows:

- *You must provide certain notices:* The Privacy Rule requires the dealership under certain circumstances to notify customers about its privacy policies and practices;

- *Your right to use Customer Information is limited:* The Privacy Rule describes conditions under which the dealership may disclose "non-public personal information" (NPI) about consumers to non-affiliated third parties; and

- *You also must allow the consumer to impose more restrictions:* Under the Privacy Rule, consumers may cut off the dealership's information disclosures to most non-affiliated third parties by "opting out" of that disclosure, subject to certain exceptions.

2. What is included in the definition of "non-public personal information"?

NPI is "personally identifiable financial information" and any list, description, or other grouping of consumers (and publicly available information pertaining to them) that is "derived using any personally identifiable financial information" that is "not publicly available."

What in the world does that mean, you ask? We're glad to see you're still awake.

It really boils down to *any* personal information you obtain about a person in connection with arranging financing or leasing for a vehicle, even if the deal unwinds or financing *cannot* be secured. A list of customers to whom you previously leased vehicles—*even just this list*—would be considered NPI. Conversely, a list of all your customers, with no mention of whether they financed, leased, or paid cash for their vehicles, would not be considered NPI subject to the Privacy Rule. (Of course, what happens to such a list still ought to be something your dealership's information security policies address.)

3. What is the Privacy Rule's definition of "consumer"?

A "consumer" is a person who obtains, or has obtained, a financial product from you that is to be used primarily for personal, family, or household purposes. A consumer may also be that person's legal representative. A consumer is not always a "customer" but a customer is always a "consumer." (Only lawyers could dream this stuff up.) This distinction is discussed in the next question.

4. *As a car dealer, must I provide an initial Privacy Notice to consumers?*

The answer is *not* clear-cut. This is perhaps one of the most convoluted questions under the Privacy Rule.

A dealership does not have to give an *initial* Privacy Notice to every person who comes through the showroom. The lines start to blur when considering whether an individual is considered a "consumer" or a "customer," as the terms are artfully crafted under the Privacy Rule.

A "consumer" is someone who gives the dealership personal information in connection with a possible credit or lease transaction. A dealership is required to provide an *initial* Privacy Notice to this individual *only* if it intends to share this information with a non-affiliated third party.

As with any complex legal analysis, exceptions apply. For example, it is OK to share this information with a non-affiliated third party, *without* providing the *initial* Privacy Notice, (i) in order to process the transaction requested by the consumer or to comply with the law (such as to send the information to a potential financing source), or (ii) if the consumer consents to the sharing (such as permission to pull a credit report).

But, without providing the *initial* Privacy Notice, it is *not* OK to share this information with joint marketing partners (as defined by the Rule) or with non-affiliated service providers who may conduct customer satisfaction surveys for you. There are also restrictions on sharing this information with your affiliates for certain purposes, including marketing (see Chapter 5). The *initial* Privacy Notice must also be given if you share this information with a non-affiliated third party for the party's own direct marketing purposes.

On the other hand, a "customer" is a consumer with whom you have a "customer relationship." A customer relationship is a continuing relationship with a consumer under which you provide one or more financial products or services. A person becomes a "customer" once you enter into a credit or lease contract or arrange for someone else to extend the credit. A dealership must give all "customers" the *initial* Privacy Notice, either before, or at the signing of, a credit or lease contract, regardless of its information sharing practices.

5. I understand that the Privacy Notice, like so many other legally mandated notices, must be "clear and conspicuous." What does "clear and conspicuous" mean as it relates to Privacy Notices?

"Clear and conspicuous" means that a Privacy Notice is reasonably understandable and designed to call attention to the nature and significance of the information in the Notice. For example, a Privacy Notice is reasonably understandable when it is presented with clear, concise sentences, paragraphs, and sections. So, when crafting such notices, try to avoid legal and highly technical business terminology. To call attention to your Privacy Notice, use plain-language headings and typefaces and type sizes that are easy to read. Also, employ wide margins and ample line spacing, as those attention-getting devices work well, too.

6. Financial institutions are required to provide annual Privacy Notices to "customers." Must I do that? You say I have to send annual Privacy Notices to a customer, even if the credit contracts with such customers were transferred to another financial institution?

No, not unless you are a buy-here, pay-here dealer or you

are not assigning some of your contracts. When the contract is assigned, the "customer relationship" is terminated, so long as you do not retain the servicing rights.

7. If I enter into a retail installment sale contract with a consumer and transfer the contract to another financial institution that will then service the contract, does the customer relationship transfer with the contract (as it applies to the Privacy Rule)?

Yes, if you transfer the servicing rights to the contract to another financial institution, the customer relationship transfers, too. The obligation to send an *annual* Privacy Notice is extinguished with the transfer of the customer relationship. However, you must still have provided the *initial* Privacy Notice to that customer.

8. What information should my customer Privacy Notices include?

Your Privacy Notice must include the following information:

- The categories of NPI that you collect.

- The categories of NPI that you disclose.

- The categories of affiliates and non-affiliated third parties to whom you disclose NPI outside of the majority of the sharing exceptions in the law. *Warning:* The category does require disclosure to third parties under the service provider and joint marketing exception (which is discussed more fully below).

- The categories of NPI about your former customers that you disclose and the categories of affiliates and non-affiliated third parties to whom you disclose NPI that are outside of the sharing exceptions in the law. *Warning:* The category does require disclosure to third parties under the service provider and joint marketing exception.

- A separate statement of the categories of information you disclose and the categories of third parties with whom you have contracted; that is, if you disclose NPI to a non-affiliated third party under the service provider or joint marketing exception, and no other sharing exception applies to the disclosure.

- An explanation of the consumer's right to opt-out of certain disclosures of NPI to non-affiliated third parties and the method by which the consumer may do so (if applicable).

- A Fair Credit Reporting Act disclosure (opt-out of disclosures of certain information among affiliates for certain purposes).

- A statement regarding your information safeguards policies and practices.

In addition to this required information, you may include any other additional information as well.

9. If I explain the contents of the Privacy Notice to a customer but do not provide a written notice, have I satisfied the Privacy Rule?

No. You must provide a written Privacy Notice. You may not provide the Privacy Notice solely by orally explaining the Privacy Notice, either in person or over the telephone.

10. OK, if I have to send a Privacy Notice, can the FTC hook me up with some sample disclosures?

Why, yes! In late 2009, the Federal Trade Commission adopted the final model privacy forms. There are three model forms for dealers: one for dealers who are not required to provide an information sharing opt-out, one for dealers who are required to provide an information sharing opt-out and want to provide an opt-out mechanism by Internet or phone, and another for dealers that want to include an additional snail-mail mechanism.

Dealers using the model notice will enjoy a "safe harbor" as long as they do not make any changes or include any variations in the model form. Plus, the FTC provided a transition period, spanning from December 31, 2009, to December 31, 2010, during which time the new model privacy notices, as well as the "sample clauses" provided under GLB, afforded dealers a "safe harbor." However, effective January 1, 2011, the "sample clauses" lost the "safe harbor," which now applies only to the new model privacy notice forms.

11. Where can I get a copy of the model notices?

There is a "form builder" available on the Federal Reserve's website at www.federalreserve.gov/bankinforeg/privacy_notice_instructions.pdf. The form builder makes developing the Privacy Notice a "fill-in-the-blanks" exercise. But, dealers will need to have a firm grasp on their information sharing practices in order to complete the forms properly.

12. Can I share NPI with a non-affiliated third party who wants the information in order to market its own products and services?

You may share NPI about a customer for this purpose only if (i) you have provided the customer an opportunity to opt-out of the disclosure in your Privacy Notice, and (ii) the customer has not directed you to not share the information. See Question 7 in this section for an explanation of what types of customer lists may be considered NPI. This question illustrates the importance of carefully writing the contents of your Privacy Notice.

13. Can I share NPI with a non-affiliated third party who provides services on my behalf (such as telemarketing or customer satisfaction surveys)?

Yes, but only in certain circumstances. The disclosure required here is commonly referred to as the "Service Provider Exception" to the Privacy Rule. You may share NPI about a customer for this purpose only if you disclosed this practice in your Privacy Notice and you have a contractual agreement that prohibits the service provider from sharing or using the information for any other purpose. Otherwise, you would be permitted to share NPI only if you have provided the customer an opportunity to opt-out of the disclosure in your Privacy Notice, and the customer has not directed you to not share the information. Again, this question illustrates the importance of carefully writing the contents of your Privacy Notice.

14. Can I share NPI with a non-affiliated third party to market my financial products and services or products and services I offer jointly with other financial institutions?

Again, yes, under certain circumstances. The disclosure required here is commonly referred to as the "Joint Marketing Exception" to the Privacy Rule. This exception comes into play when you use non-affiliated third parties to market either your products or services, or financial products and services offered jointly by you and other financial institutions, which each financial institution agrees by contract that it jointly offers, sponsors, or endorses. You may share NPI about a customer for this purpose only if you disclose this practice in your Privacy Notice, and you have a contractual agreement that prohibits the non-affiliated third parties (including non-affiliated financial institutions) from sharing or using the information for any other purpose. Otherwise, you would be permitted to share NPI only if you have provided the customer an opportunity to opt-out of the disclosure in your Privacy Notice, and the customer has not directed you to not share the information. Once again, the carefully written Privacy Notice is critical.

15. As is true of most federal regulations, the Privacy Rule addresses its effect on state law. What is the general rule to follow?

The GLB Act and its corresponding regulations are not meant to trump state law. The general rule is that both federal and state law will co-exist *except* to the extent that such state statute, regulation, order, or interpretation is inconsistent with the federal law, and then only to the extent of the inconsistency. Just because a state law affords greater protection won't render the state law inconsistent. Also, you cannot just haphazardly decide that the laws don't work together. It is up to the FTC to make an informed determination on its own motion or upon the petition of any interested party. You should always contact your compliance attorney, who may have an idea as to how to reconcile the law or who may know if the FTC has made a determination.

Part Three: Sixteen Things You Should Know About the Safeguards Rule

1. What are the objectives of the Safeguards Rule?

As mentioned earlier, the Safeguards Rule addresses how your dealership protects information about its finance and lease customers. The Safeguards Rule sets forth three main objectives: (i) to insure the security and confidentiality of Customer Information, (ii) to protect against any anticipated threats or hazards to the security and/or integrity of Customer Information, and (iii) to protect against any unauthorized access to or use of Customer Information that could result in substantial harm or inconvenience to any customer.

2. What types of information does the Safeguards Rule cover?

The Safeguards Rule applies to "Customer Information." And, "Customer Information" means "any record containing 'non-public personal information' about a customer of the dealership, whether in paper, electronic, or other form, that is handled or maintained by or on behalf of the dealership or its affiliates." While the Safeguards Rule does not apply to mere "*consumer* information" (here's that pesky and confusing distinction again between folks who are your customers and those who are just consumers), most financial institutions choose not to distinguish between the different types of information, and they apply the higher level of safeguarding controls to all personal information in their possession.

3. What does this really mean?

When determining what information is considered Customer Information for the purpose of this requirement, think about the types of information you gather about a customer seeking to lease or finance a vehicle through you. This could include, for example, Social Security Numbers, account numbers, a credit report, a credit score, and so on. It may also include a list of names of customers who have leased or financed their vehicles through your dealership. It doesn't stop there— limitless types of information could be considered Customer Information for purposes of the Safeguards Rule. Note that it may be difficult and time consuming (not to mention expensive) to separate protected information from other, non-protected information for safeguarding purposes. It is a "best practice" to subject *all* customer and consumer data to the protections set forth in the Safeguards Rule.

4. To whom do I have an obligation under the Safeguards Rule?

The Safeguards Rule applies to all Customer Information in your possession, regardless of whether such information pertains to individuals with whom you have a customer relationship or customers of other financial institutions (including other dealerships) that have provided such information to you.

5. What is an information security program?

An information security program is composed of the administrative, technical, or physical safeguards you require to access, collect, distribute, process, protect, store, use, transmit, dispose of, or otherwise handle Customer Information. The Safeguards Rule requires dealers to develop, implement, and maintain a comprehensive *written* information security program. An "information security program" is the same thing as a "Safeguards Policy," and we will use the two phrases interchangeably.

6. What are the required elements of a Safeguards Policy?

The Safeguards Rule requires five elements to your dealership's information security policy. Those elements are:

- You must designate an employee or employees to coordinate your information security program.

- You must identify reasonably foreseeable internal and external risks to the security, confidentiality, and integrity of Customer Information that could result in its unauthorized disclosure, misuse, alteration, destruction, or other compromise, and you must assess the sufficiency of any safeguards in place to control these risks. At a minimum, your risk assessment should include consideration of risks in each relevant area of your operations, including (i) employee training and management; (ii) information systems, including network and software design, as well as information processing, storage, transmission, and disposal; and (iii) detecting, preventing, and responding to attacks, intrusions, or other systems failures.

- You must develop and implement Customer Information safeguards to control the risks you identify through the risk assessment and you regularly must audit these safeguards to ensure their effectiveness.

- You must oversee service providers who take possession of Customer Information, even for a minor task.

- You must evaluate and adjust your information security program.

7. What is a program coordinator?

This person manages your compliance obligations under the Safeguards Rule. The program coordinator will be responsible for coordinating your safeguards policy throughout your dealership or family of dealerships. The program coordinator must be an employee of the dealership and he or she must be empowered with the authority and resources to design, implement, maintain, and enforce the safeguards that he or she deems necessary. In most dealerships, the program coordinator should be someone fairly senior in the management chain.

8. What do you mean by "identifying reasonably foreseeable risks" to Customer Information?

The Safeguards Rule requires you to conduct a risk assessment of your dealership's operations to determine where there is a "reasonably foreseeable" risk that Customer Information may be compromised. "Reasonably foreseeable" can mean different things for different dealers, and information security programs will vary to reflect these risks. In other words, if you bought an "off-the-shelf" information security program from your trade association, three-hole punched it, and slapped it into a binder, you are falling short of the requirement, because you never conducted a risk assessment of your dealership.

At a minimum, such a risk assessment should include consideration of risks in each relevant area of your operations, including (i) employee training and management; (ii) information systems, including network and software design, as well as information processing, storage, transmission, and disposal; and (iii) detecting, preventing, and responding to attacks, intrusions, or other systems failures.

Don't know where to start? Consider things like the physical layout of the dealership and information systems used at the dealership. Also, consider things like file storage, office access, and employee training. Keep in mind that there are many vendors out there that can help you perform your risk assessment and maintain your information security program.

9. What does it mean to design and implement Customer Information safeguards to control the risks identified in my risk assessment?

Once you've identified the "risks" in your dealership, you need to develop ways to reduce them. Some may be simple, like adding locks to doors and file cabinets or adding password protection to computers. Others may be more complex, like implementing certain technology or developing formal privacy training materials for existing and new employees. The proper "fix" will vary depending on the size and nature of your dealership.

10. How often do I have to test my safeguards?

How often you test your safeguards likely depends upon the size and complexity of what you are monitoring. For example, you may want to check for unlocked doors and messy sales areas daily. But, you may wish to quiz your employees semi-annually. The important thing is that you do, in fact, periodically test your safeguards. Your policy also should call for retaining records of what you've done, documenting protective measures, testing, training, and so on.

11. What does the Safeguards Rule say about service providers?

The Safeguards Rule requires you to oversee your service providers by taking reasonable steps to select and retain service providers that are "capable of maintaining appropriate safeguards" for your Customer Information. Also, the Safeguards Rule requires you to obtain the contractual agreement of your service providers to "implement and maintain such safeguards."

Consider service providers used by your dealership, such as DMS and CRM providers, as well as parties you outsource functions to, such as billing, mailing, or shredding companies. Think about any vendors that could possibly have access to Customer Information, such as the janitors who clean your dealership's business office after you've gone home.

12. Do I ever have to change and adjust my safeguards policy?

Yes. Your safeguards policy is intended to be somewhat "organic" and should be revised periodically to reflect changes in technology and the results of your periodic audits. For example, you may need to revise your policy to address risks inherent to new technology implemented in the dealership. Also, as you make adjustments to your practices based on internal audits of your safeguards policy, these adjustments should be reflected in the written policy.

13. What standard will the FTC apply when determining whether my dealership's safeguards policy complies?

The FTC will use a flexible standard. The FTC understands that no two dealerships are alike. The Safeguards Rule is designed to give individual dealerships the flexibility to adopt safeguards appropriate for that dealership, and it requires that your safeguards be appropriate to the size and complexity of your dealership, the nature and scope of your financing and lease activities, and the sensitivity of the Customer Information you collect, store, transmit, and so on. On this last item, to the extent that you collect credit applications from consumers and pull credit bureaus, you are in possession of some of the most sensitive information available.

Be aware that, although the Safeguards Rule will permit dealerships to develop appropriate safeguards based on the size and complexity of their operations, each dealership's policy must contain the five required elements discussed in Question 6 in this section.

14. What is the Disposal Rule?

The Disposal Rule requires entities that possess consumer information (or any compilation of consumer information) to properly dispose of such information by taking reasonable measures to protect against its unauthorized access to, or use of, this information (in connection with its disposal).

For the purpose of the Disposal Rule, consumer information is "any record about an individual whether in paper, electronic, or other form, that is a consumer report or is derived from a consumer report." The information has to identify, or give one the means to identify, a consumer—if it does not, it is not a consumer report.

15. Why are we talking about the Disposal Rule in the GLB chapter?

Yes, we addressed it already in Chapter 5. However, it's such a darn good fit in this chapter that we decided to talk about it again. It would make sense that any safeguards policy developed by your dealership would address how to protect consumer information in connection with its disposal.

Nevertheless, as a technical matter, the Disposal Rule is not part of GLB or the Safeguards Rule. It is actually part of the Fair Credit Reporting Act, which is discussed in Chapter 5.

16. Where can I get additional information about complying with the Safeguards Rule?

There are countless resources out there to help dealers comply with the Safeguards Rule. A good place to start would be the NADA Management Guide's *A Dealer Guide to Safeguarding Customer Information,* available from NADA for $25 (members) or $50 (non-members). Yes, we wrote the guide with NADA, and we're pretty proud of it. And, no, we don't make any money off the sales. Rats.

CHAPTER 11

The USA PATRIOT Act & OFAC Requirements

By Nicole Frush Munro

Terrorist 101—Find 'Em and Report 'Em: Eighteen Things Dealers Should Know About Bad Guys

From the first days of tribal warfare, there have been terrorists. Societies have always been at risk. But, it wasn't until September 11, 2001, that terrorists caused a tragedy forever changing this nation's core. While we may never know the invisible and lasting impact of September 11, 2001, on our lives, now more than ten years later, the impact of that day on the way we do business continues.

In response to heightened risks of terrorism in the United States, government agencies stepped up enactment and enforcement of laws designed to battle terrorism and to catch terrorists before they could strike again. Today, these enforcement actions not only touch the big industry players, they also reach right into Mom and Pop's Auto Sales and Repair Shop. Such is the personal nature of national policy since 9/11.

Two federal anti-terrorism tools that affect dealers include (i) the USA PATRIOT Act (Uniting and Strengthening America by Providing Appropriate Tools Required to Intercept and Obstruct Terrorism Act of 2001) and (ii) the requirement that dealers check the Specially Designated Nationals list (the "SDN list") maintained by the Treasury Department's Office of Foreign Assets Control (OFAC). The OFAC requirements were strengthened in 2001, but they have been around for decades. Enacted in 2001, the USA PATRIOT Act directly responded to the attacks on 9/11.

This chapter addresses the requirements that these two federal anti-terrorist schemes impose on dealers.

1. What is OFAC and what does it do?

OFAC, an agency within the U.S. Department of the Treasury, administers and enforces economic sanctions against hostile targets to advance U.S. foreign policy and national security objectives. These sanctions programs target certain individuals, foreign governments, financial institutions, organizations, and "specially designated nationals," or "SDNs," to deprive those persons of access to the U.S. financial system and the benefit of services involving U.S. markets. OFAC gets its authority from statute and, more recently, a post-9/11 Presidential Executive Order.

On September 24, 2001, by Presidential Executive Order (Executive Order 13224), President George W. Bush significantly expanded OFAC's powers and the list of SDNs. That Order expressly mandated that "all property and interest in property of the [SDNs] that are in the United States, or that hereafter come within the United States, or hereafter come within the possession or control of United States persons, are blocked."

Further, the Order provided that "any transaction or dealing by United States persons or within the United States in property or interests in property blocked pursuant to this order is prohibited, including but not limited to, the making or receiving of any contribution of funds, goods, or services to, or for the benefit of, those persons listed in the Annex to this order or determined to be subject to this order."

OFAC determines which names appear on the SDN list. Businesses and individuals are prohibited from dealing with, or transacting business with, any individual or entity that is the subject of Executive Order 13224, and whose name appears on the list. Don't take it personally—it's not just dealers that are supposed to check the list before transacting business with someone. Everyone must, whether you're IBM or Microsoft, or the hot dog vendor with the pushcart on the corner!

2. Do the OFAC rules and regulations apply to me?

Yes. The OFAC prohibition applies to all U.S. persons and all business transactions. For a dealership, this means that it applies to new and used car sales, car parts sales, sales of services, and car rentals. It also applies to those persons the dealership does business with, including its employees and vendors. It applies to all transactions regardless of the amount of the transactions. For example, the prohibition covers the sale of a 99-cent washer in the parts department (assuming anything still sells for 99 cents).

3. What do you mean by "SDN"?

SDN is the acronym for "specially designated national." OFAC keeps the list. SDNs are individuals, companies, or other entities identified as being owned or controlled by, or acting for, or on behalf of, the governments of certain target countries, or associated with international drug trafficking, terrorism, or some other illegal activity. Businesses and individuals are prohibited from dealing with, or transacting business with, any individual, company, or other entity listed by OFAC as an SDN.

4. When do I check the SDN list?

OFAC has issued statements through various publications and guidance materials suggesting that businesses create a risk-based compliance program. OFAC has stated "[e]very organization has a different level of risk that must be assessed to determine the best way to ensure that it does not do business with a sanctions target." English translation: "Every business must determine the best way to make sure it doesn't do business with an SDN." In November 2009, OFAC published Economic Sanctions Enforcement Guidelines, which include an OFAC risk matrix as an annex. Dealers can use the matrix to evaluate their compliance program. Dealers can access the Guidelines and OFAC risk matrix through the link maintained for us to the Federal Register at www.federalregister.gov/articles/2009/11/09/E9-26754/economic-sanctions-enforcement-guidelines.

OFAC's programs and the SDN list change frequently, but in an irregular way, which makes compliance more difficult. The SDN list can remain unchanged for two weeks and then change three times in five days. It is important that the SDN list you are checking is current and you have complete information about OFAC's current restrictions. With respect to sales transactions, you must check the list as it appears on the date of the transaction. If you have a continuing business relationship with a person, such as an employee or a vendor, the only way to be safe is to check your list of such persons against the SDN list every time the SDN list changes. If you are a buy-here, pay-here dealer, holding and collecting your own contracts, you should check the list every time you accept a payment from a customer. Because these checks on a continuing relationship are impractical to do manually, you should employ a mechanism to "scrub" the names of those you employ, do business with, or deal with on a regular basis in any way against OFAC's SDN list. The list should be re-scrubbed for such continuing relationships each time OFAC updates the list.

5. How do I check the SDN list?

Try the link maintained for us to the OFAC website at www.dealerdeskbook.com/resources/sdnlist/, where OFAC publishes its SDN list and each update. Also, several commercial services offer various kinds of electronic solutions to assist dealers in meeting their OFAC obligations. You can find these companies by searching "OFAC" in your web browser.

6. What if my customer's name matches one on the SDN list?

If any transaction produces a potential "hit," you should evaluate the validity of the "hit" and avoid reporting false positives. OFAC suggests the following due diligence procedures:

- Ensure that the "hit" matches OFAC's SDN list, as opposed to another agency's SDN list.

- Evaluate the quality of the "hit" (manually compare the consumer's name with the name on OFAC's SDN list).

- Collect more information from the consumer if his or her name matches exactly or contains many similarities to a name on the list. More information may determine whether there is an exact match, as most entries on the OFAC SDN list include full name, address, nationality, passport, tax ID, place of birth, date of birth, former names, and aliases.

Once you complete your evaluation, if there are a number of similarities or exact matches, call the OFAC hotline at 1.800.540.6322. Unless you find an exact match, OFAC recommends you call the hotline before you block the transaction. If there is an exact match or OFAC verifies a match, you must block the transaction (yes, stop the sale!), and file a report with OFAC within 10 business days. Consider the timing involved—you should scrub your customer's name at the *outset* of the transaction (again, the rule applies to any transaction—sale, service, finance, etc.). If you get a "hit," you must block the transaction before it is consummated. In your report to OFAC, you must include the name of the blocked customer, property, location of property, account information, estimated value, date blocked, a photocopy of the payment, and the business name and phone contact for the representative making the report. Your Adverse Action Notice may indicate OFAC hit as the reason for credit denial.

7. How do I report a match?

Within 10 business days following the date you determine a match, you must file the following information in a written report to OFAC: the name of the blocked customer, property, location of property, account information, estimated value, date blocked, a photocopy of any payment, the business name, and the phone contact for the representative making the report.

8. After I report, can I sell the car to someone whose name appears on the SDN list?

Absolutely not. If you have done your due diligence and found that your customer's name is similar to, or an exact match to, a name on the OFAC SDN list, you must block the transaction and file a report with OFAC within 10 business days following the date that you blocked the transaction.

9. Where can I find help?

Try the link we maintain to the OFAC's website at www.dealerdeskbook.com/resources/ofac/ for more information about OFAC compliance. For answers to frequently asked questions, see www.dealerdeskbook.com/resources/ofacfaq/.

10. What are my recordkeeping responsibilities?

Businesses must retain records of blocked accounts or deals for five years. Further, businesses must submit an annual report if they have any blocked accounts or deals as of June 30 of each year. Also, businesses involved in litigation, arbitration, or other binding alternative dispute resolution proceedings regarding blocked property must report on those proceedings within 10 days of filing to OFAC's general counsel.

11. "Money laundering"—What's that?

When money is derived from illicit activities, it's "dirty." Dirty money, usually in the form of cash, is easily confiscated by the authorities. When dirty money is converted into assets like cars, it is cleaned up a bit, or "laundered." Property bought with dirty money remains subject to seizure by the authorities, but difficulty tracing the laundered money inhibits seizure.

12. Who is "FinCEN"?

FinCEN is the Treasury Department's Financial Crimes Enforcement Network. FinCEN's mission is "to enhance U.S. national security, deter and detect criminal activity, and safeguard financial systems from abuse by promoting transparency in the U.S. and international financial systems." FinCEN gathers and analyzes information under laws, such as the Bank Secrecy Act, to support financial crimes investigations.

13. Do the USA PATRIOT Act's cash reporting requirements apply to me?

Yes. The USA PATRIOT Act imposes a cash-reporting requirement found in Section 365 of the Act on dealers. Dealers already were subject to cash reporting requirements under the Internal Revenue Code, but Section 365 expanded the scope of entities required to file reports of large cash transactions to FinCEN to include anyone involved in a trade or business who receives more than $10,000 in cash in a single transaction, or who receives $10,000 in cash in two, or more, related transactions.

Section 365 also requires that those entities establish procedures to track cash transactions, to make sure reports are filed when required, and prohibits the structuring of transactions to avoid the application of the cash reporting rules. The reporting form for cash transactions is "IRS Form 8300/FinCEN Form 8300," a form nearly identical to the required IRS form for reporting cash transactions. For a discussion of the IRS requirements, see Chapter 13.

14. Do the "know your customer" money laundering parts of the USA PATRIOT Act apply to me?

Not yet. The USA PATRIOT Act contains a provision requiring "financial institutions" to establish an anti-money laundering program. The term "financial institution" includes a dealer or finance company. At a minimum, an anti-money laundering program must include the development of policies, procedures, and controls to guard against money laundering, the designation of a compliance officer, and the establishment of an ongoing training program. The program must contain an independent audit function to test the program. Regulations

239

applicable to dealers implementing this program requirement have not yet been enacted.

The "know your customer" requirements of the USA PATRIOT Act, originally scheduled to become effective in April 2002, were delayed until October 2002, and then they were delayed again for an indefinite period. The delays allow FinCEN to consider whether car dealers ought to be subject to these rules, and if so, what the rules for car dealers ought to look like. During that time, FinCEN temporarily exempted certain financial institutions, including vehicle sellers, from the requirement to establish an anti-money laundering compliance program.

On February 24, 2003, FinCEN published an "Advance Notice of Proposed Rulemaking" in the Federal Register. FinCEN asked for comment on five questions:

- What is the potential money laundering risk posed by vehicle sellers?

- Do money laundering risks vary by (i) vehicle type (for example, boat, airplane, automobile); (ii) market (wholesale versus retail); or (iii) business line (international sales, sales to governments)?

- Should vehicle sellers be exempt from coverage under sections 352 and 326 of the USA PATRIOT Act?

- If vehicle sellers, or some subset of the industry, should be subject to the anti-money laundering program requirements, how should the program be structured?

- How should a vehicle seller be defined? Should there be a minimum threshold value in the definition? Should it include wholesale and retail sellers? Should sellers of used vehicles be included?

The comment period expired, and the Treasury Department has yet to issue regulations dealing with these issues. Until it does, dealers need not comply with USA PATRIOT Act money laundering obligations. Dealers must still comply with the IRS/FinCEN cash reporting requirements.

15. What other requirements does the USA PATRIOT Act impose on dealers?

One provision of the USA PATRIOT Act required dealers to respond to information requests from federal government law enforcement agencies. However, Treasury placed a "brief moratorium" on the "Special Information Sharing Procedures to Deter Money Laundering and Terrorist Activity" ("Information Sharing Rules"). The Information Sharing Rules were published on September 26, 2002, and were effective as of that date.

Under the rules, law enforcement officials who had "credible evidence" of a suspect's involvement in money laundering or terrorism activities could send a request to banks and other financial institutions (including dealers), requesting that the recipient search its records for account or transaction information concerning the individual or entity named in the request.

Treasury granted dealers a grace period under these rules. Treasury indicated initially that it would send such requests only to financial institutions required to have anti-money laundering programs in place. Since dealers had escaped the money laundering requirements, they received a temporary pass. But Treasury also advised that all financial institutions were "on notice" that they might be contacted to provide the information. After Treasury overwhelmed banks with information requests, the banks complained, and on November 19, 2002, Treasury agreed to institute a "brief moratorium" on such requests. Treasury then implemented a revised reporting system.

Although we are unaware of any information requests directed to dealers, dealers should not ignore the Information Sharing Rules. Dealers are "on notice" that they could receive such requests when the moratorium ends, so you should make sure that you can respond in a timely manner to any such requests you receive. As a best practice, develop formal written procedures to respond to such requests. That should make receiving one a much easier experience.

16. What are the penalties for violations?

The penalties for failing to comply with OFAC's requirements are very, very harsh, indeed—including 30 years in jail, fines up to $10 million against corporations and $5 million against individuals, and civil penalties ranging from $250,000 or twice the amount of each underlying transaction up to $1,075,000 for each violation. With penalties like these, you've got to comply with OFAC—this isn't one of those "we'll take the risk" deals, where you can try to fly under the radar. Another thing—you don't want to be the dealer that sold a car or truck to a known terrorist who happens to use the vehicle in a terrorist attack.

17. Do I have any defenses against enforcement?

For OFAC violations, the answer is "no." If you do business with someone listed on the SDN list, you're out of luck. OFAC has levied stiff fines for violations, even in situations in which the violator self-reports the violation. The 2009 Economic Sanctions Enforcement Guidelines, published by OFAC, explain that voluntary self-disclosure of an apparent OFAC violation will be considered in determining the appropriate agency response, and in cases where civil penalties apply, the amount of the penalty. Voluntary self-disclosure will result in a base penalty amount of at least 50% less than the base penalty amount if you're caught with an apparent violation. The Guidelines do provide a little incentive to keep you honest.

The Guidelines also provide other mitigating factors considered by OFAC in assessing its enforcement response, including cooperation with an OFAC investigation, the value of the apparent violation, the commercial sophistication of the business, the timing of the apparent violation (particularly if the apparent violation occurred after the addition of a new name to the SDN list), and the remedial response to the apparent violation.

18. What can I do to help fight terrorism?

OFAC

Ensure that your sales, F&I, and service departments check every customer against the SDN list. Require your HR department to run current and potential employees' and contractors' names for matches. In addition to these requirements, OFAC suggests the following procedures to ensure compliance:

- Designate a "Compliance Officer" responsible for monitoring compliance.

- Use "interdict" software to scan transactions and scrub against OFAC's SDN list.

- Conduct an in-depth audit of the business once a year.

- Establish compliance-training programs for employees.

Anti-Money Laundering

Look for Treasury to issue its long-delayed rules requiring dealers to develop "know your customer," anti-money laundering programs. Be on alert for information requests from the government, and prepare a policy for complying with such requests before you receive one. Pay attention to your responsibilities because they may change at any moment.

The IRS
Form 8300
Cash Reporting
Rule

By Catharine S. Andricos

CHAPTER 13

Thirty-One Things a Car Dealer Needs to Know About the IRS 8300 Reporting Rule

When Sally Smith graduated from high school, her parents bought her a new car. Way to go Sally! Better yet, they bought it from your store. Not wanting to be saddled with endless monthly payments, the Smiths decided to put $15,000 down. They had traveler's checks of $6,000, which they decided to use, and the remaining $9,000 downpayment, they paid in cold hard cash. Your GSM delivered the keys personally, and the Smiths drove off. The deal was filed away and everybody was happy.

Everybody?

Nope. If that's where the deal ended, one unhappy camper in the above scenario is the IRS. Another one will be you, when they find out. That's because the IRS's 8300 Reporting Rule ("the Rule") requires any person in a trade or business who receives more than $10,000 in cash in a single transaction, or in related transactions, to file combined IRS and FinCEN Form 8300. It's like the IRS is saying, "Show me the money!"

Why does the IRS care about large cash payments? Drug dealers and smugglers often use large cash payments to "launder" money from illegal activities. That is, they convert "dirty" money (illegally gained money) to "clean" money by using it in a legal transaction. The government can trace this laundered money through the payments that businesses like yours are required to report. As a side note, the USA PATRIOT Act of 2001 increased the scope of these laws to help trace funds used for terrorism. (See Chapter 12 for a discussion of OFAC and terrorism-related requirements that apply to your business.)

So, why should you care about the IRS 8300 Rule? That's simple: If your dealership accepts cash, the Rule (and its penalties) applies to you. If you want to read the rule, you can find it at www.dealerdeskbook.com/resources/form8300/.

1. Who must file Form 8300?

Generally, any person in a trade or business who receives more than $10,000 "cash" in a single "transaction" or in "related transactions" must file Form 8300. These words mean something different than what you would ordinarily think, so be sure you read on!

2. What is "cash"?

It's the green stuff that you use to pay for things. The Benjamins. The Dead Presidents. But for purposes of the Rule, it's currency and coin of the United States and any other country. "Cash" *also includes* certain money instruments—a cashier's check, bank draft, traveler's check, or money order—if they have a face amount of $10,000 or less and are not otherwise excepted from the definition (see Question 4, on the next page).

The reason you have to report these instruments if they are $10,000 or less is so that the IRS will be able to figure out if someone is using these instruments in a way that is circumventing the reporting requirement. For example, they're worried about folks who pay cash for multiple money instruments in amounts under the $10,000.01 reporting trigger, in order to avoid the reporting requirement.

3. What about personal checks?

Personal checks are not considered "cash" for purposes of the Form 8300 Rule.

4. Are there any exceptions to the definition of "cash"?

Sure there are. Cashier's checks, bank drafts, traveler's checks, or money orders that you receive are not considered cash if they have a face amount of *more than* $10,000. They are also not cash if one of the following exceptions applies:

- If the item is part of the proceeds of a bank loan. As proof that it's from a bank loan, you may rely on a copy of the loan document, a written statement or lien instruction from the bank, or something similar; or

- If it is received on the payment of a promissory note or an installment contract, if:

  - You use similar notes or contracts in other sales to ultimate consumers (retail sales) in the ordinary course of your business; and

  - The total payments for the sale that you receive on or before the 60th day after the sale are 50% or less of the purchase price.

5. What is a "transaction"?

The Rule lays out many fact patterns, each of which constitutes a "transaction." Relevant to you, a "transaction" occurs when goods, services, or property are sold—you sell a car or someone pays for body or other repair work.

6. What is a "related transaction"?

Transactions between a buyer and a seller that occur within a 24-hour period are "related transactions." For example, if you sell two cars, each for $6,000, to the same customer in one day, and the customer pays you in cash, these are related transactions. Because they total $12,000, you must file Form 8300.

Transactions more than 24 hours apart are related (and therefore, reportable) *if* you know, or have reason to know, that each transaction is one of a series of connected transactions. For example, a customer pays you $8,000 in cash for a vehicle one day, indicating his plan to come back and get the rust-proofing. Three days later, he comes in and pays another $3,000 to add your deluxe rust-proofing package. That's $11,000, and you knew, or had reason to know, that the sale of the vehicle and the subsequent transactions were a series of connected, or "related transactions." You must file Form 8300 to report these transactions.

7. *Exactly what payments must be reported?*

You must file Form 8300 to report cash paid to you if it is:

- *More than* $10,000 in "cash";

- Received as (i) one lump sum of more than $10,000; (ii) installment payments that cause the total cash received within one year of the initial payment to total more than $10,000; or (iii) other previously unreportable payments that cause the total cash received within a 12-month period to total more than $10,000 (for example, 10 monthly cash payments of $500 each, followed the next month by a cash payment of $6,000);

- Received in the course of your trade or business;

- Received from the same buyer; or

- Received in a *single transaction* or in *related transactions.*

8. Does the 24-hour period mean one day, such as all day Monday, or is it literally 24 hours around the clock?

A 24-hour period is 24 full hours around the clock. It doesn't necessarily have to be a calendar day or a banking day. So, 9 a.m. on Tuesday to 9 a.m. on Wednesday is considered a 24-hour period. Start of business on Tuesday to close of business on Tuesday is not a 24-hour period.

9. What, where, and when do I file?

IRS Form 8300 is what you file. How much you receive and when you received it will determine when you must file. Usually, you must file within 15 days after receiving a cash payment. If the Form 8300 due date (the 15th day or last day you can timely file the Form) falls on a Saturday, Sunday, or holiday, you get until the next day that isn't a Saturday, Sunday, or holiday. You can file it by mailing it to the address given in the Form 8300 instructions.

10. What if I receive more than one payment, like in an installment payment arrangement?

In cases like this, if the first cash installment is more than $10,000, you must file the form within 15 days of receipt of that payment. If the first cash payment is not more than $10,000, you add that payment and any later cash payments made within one year of the first payment. When the total cash payments add up to $10,000, you must file within 15 days.

11. That multiple-payment scenario sounds complicated. How about an example?

Glad you asked. Say that on January 10, you receive a cash payment of $11,000. You receive additional cash payments on the same transaction of $4,000 on February 15, and payments of $5,000 on March 20, and $6,000 on May 12. Here's how your filing schedule would look: By January 25, you must file Form 8300 for the $11,000 payment that was made on January 10. By May 27, you must file an additional Form 8300 for the additional payments that total $15,000. That second filing is for the $4,000, $5,000, and $6,000 payments you received. Again, since they were all a part of the same transaction, and they all happened within one year, you must file once for the first $10,000, and then again within 15 days after the subsequent payments total $10,000.

12. When I file Form 8300, do I have to tell the buyer about it?

Yes. A business must notify its customer of the filing in writing (which also can mean electronically, if the customer agrees to get it in that format) by January 31 of the subsequent calendar year.

13. What goes on that statement?

Include the name and address of your business, the name and phone number of a contact person (your comptroller or secretary/treasurer are good contact people), and the total amount of reportable cash you received from the person during the year. In addition, it must state that you are also reporting the information to the IRS.

14. There's a space on Form 8300 for the buyer's Taxpayer Identification Number. What is a Taxpayer Identification Number?

A Taxpayer Identification Number (TIN) is *required* for Form 8300. For individuals and sole proprietors, the TIN is the person's Social Security Number. For non-resident alien individuals who need a TIN, but can't get a Social Security Number, the TIN is an IRS Individual Taxpayer Identification Number (ITIN). The TIN for other persons, including corporations, partnerships, and estates, is the Employer Identification Number.

15. My customer is a non-resident alien and doesn't have a TIN. What should I do?

No TIN is necessary for an individual if *all* of the following are true:

- The individual does not have income effectively connected with the conduct of a business in the United States, or an office, or place of business, or is a fiscal or paying agent in the United States, at any time of the year;

- The individual does not file a Federal tax return; and

- In the case of a *non-resident alien individual,* the individual has not chosen to file a joint federal income tax return with a spouse who is a U.S. citizen or resident.

To repeat: If *all* of the above conditions are true, no TIN is needed, and you can file Form 8300 without it.

16. My customer is a foreign corporation without a TIN. What should I do?

Exactly what you did for the *non-resident alien individual.* The same rules apply.

17. Does the statement have to be a separate form, or can I just use the sales invoice, if I add the part about reporting the payment to the IRS to it?

There is nothing in the Internal Revenue Code or regulations that requires a specific format for the customer statement. As long as the statement contains all of the required information, it shouldn't matter what form the notice takes. So, whether you create a separate notification letter, use the sales invoice, or use another sale document (being careful to add language informing the customer that you are reporting the information to the IRS), you should be in compliance. What ever you do, you should have a written policy and make sure that everyone follows it!

18. Do I have to keep that statement, or can I throw it away?

Like many other dealership records, you have to keep the form for five years. That's the federal requirement. State law may impose different recordkeeping requirements.

19. Will I get into trouble if I don't file the forms on time, or at all?

It's the IRS. What do you think? There are civil penalties for not filing a correct Form 8300 by the due date and for not providing the required statement to the people who made those payments. If you purposely disregard the Reporting Rule, the penalty is the greater of $25,000 or the amount of cash you received that you were required to report (up to $100,000). That's a whole lotta green. Keep in mind that this all ties in with anti-money laundering and anti-terrorism efforts—the federal government takes this very seriously.

There are also criminal penalties for purposely not filing

Form 8300, purposely filing a false or fraudulent Form 8300, stopping or trying to stop a Form 8300 from being filed, and for setting up, helping to set up, or trying to set up a transaction in a way that would make it seem unnecessary to file a Form 8300 (such as breaking a big transaction up into little transactions).

The IRS will slap some pretty big penalties on you for these things—you can be fined up to $500,000 ($1,500,000 if your gross receipts exceed $5 million) or sentenced to up to five years in prison, or both. Unless you've always wanted to wear a stylish orange jumpsuit and spend your days pounding out license plates (for the cars a dealer who complied with the Rule is still out there selling), file the Form correctly and on time.

20. I looked at Form 8300, and there's something on there called the Suspicious Activity Box. What is that?

That's the box you check when a customer offers you $1,000 over sticker price and the car isn't hot (as in very desirable, not stolen). It's also the box you check when you receive $10,000 or less in cash and feel like something just isn't right.

When a transaction is suspicious, it means that you suspect something strange is going on—perhaps it appears as though the customer is trying to cause you not to file Form 8300 or is trying to cause you to file a false or incomplete Form 8300. In that case, you can choose to file Form 8300. You can also call the IRS Criminal Investigation Division to report suspicious activity. Don't worry—since filing a Form 8300 for suspicious activity is voluntary, you don't have to notify the customer that you've filed the form. Customer notification is only required when filing the form is required. *In fact, your business is prohibited from informing the buyer that the Suspicious Activity Box was checked.*

21. Are the reporting rules different for wholesalers, as opposed to retailers?

Yes. A wholesaler is required to file Form 8300 only if it receives payments in legal tender or coins—it's all about the Benjamins. A wholesaler doesn't have to report payments received in cashier's checks, bank drafts, traveler's checks, or money orders, unless the wholesaler knows that the payer is trying to avoid the reporting of the transaction on Form 8300.

22. I'm a retailer, but I also do some wholesaling on the side. What do I have to report?

If your business principally is retailing—selling to ultimate consumers—then all sales, including wholesale transactions, are considered "retail sales" and are subject to the Form 8300 reporting requirements.

23. If I sell to wholesalers, do I have to accumulate all of the sales to a wholesaler over a one-year period like I would if selling to retail customers?

No, you don't. Each transaction in that scenario stands alone. But, if you know that any of the individual purchases are related, you'll have to file the form.

24. I have a lot of repeat business throughout my dealership. What if a customer buys a vehicle one day, and then a few weeks later, the same customer buys something else from me? Do I have to add these amounts together for filing purposes?

No. If the payments made on these two vehicles are for separate, unrelated transactions, you don't have to aggregate the amounts. Just make sure that the two transactions really are unrelated and separate.

25. What if a customer wire transfers money from his account into the dealership's account? Do I have to report the transfer?

No. Wire transfers represent money already in the system; the Rule is intended to capture cash entering the system to be laundered. So, no reporting is necessary for wire transfers. Even if a customer wires $15,000 to your dealership's account, you're off the hook. The same situation applies if a customer wires $9,000 into your dealership's account and presents $5,000 in cash. Only the $5,000 is treated as cash, so no reporting is necessary.

26. I know that if a customer makes weekly or monthly payments under an installment sale contract to the dealership, I have to add up all of the relevant payments over the one-year period. What about lease payments?

Lease payments are treated just like installment payments or other payments. In the IRS's eyes, the lease of the vehicle is the same as the purchase of a vehicle. So, each time the total amount exceeds $10,000 in cash, the dealership must file a Form 8300 within 15 days of the payment that causes the payments to total more than $10,000.

27. What if a husband and wife buy two cars at the same time from my store, and the total cash received at the time is $10,500. How many Form 8300s should I file?

One or none. This transaction can be viewed as either a single transaction or two related transactions. Worst case, only one Form 8300 must be filed.

28. My body shop does a lot of business, and sometimes we take in more than $10,000 for repairs to a single vehicle. Do I have to file Form 8300 for service repairs?

Yes. The reporting rule applies to goods and services alike. But note that for *service and related repairs,* the expanded definition of cash (cashier's checks, travelers' checks, money orders, etc.) doesn't apply, so *you only have to file if you receive cold hard cash.*

29. What if I have a customer who buys multiple cars from me over a year, all at different times, and I receive payments from him in cash totaling $15,000?

First, give this guy some free oil changes to keep him coming back!

These are separate transactions. No filing is necessary, unless one of his cash payments exceeded $10,000. Say that the customer buys Car #1 on Saturday, and he buys Car #2 two weeks later. These are separate transactions, *unless* you negotiated the purchase of Car #2 at the same time as you negotiated the sale of the first car. If that's the case, the transactions are related and reportable.

30. I sold a car and took in more than $10,000 cash on the deal, but three days later, the deal was unwound, because we couldn't get it financed. We returned the cash to the customer. Now what?

You still have to file the Form 8300. Once the dealership receives the cash, the Form must be filed. The IRS reasons that the deal not going through may in fact be an attempt to launder illegal funds. (It could just be because of bad credit, but in light of the civil and criminal penalties for non-compliance, just do what the IRS tells you.) And remember, even if you took in less than $10,000 cash and the deal was cancelled, you can still choose to file the Form 8300 if you feel that something suspicious is going on.

31. What should I do if a customer wants to know about the 8300 reporting rule?

You can tell a customer anything about the law. And remember that you have to notify a customer in writing when you report information to the IRS. What you can't do is help a customer in structuring a deal to prevent a Form 8300 from being filed. However, remember that if you file a voluntary Form 8300 because of suspicious activity, you are prohibited from informing the customer of that.

Chapter 14

Federal
Do-Not-Call Rules:
FTC Telemarketing
Regulation &
FCC Regulation of
Telephone Calls &
Rule Restricting Calls
to Cell Phones

By Alicia H. Tortarolo,
L. Jean Noonan, and
Michael A. Goodman

Sixteen Things a Car Dealer Needs to Know
About Federal Do-Not-Call Regulations

When the national do-not-call list was established in 2003, it became one of the all-time most popular accomplishments of the federal government. Can you think of anything else Uncle Sam has done that comes close?

However, one group does not think the do-not-call list is the greatest thing since sliced bread—that group makes a living by telemarketing.

But, telemarketers need not despair. Even though there are 217 million numbers on the do-not-call list today, there are still millions and millions of numbers that you—as a car dealer—can call. Moreover, there are a handful of exemptions to the do-not-call list that dealerships should be able to take advantage of—at least for some of their calls.

As a preliminary matter, it is important to understand that federal regulation of telemarketing is more than just the do-not-call list. Two federal agencies—the Federal Trade Commission and the Federal Communications Commission—have enacted telemarketing regulations. In some areas, these regulations are identical. In other areas, they are similar but different. And in yet other areas, they address totally different topics. (Your tax dollars at work.)

This chapter should make your life a little easier. Once we identify the types of calls that are most common for dealerships, we find that many telemarketing regulations do not apply. Dealerships use telephone calls as the first step in a long road of customer development. Dealers don't complete a sale over the phone. Instead, they use the call to invite consumers to visit the dealership, where the main sales pitch will be made. The preliminary nature of that type of phone call automatically qualifies the dealership for an exemption from many federal telemarketing provisions.

So, please note that this chapter only considers telephone calls in which the sale of goods or services is not completed, and payment is not required, until after a face-to-face sales presentation.

With that background, here are 16 things that we think dealers need to know about federal do-not-call regulations.

1. I love avoiding telemarketing calls as much as the next person, but the calls placed by my dealership don't seem like telemarketing to me. Do we really have to worry about the do-not-call list?

Yes, in many cases, but not always. The Federal Trade Commission (FTC) and the Federal Communications Commission (FCC) have indicated that calls inviting a consumer to visit a retail operation for a sales pitch clearly are telemarketing calls, subject to the national do-not-call list.

However, there are exceptions. For example,

- Calling your existing customers, or

- Calling consumers who have expressed an interest recently (see Question 3) in your products and services.

In the above instances, compliance with the do-not-call list is not required.

2. *For starters, can you tell me the federal laws that apply to my calls?*

The first federal law was the Telephone Consumer Protection Act (TCPA), enacted in the early 1990s. The TCPA directed the FCC to write federal telemarketing regulations. Today, the FCC's rules regulate telemarketing and also the use of certain kinds of technology to call consumers, even if there is no sales pitch during the call.

The TCPA is available through our link at www.dealerdeskbook.com/resources/tcpa/. The FCC's rules implementing the TCPA are available at www.dealerdesk book.com/resources/fccrulestcpa/.

In the mid-1990s, Congress passed a second telemarketing law, the Telemarketing and Consumer Fraud and Abuse Prevention Act (TCFAPA). This law directed the FTC to write more comprehensive telemarketing rules. The resulting FTC Telemarketing Sales Rule applies only to interstate telemarketing.

The TCFAPA is available at www.dealerdeskbook.com/resources/tcfapa/ and the FTC's Telemarketing Sales Rule is available at www.dealerdeskbook.com/resources/telemarketing salesrule/.

3. *Let's talk about the 800-pound gorilla in the room—the national do-not-call list—what do I need to know?*

You need to know a place that sells very large bananas. (Just kidding.) The federal government heard loud and clear from the public that many people hate most telemarketing calls. However, the public also said that it did not resent telemarketing calls from companies it does business with. As a result, the national do-not-call list applies broadly to calls with a sales purpose, but does not apply when a business calls its customers or other people who have recently expressed an interest in the business' goods and services.

For dealers, there is good news and bad news here. The good news is that you can call your current customers and your former customers for 18 months after your relationship with them ends, even if they are on the national do-not-call list. For example, you can call a customer for 18 months after he or she buys a car from you or even after he or she asks you to rotate the car's tires.

More good news is that you can also call consumers who haven't bought anything from you yet, but who have recently expressed an interest in what you're selling. If a consumer visits your dealership and leaves her name and number on a sign-in sheet, you can call her back for three months after her visit. If a consumer leaves her name, but not her number, however, the safest course is not to call her without checking to see if the number you come up with for her is on the do-not-call list.

The bad news is that a dealer's call is a *telemarketing call,* even if you're simply inviting the consumer to visit your dealership or you received the consumer's name and number from a customer of yours. For example, if a customer suggests that you call his mother because her car is on its last legs, *you cannot make that call without checking* the do-not-call list. No one can give you permission to call someone else.

You can find out more information about the national do-not-call list at www.dealerdeskbook.com/resources/donotcall/.

4. Assuming all my calls are to invite consumers to visit my dealership, what do I need to know about the FTC's Telemarketing Sales Rule?

First, remember that both the FTC and the FCC regulate telemarketing calls. The FTC's Telemarketing Sales Rule gives favorable treatment to calls that are designed to be followed by a face-to-face presentation before a sale is completed. Not many dealers are selling a car completely over the phone, so this chapter assumes that you call consumers to invite them to visit your dealership to receive your sales pitch. Also, note that the FTC's Telemarketing Sales Rule applies only to interstate calls, not calls made to consumers within the same state. That's great if you place calls to local consumers directly from your dealership, but be careful if you use a third party to make calls for you. They may be using an out-of-state call center to originate calls to consumers in your state. Also be wary if you draw business from neighboring states or make calls from home and your home is across state lines.

The only provisions of the FTC's Telemarketing Sales Rule that apply to a dealer's typical interstate calls are the following:

- You may not use threats, intimidation, or profane or obscene language in your calls.

- You must transmit caller ID information in your calls.

- You must not call someone repeatedly or continuously with intent to annoy, abuse, or harass him or her.

- You must not interfere with anyone's do-not-call rights. That means you must process and honor consumers' requests that you not call them again.

- You must not call someone on the do-not-call list unless you have an exception that allows you to do so.

- You must not call consumers unless you can immediately connect them to a live sales representative. (Some telemarketers use technology that calls many consumers at once; if no sales representative is available, the consumer is hung up on or placed on hold.)

- You must not call consumers with a prerecorded sales message unless you have the person's express agreement (see Question 8 for details) and your messages provide a way for the person to tell you not to call again.

- You must not use a do-not-call list for any purpose other than compliance with the law.

- If you are required to comply with the do-not-call list, you must register for the list, pay the required fee, and comply with all regulations applicable to the list. Your lawyer can give you more information on the details of complying with the do-not-call list requirements and prohibitions.

- You must not call a consumer before 8 a.m. or after 9 p.m.

This may seem like a long list of dos and don'ts, but there are plenty of other provisions in the FTC's Telemarketing Sales Rule that do not apply.

5. What do I need to know about the FCC's TCPA telemarketing regulations?

One useful tip is that some of the FCC's TCPA regulations apply to *all telephone calls,* not just telemarketing calls. Also, the FCC's TCPA regulations apply to *both* interstate calls and intrastate calls. That said, here's the list:

- Unless you have the called party's advance permission, you cannot call that person's cell phone using autodialing technology or a prerecorded message. This permission must be express (not implied); so, if you request consumers' telephone numbers on a sign-in sheet at the dealership, you should *explain* at the top of that sign-in sheet that *you will call them back using the number they provide,* and that sign-in sheet should be the document that dictates making such calls. Note for sales calls: Effective October 16, 2013, this permission must be obtained by "prior express written consent," which is consistent with the FTC Telemarketing Sales Rule's "express agreement" standard for prerecorded sales messages.

- Unless you have the called party's advance permission, you may not "cold call" consumers at home to deliver a *prerecorded sales pitch* (even one inviting them to your dealership). Again, this permission must be express (not implied). Effective October 16, 2013, this permission must be obtained by "prior express written consent."

- You must not call consumers unless you can immediately connect them to a live sales representative. (Some telemarketers use technology that, to maximize sales reps' time on the phone, calls many consumers at once; if no sales representative is available, the consumer is hung up on or placed on hold.) The FCC says you can connect called consumers to a prerecorded message instead of a live sales representative only *if* you have their "prior express written consent."

- When you are permitted to contact consumers with a prerecorded message, at the beginning of the message you must identify the party responsible for the call. During or after the message, you also must provide that party's call-back number. The number provided must allow consumers to call back to make a do-not-call request. And, effective January 14, 2013, prerecorded sales messages must incorporate a do-not-call/opt-out mechanism.

- Unless you are calling a customer or someone who has recently expressed an interest in your dealership, you may not call before 8 a.m. or after 9 p.m. Bear this in mind, particularly, if you call across time zones.

- Unless you are calling a customer or someone who has recently expressed an interest in your dealership, you may not call anyone on the do-not-call list. Your lawyer can give you more information on the details of complying with the do-not-call list requirements and prohibitions and help you to assure that third parties, if any, providing names for you to call also comply.

- If you make telemarketing calls, you must have your own internal, written do-not-call policy that is available to consumers who ask for it; you must train your callers to comply with the law; and you must process and honor do-not-call requests.

- In all telemarketing calls, you must identify the party responsible for the call (the individual caller or the dealership) and that party's telephone number or address.

- In all telemarketing calls, you must transmit caller ID information. You may arrange for the transmitted information to be a customer service telephone number rather than the specific line that was used to place the call. You are prohibited from knowingly causing any caller identification service to transmit or display misleading or inaccurate caller identification information with the intent to defraud, cause harm, or wrongfully obtain anything of value (otherwise known as "caller ID spoofing").

• If you use autodialing technology, you must comply with a series of technical requirements. Your lawyer can help you with the specifics of these standards.

6. My dealership is part of a larger corporate structure—I have affiliates and parent companies within this structure. Will do-not-call requests apply across my corporate structure?

This is the situation in which the classic lawyer response applies: It depends. The FCC says a do-not-call request to your dealership applies only to your dealership and not to entities affiliated with you, unless the consumer reasonably would expect your affiliates to be included in the do-not-call request. Whether a consumer would reasonably expect your affiliates to be included in the request depends on whether you and your affiliates have similar names and sell similar merchandise. The more different the name and offering, the less likely it is that the request will extend to your affiliates. The FTC basically says the same thing.

7. If I call a consumer and she tells me not to call again, how quickly must I process that request? And how long do I need to keep her name on my company do-not-call list?

The FCC says you must honor these do-not-call requests within 30 days. Do-not-call requests must be honored for five years. Registration on the national do-not-call list is permanent, unless the consumer removes his or her number from the list or the number is disconnected or reassigned.

8. I'd like to use a prerecorded message for marketing to leads and current customers. Is that allowed?

Not anymore. The FTC's Telemarketing Sales Rule now prohibits all prerecorded sales messages unless you have the called person's "express agreement." That agreement must be in writing (electronic form is also OK), signed by the person, and must include the person's telephone number. In collecting this agreement, you must clearly and conspicuously explain what the person is agreeing to, and you must identify yourself as the company receiving the agreement. You cannot require a person to provide this agreement as a condition of a purchase by that person.

When you get this required agreement, your message must begin within two seconds of the person's greeting, and you must comply with complex standards for giving people an easy way to tell you not to call again. You must also allow all unanswered calls to ring for at least four rings or 15 seconds if you place prerecorded sales calls.

In 2013, two sets of FCC rule amendments will take effect so that, ultimately, the FCC's regulation of prerecorded sales messages will resemble the FTC's approach. The standards will be similar but not identical, so you will need to proceed carefully here. Beginning on January 14, 2013, the FCC will require prerecorded sales messages to include a particular form of do-not-call/opt-out mechanism, like the FTC currently requires. Beginning on October 16, 2013, the FCC will require a specifically-regulated "prior express written consent" for prerecorded sales messages that differs from the FTC's approach.

These are tricky standards, so if you are interested in prerecorded message telemarketing, you should discuss these standards with your lawyer.

9. My dealership likes to be on the cutting edge of marketing techniques. Do these telemarketing regulations apply to text messages?

The FCC says that its telemarketing regulations apply to text messages that are delivered without using the Internet. For example, "short messages"—which are sent from one mobile phone to another without using an Internet address— are regulated by telemarketing regulations. In other words, the FCC has said that a phone call is a phone call, whether the call involves a voice communication or a text communication.

Therefore, you should avoid using autodialing technology to deliver "cold call" text messages in bulk. You should also avoid sending phone-to-phone text messages to consumers on the do-not-call list. You can send text messages with the recipient's permission and, if you are not using a dialer, to people with whom you have an established business relationship (based on a purchase or an inquiry or application).

For a discussion of federal regulation of email messages, including text messages delivered via the Internet, see the Do-Not-Email discussion in Chapter 16.

10. Are there any recordkeeping requirements?

The FTC Telemarketing Sales Rule recordkeeping requirements do not apply to telephone calls in which the sale is not completed until after a face-to-face sales presentation by the seller. However, you are still required to keep records of do-not-call requests. Also, the FTC does not require callers to keep records showing that calls were based on an established business relationship, but keeping such records makes good business sense. If you call a former customer and he complains to the FTC that the call was illegal because he is on the do-not-call list, you will want to be able to produce a record of the existence of that business relationship. Better still is a written calling procedure that demonstrates where the names and numbers to call *come from*. That way, the dealership can confirm that an individual call was legal and that its procedure is designed to ensure that all such calls are legal.

Similarly, the FCC's TCPA regulations do not include distinct recordkeeping requirements, but these regulations call for written policies of do-not-call compliance efforts. Accordingly, you will always want to have documentation of defenses and safe harbors available to you, such as the existence of an established business relationship or advance permission from a called consumer.

11. Are there any available defenses if I get sued?

There are defenses and safe harbors built in to many of the federal telemarketing provisions.

With respect to the FTC's Telemarketing Sales Rule, you can call someone on the do-not-call list if they give you written and signed permission. You also can call someone on the do-not-call list based on an established business relationship (which may be based on a purchase or a simple inquiry). If you call someone on the do-not-call list by accident, you haven't broken the law as long as you comply with the following:

- You have a written do-not-call compliance policy.

- You train employees on the policy.

- You monitor and enforce compliance.

- You keep a dealer-specific do-not-call list.

- You have a process in place for complying with the national do-not-call list.

Also, there is a safe harbor available if you use autodialing technology and, on rare occasions, no live sales representative is available to speak with a live consumer who answers your call. Your lawyer can assist you with the details of this complex safe harbor.

The FCC's defenses and safe harbors under its TCPA regulations are similar, with a key difference that takes effect in 2013. The do-not-call list safe harbor requires a showing of *all of the following:*

- A call to a number on the do-not-call list was the result of error.

- The caller had a written compliance policy and trained its callers on that policy.

- The caller maintained an internal do-not-call list.

- The caller had a process for complying with the do-not-call list.

Additional do-not-call exemptions are available based on an established business relationship or a personal relationship. Beginning on January 14, 2013, the FCC's safe harbor for autodialing technology when no sales representative is available will look a lot different from the FTC's approach. Again, you should work with your lawyer on this complex issue, but you should note that your safe harbor message will need to include the same do-not-call/opt-out mechanism as in your prerecorded sales messages. The FTC does not require this.

12. *Let's say my telemarketing violates the law. Who can come after me?*

The FTC and state law enforcement can sue for violations of the FTC's Telemarketing Sales Rule. The Consumer Financial Protection Bureau can also bring an enforcement action for violations of the Rule with respect to the offering or provision of a consumer financial product or service by dealers who are subject to the Dodd-Frank Wall Street Reform and Consumer Protection Act of 2010 (Dodd-Frank Act; see Chapter 19). Theoretically, consumers can also sue, but the standard is very high, and no one has ever brought a private suit based on the FTC's Telemarketing Sales Rule.

The FCC, state law enforcement, and individual call recipients can sue for violations of the FCC's TCPA regulations. And, in the telemarketing arena, private suits have been brought with some frequency and success.

13. *But I'm not some notorious telemarketer. Is anyone really going to come after me if I break these laws?*

The federal agencies typically focus their telemarketing enforcement efforts on actions that result in consumers' losing money. However, they are also determined to protect the utility of the national do-not-call list. To that end, the federal agencies have sued companies for failure to comply with the do-not-call list, even if consumers did not sustain substantial money losses.

Recently, it appears that the federal agencies have also filed suits in an attempt to bring an enforcement action for each possible violation. For example, recent suits have targeted failure to transmit caller ID information, failure to use autodialing technology properly, and failure to maintain and honor a company-specific do-not-call list.

The federal agencies don't go out of their way to sue small-time violators, as opposed to people who do the most harm, but they do try to vary their prosecutions in a way that sends signals to different industries that they—the feds—are on the prowl. The bottom line is that the best way to avoid being sued is to implement a robust compliance program, make sure it is followed, update it as needed, and take all complaints from consumers seriously. Failure to address consumer complaints yourself is one way those complaints wind up with a federal regulator.

14. I use a professional call center to make my calls for me. Which one of us is responsible if calls violate federal telemarketing laws?

Both of you. The FTC and the FCC have clearly indicated that both the business promoted in the call and any third party placing calls on behalf of a business face liability for violations of federal telemarketing regulations. In announcing a $5.3 million penalty against DirecTV, the FTC chairman stated, "Sellers are on the hook for calls placed on their behalf." The FTC's suit against DirecTV targeted both the business being promoted and the callers hired by the business. If you use a third party to place calls for you, you must monitor its telemarketing activities and respond promptly to consumer complaints. Your contract with such a call center must address these issues, but merely addressing responsibility for legal compliance in your contract with a call center will not provide you with a defense in a federal enforcement action.

15. If I get sued, what penalties can I face?

For violations of the FTC's Telemarketing Sales Rule, courts can award up to $16,000 for each violation of the Rule. For dealers subject to the Dodd-Frank Act, courts or the CFPB may award anywhere from $5,000 to $1 million for each day a violation continues.

The FCC can ask for the same penalty for violations of its TCPA regulations, but it usually fires a warning shot before it does so. A separate penalty structure—up to $10,000 per violation or three times that amount for each day of a continuing violation—applies for violations of the prohibition on caller ID spoofing. State law enforcement and individual call recipients can obtain up to $500 for each violation (and triple that amount for willful or knowing violations).

16. What about state telemarketing laws? Do I have to comply with them too? Or do the federal laws preempt state laws?

The FTC's Telemarketing Sales Rule does *not* preempt any state telemarketing law.

The FCC's TCPA regulations *do* preempt *some* state telemarketing laws. The FCC's regulations preempt state laws regarding technical and procedural standards governing the use of automated dialing technology and disclosure requirements for prerecorded messages.

However, you should be aware that many states' telemarketing laws address issues not raised at the federal level, such as the obligation to register with the state before engaging in telemarketing. Because this is a complex issue, you should discuss it with your lawyer.

Federal Communications Commission: The Do-Not-Fax Rule

By L. Jean Noonan,
Alicia H. Tortarolo, and
Michael A. Goodman

Nineteen Things a Car Dealer Needs to Know About Federal Do-Not-Fax Regulations

Facsimile machines have been with the industry for many years, mostly to enable F&I and lender personnel to trade credit applications, credit approvals, and other related documents quickly and expeditiously.

Federal regulation of faxed ads began with a quiet 12 years from 1991–2003. Under the federal Telephone Consumer Protection Act (47 U.S.C. § 227) (TCPA), junk fax advertising was prohibited, and recipients had a private cause of action against the businesses that sent junk faxes. You can find the TCPA at the link we maintain for your convenience at www.dealerdeskbook.com/resources/junkfaxlaw/. This federal ban, of course, preempted any lesser stringent do-not-fax rules on the state level.

In 2003, however, at the same time that the federal government was establishing the national do-not-call list, the Federal Communications Commission (FCC) decided to tinker with its regulation of faxed ads by proposing to make *all faxed ads illegal unless the sender had the recipient's advance written permission.* This was a "heart attack" for fax machine manufacturers.

Before this proposal could take effect, businesses that make it a practice to send faxed ads loudly took their grievances about the FCC to Congress. The FCC agreed to shelve its proposal while Congress considered how to resolve this dispute. In July 2005, Congress took action by passing the Junk Fax Prevention Act (JFPA). You can find the JFPA at www.dealerdeskbook.com/resources/jfpa/.

The JFPA resolved the uncertainty surrounding federal

regulation of faxed ads once and for all. This Act restored the original approach: Faxed ads are permitted if they are based on an established business relationship or the recipient's advance permission. Junk faxes remain prohibited, but senders did not need advance permission to send the fax, so long as there was an established business relationship with the recipient.

However, the Act also imposed new requirements: All faxed ads must include a notice explaining how recipients can opt-out of receiving future faxed ads from the sender.

With that background, here are 19 things that we think dealers need to know about federal do-not-fax regulations.

1. What do you mean by "do-not-fax"?

Since the earliest federal regulation of faxed ads, unsolicited ads have been prohibited. Delivery of these ads imposes significant and unavoidable costs on recipients—they must pay for the paper and toner to print the sender's ad. Even the earliest regulation, however, recognized that recipients didn't mind faxed ads from companies they did business with, compared to blasts of faxed ads from vendors they did not know or from fly-by-night operations.

Congress preserved favorable treatment for faxed ads, based on an established business relationship or the recipient's consent, when it passed the JFPA in July 2005. In that respect, Congress resolved faxed ad senders' biggest concern in their favor.

However, in recognition of the costs that recipients of all faxes bear—even faxes sent based on an established business relationship or the recipient's consent—the JFPA requires *all* faxed ads to include an opt-out disclosure, and the JFPA requires senders to honor recipients' do-not-fax requests. This means that, even if you have a golden ticket from Willy Wonka inviting you to send him faxed ads, you still must include an opt-out notice in those ads, and you must take Willy off of your faxing list if he asks you to.

2. Where do I go to find out what I'm supposed to do?

Three federal laws and two federal regulations address faxed ads. But relax: This book tells you what you need to know, not what you might want to know. And what you need to know is contained in two federal regulations issued by the Federal Communications Commission (FCC). They provide the federal "dos" and "don'ts" of faxed ads.

The primary regulation contains the new opt-out provisions and definitions of useful terms. The secondary regulation requires the disclosure of certain information about the sender and the transmission in every fax.

These regulations are available at www.dealerdesk book.com/resources/optout/ and www.dealerdeskbook.com/ resources/disclosure/.

3. What do the FCC's faxing regulations say?

These regulations prohibit faxed ads, unless there is an established business relationship between the sender and the recipient or the recipient has provided advance permission.

Assuming a faxed ad is permitted, the first page of the ad must include a clear and conspicuous notice explaining that the recipient has the right to opt-out of receiving future faxes and the method the recipient must use to opt-out.

All faxes must disclose the date and time the fax is sent and the name and telephone number of the entity responsible for the fax.

4. To whom do these regulations apply?

The FCC's faxing regulations apply to all entities sending faxed ads. The regulations apply equally to faxes sent across the street, across the country, and to faxes sent to individual consumers, enormous corporations, and Willy Wonka.

The FCC considered, but rejected, an exemption for non-profit organizations and associations communicating with their members.

5. I hire a fax broadcaster to handle my faxes for me. Does that mean I'm off the hook?

No. The FCC regulations recognize that many businesses hire a third-party fax broadcaster to send faxes on their behalf. The FCC permits this action, but maintains that the business being promoted in a faxed ad must comply with the notice requirement and honor opt-out requests and comply with all other applicable provisions.

Businesses may hire a third party to process opt-out requests on their behalf, but they are still responsible for compliance.

6. Most of my faxes are sent to companies I do business with. They are not "spam faxes" sent to consumers. Does that mean I'm off the hook?

Yes and no. Again, the FCC's regulations permit you to send faxed ads to recipients based on an established business relationship, so you're off the hook with respect to the ban on unsolicited faxed ads.

However, these regulations require you to comply with the new opt-out provisions—you must disclose the opt-out rights to recipients, and you must honor their opt-out requests.

The FCC doesn't care if the receipt of your faxed ads is the highlight of someone's day. You still must give that person the opportunity to opt-out of getting more of your faxed ads in the future.

7. When I send faxes to consumers, it's because they ask for them. Am I off the hook?

Again, yes and no. The FCC allows you to send faxed ads to someone who has asked for them. However, your faxes must include the opt-out notice, and you must honor recipients' opt-out requests.

8. Are any types of faxed advertisements excluded from these regulations?

No. The new opt-out notice requirements apply to all faxed ads. The FCC has indicated that even those faxes that advertise goods or services for free may still be a faxed ad, if the free offer is meant to promote goods or services offered for a fee. However, faxes that contain only information, such as news articles or employee benefit information, are not regulated by these new requirements.

9. OK. Let's get down to nuts and bolts. What exactly do my disclosures need to say and where do they need to go?

The FCC's regulations require all faxed ads to include a notice with three specific disclosures:

- All faxes must clearly mark, in a margin at the top or bottom of each page, or on the first page, the date and time the fax was sent.

- All faxes must clearly mark, in a margin at the top or bottom of each page, the identity of the entity or individual responsible for the fax and that entity's or individual's telephone number.

- According to the JFPA, all faxed ads must also include the opt-out notice clearly and conspicuously on the first page of the ad. "Clear and conspicuous" has a particular definition in this last context. It means an opt-out notice that would be apparent to the reasonable consumer, separate and distinguishable from the advertising copy or other disclosures, and placed at either the top or bottom of the fax.

The FCC does not set any specific font type or size requirements, but it does indicate that the opt-out notice should use bolding, italics, a different font, or similar techniques to be distinguishable from other content on the same page.

No specific wording is required, but to ensure compliance, it makes sense to stick as closely as possible to the wording used in the regulation. For example, the following opt-out disclosure language would comply with the regulation:

> The recipient of this fax may make a request to the sender not to send any future advertisements to that recipient. A sender's failure to comply with such a request within 30 days is unlawful. A recipient may submit an opt-out request by calling [(xxx) xxx-xxxx] or sending a fax to [(xxx) xxx-xxxx]. A recipient's opt-out request must identify the telephone number(s) of the fax machine(s) to which the request relates and be made to the telephone number or fax number identified in this advertisement.

Note several elements of this sample disclosure:

- The notice must disclose the recipient's right to opt-*out* and that failure to honor an opt-out request is unlawful.

- The notice must explain what the recipient must do to submit a valid opt-out request.

- The notice must be on the first page of the fax's *advertising* material. If a cover page precedes that material, the FCC encourages (but does not require) the notice to appear on the cover page as well.

- The notice must include an opt-out telephone number *and* fax number. If neither of these numbers is a toll-free number, the notice must include a cost-free option for submitting an opt-out request, such as a website address or email address.

10. Tell me how the opt-out mechanism needs to work.

Your opt-out mechanism must include a telephone number and a fax number that recipients may use to submit opt-out requests. If neither of these numbers is toll-free, then you must also provide a website address or email address where recipients may submit an opt-out request at no cost.

All contact points for submitting an opt-out request must be available 24 hours a day, 7 days a week.

The FCC requires senders to honor opt-out requests within "the shortest reasonable time." This period of time must be no longer than 30 days.

11. Does the new regulation address the format for submitting opt-out requests? What if a consumer sends me an opt-out letter by U.S. mail?

A recipient's opt-out request must identify the fax number(s) to which the request relates and be made using a mechanism provided in the sender's opt-out notice. You are not required to honor an opt-out request that does not meet these standards. However, an established customer that goes to the trouble of writing to ask you not to send unsolicited faxes really ought to be heeded, just as if his notice by mail was binding.

Note that an opt-out request terminates an "established business relationship" for purposes of being able to send unsolicited faxed ads. A sender may resume sending faxed ads to a recipient who previously opted-out, if the sender subsequently receives the recipient's express invitation or permission.

12. What constitutes an "established business relationship"?

The FCC's regulations include a special definition of "established business relationship" (EBR) that applies only to faxed ads. This definition is special in the faxing context, because the EBR never expires. This relationship may be created by either a purchase or an inquiry or application. And remember that, while EBRs do not expire with the passage of time, they do terminate if the recipient opts-out.

As a general rule for fax transmissions, an EBR typically means that someone has bought something from you or has expressed an interest in buying something from you.

13. Does the FCC regulation address where I get the fax numbers of my EBR recipients?

Yes, when the faxed ad is based on an established business relationship. The regulation says faxed ads based on an EBR are permitted only if (i) the recipient voluntarily provided his fax number to the sender; or (ii) the recipient's fax number was voluntarily made available to a publicly available directory, advertisement, or website.

If a sender obtains a recipient's fax number from other sources, the sender must take reasonable steps to verify that the recipient made the fax number publicly available.

Please note that this restriction includes a grandfather clause: With respect to any EBR that existed before July 9, 2005, it does not matter where the sender obtained the recipient's fax number as long as the sender had the recipient's fax number before July 9, 2005.

14. What constitutes "prior express invitation or permission"?

This term is used in the FCC's definition of "unsolicited advertisement." A faxed ad is unsolicited, *unless* it is sent in response to a recipient's "prior express invitation or permission."

What constitutes "prior express invitation or permission" is a source of some confusion, because the FCC has not directly stated what is, and is not, sufficient. Congress clarified one issue in the JFPA by stating that the invitation or permission need *not* be in writing. A recipient's oral or electronic consent may be sufficient. But note, if a sender is sued for non-compliance, he may have to prove the existence of a recipient's invitation or permission. A written document (or a recording of a telephone conversation) would be the best verifiable source of such proof.

The FCC has given some guidance on this standard. The invitation or permission must include the fax number to which ads may be sent. It cannot be in the form of a "negative option." (*I can fax to you unless you tell me "no."*) And, of course, it must be "express" and must be given prior to the sending of any faxed ads.

The FCC advises that a sender requesting a fax number on an application form could include a clear statement that, "by providing such fax number," the applicant agrees to receive faxed ads. Submission of an application, including a fax number, would create an established business relationship for purposes of this regulation. This also may suggest that an application would not constitute sufficient express permission if the form requested a fax number, but did not also state that the recipient agrees to receive faxed ads at that number.

Incidentally, you also may not fax a person in order to request his or her consent to receive faxed ads.

15. Do the FCC's faxing regulations impose any recordkeeping requirements?

These regulations do not include recordkeeping requirements, but the FCC has stated that senders relying on a recipient's prior express invitation or permission must be prepared to demonstrate that all invitations and permissions were in fact "prior" and "express." The FCC also strongly encourages senders to "promptly document" that they received a recipient's invitation or permission.

16. Do the federal faxing laws and regulations address preemption? What do I do about state laws that are inconsistent with the federal approach?

The federal requirements to disclose the date and time of each fax and the name and telephone number of the party responsible for the fax would "preempt," or invalidate, any inconsistent state law.

The federal law does not always preempt other state laws regarding faxes. However, one recent court decision found that a California law inconsistent with the JFPA was preempted. This state law would have required the recipient's consent before any faxed ad could be sent. The court refused to apply this restriction to interstate faxes, but it did allow this restriction to apply to faxes sent from California senders to California recipients. Similarly, a state law requiring more disclosure than the federal law probably would not be preempted.

Based on this information, it is unclear when the federal regulation of faxes will preempt inconsistent state laws. You should confirm whether any such laws apply to your customary business advertisement faxing practices, and consult your lawyer whenever you encounter an inconsistent state law.

17. What is the penalty for violations?

The FCC's typical approach is to issue a "Citation" alleging violations of the law. If violations continue, the FCC may issue a "Notice of Apparent Liability," which sets a proposed fine amount. The FCC may fine a sender up to $16,000 for each faxed ad that violates the law. Senders receiving a Notice of Apparent Liability have 30 days to either pay the proposed fine or file a statement seeking a reduction or cancellation of the proposed fine.

In one recent Notice of Apparent Liability, the FCC proposed a fine of $4,500 for each unlawful unsolicited faxed ad and $10,000 for each unsolicited faxed ad sent to a recipient who had previously submitted an opt-out request.

18. Who can enforce violations of the FCC's faxing regulations?

The FCC can enforce its own regulations. State law enforcement officials can also bring law enforcement actions and can obtain up to $500 per violation (and up to $1,500 for willful or knowing violations). Recipients of unlawful faxed ads have a private right of action and can obtain up to $500 per violation (and up to $1,500 for willful or knowing violations).

19. Are there any available defenses if I get sued?

There is no formal defense or safe harbor if you get sued for sending faxed ads improperly. You should be prepared to document why your faxes did not violate the law. This would include records of any recipient consent, established business relationships (including evidence that recipients provided fax numbers voluntarily), and functional opt-out procedures. Your office procedures should include regular maintenance of these types of records.

CHAPTER 15

Federal Trade Commission: The Do-Not-Email Rule

By L. Jean Noonan,
Alicia H. Tortarolo, and
Michael A. Goodman

Twenty-Two Things a Car Dealer Needs to Know About Federal Do-Not-Email Regulations

Many of us have differing definitions of email "spam," but most of us agree on one thing: We hate it. In 2003, Congress cut through all the confusion about what is, and is not, spam by creating its own definition, along with the rules of the road for email marketing in the CAN-SPAM Act. Ironically, the only place the word "spam" appears in this Act is in the title.

The first lesson of CAN-SPAM compliance is that this law does *not* outlaw unsolicited commercial email. You can blast email marketing all day and all night. But, you must stop sending commercial email to recipients who tell you to stop. You also must be truthful in your "from" line and "subject" line, and you must make certain disclosures in all commercial messages.

With that background, here are 22 things dealers should know about federal "Do-Not-Email" regulations.

1. So what does "CAN-SPAM" stand for anyway?

"CAN-SPAM" stands for the Controlling the Assault of Non-Solicited Pornography and Marketing Act of 2003. Congress loves acronyms.

Because the CAN-SPAM Act allows you to send unsolicited commercial email messages, some jokers refer to this law as the "(You) Can Spam Act."

The text of the CAN-SPAM Act is available at www.dealerdeskbook.com/resources/canspamact/.

2. In the introduction, you said that there are lots of different definitions of spam, but Congress picked just one. What is Congress' definition?

In the CAN-SPAM Act, instead of defining spam, Congress defined the term "commercial electronic mail message." *These* are the messages that have to comply with all provisions of the Act. Congress also defined "transactional or relationship email messages." More on the latter messages in Question 3.

The term "commercial electronic mail message," or "commercial email message," means a message whose primary purpose is the advertisement or promotion of a product or service. In other words, an email message is commercial if its *primary purpose* is to advertise something. Notice what Congress left out of the definition:

- There is no bulk distribution list requirement (even a single commercial message must comply);

- There is no exception for permission-based messages; and

- There is no exception for business-to-business messages.

3. Does CAN-SPAM apply to email messages with a primary purpose that is not commercial?

Yes. CAN-SPAM also regulates "transactional or relationship email messages." These are messages that build on a pre-existing relationship between the sender and the recipient of an email message and concern that pre-existing relationship. Examples:

- Messages that confirm a transaction between the sender and recipient;

- Messages providing warranty or product recall information; and

- Messages delivering goods or services to a recipient who previously agreed to receive such messages from the sender.

However, only one CAN-SPAM provision applies to transactional or relationship email messages. The rest of CAN-SPAM applies only to commercial email messages covered in Question 6.

4. I might want to send messages that advertise my dealership and concern a pre-existing relationship I have with a customer. How would those messages be treated?

It will depend. This is one of the tricky parts of CAN-SPAM. We'll walk through this together. Take it slow.

First, Congress told the FTC to figure out how to answer this question. The FTC issued criteria to help people determine the "primary purpose" of an email message. If a message has a "commercial" primary purpose, it is considered a commercial email message. If it has a "transactional or relationship" primary purpose, it is considered a transactional or relationship email message. If the primary purpose is *neither,* then the message is not covered by CAN-SPAM.

Second, the FTC divided the universe of possible email messages that could be covered by CAN-SPAM into four categories:

- Some messages have *only commercial content.* These messages automatically have a commercial primary purpose and are considered "commercial email messages" under CAN-SPAM.

- Some messages have *only transactional or relationship content.* These messages automatically have a "transactional or relationship" primary purpose and are considered "transactional or relationship email messages" under CAN-SPAM.

Sounds easy so far, right? Here comes the tricky part.

- Some messages have *both commercial content and "transactional or relationship" content.* These messages have a "transactional or relationship" primary purpose if the "subject" line of the message refers only to the message's "transactional or relationship" content AND the message's "transactional or relationship" content is placed at the start of the message. To say it another way, if your message has both types of content, and it refers to the commercial content in the "subject" line, OR it begins with the commercial content, then it has a commercial primary purpose and will be considered a commercial email message under CAN-SPAM.

- Some messages have *both commercial content and some other type of content* (for example, a weather report or news update). These messages have a commercial primary purpose and are considered commercial email messages under CAN-SPAM if the "subject" line refers to the commercial content OR the message's recipient believes that the primary purpose of the message is commercial.

The recipient!?! Note well: If satisfying your compliance burden depends on an email message being commercial or unregulated by CAN-SPAM, remember that determination could be in the hands of a recipient. The FTC suggests that a recipient will believe a message has a commercial primary purpose if the commercial content is the most prominent content in the message.

The FTC's CAN-SPAM rules are available at www.dealer deskbook.com/resources/canspamrules/.

5. Why should I care what the "primary purpose" of my message is?

You should care, because commercial email messages are heavily regulated by CAN-SPAM; transactional or relationship email messages are lightly regulated; and other types of email messages are not regulated by CAN-SPAM at all.

6. What do you mean "CAN-SPAM heavily regulates or lightly regulates" email messages? What do I need to know to ensure that I comply with the law?

You may be sure that you comply if you do all of the following:

- Verify the accuracy of your "from" and routing information. Let's start with the one provision that applies to both commercial and transactional or relationship email messages: CAN-SPAM says all such messages must have accurate information in the "from" line and in the routing information (which shows the path a message took between the sender and the recipient).

CAN-SPAM's other provisions apply only to commercial email messages:

- Make sure the "subject" line is true. Commercial email messages must have truthful "subject" lines.

- Include a way to opt-out. Commercial email messages must include an opt-out mechanism.

- Always honor opt-out requests.

- Be sure that your ads say that they are ads. Commercial email messages must identify themselves as advertisements.

- Include the sender's address.

7. Let's start with the "from" line and routing information. How do I make sure I comply with this provision by providing accurate information?

CAN-SPAM prohibits senders from using misleading "from" line information or routing information. Congress knew spammers routinely used fake information in these places so they couldn't be found.

CAN-SPAM says this information is misleading if it hinders law enforcement's ability to find the actual sender. CAN-SPAM also says that a message automatically complies with this provision if the "from" line identifies any person who was responsible for transmitting the message. The "from" line should either identify the dealership responsible for the message or an email service provider used by the dealership to transmit the message.

8. Next, how do I make sure I comply with the "subject" line regulation?

CAN-SPAM prohibits commercial email messages from using a "subject" line likely to mislead a recipient about the contents or subject matter of the message. Congress added this provision because spammers routinely used deceptive "subject" lines to get recipients to open messages they otherwise would have deleted.

For example, a "subject" line that says "Urgent public safety message from the federal government" is illegal if the commercial email message then advertises herbal products that are supposed to change the appearance of a body part. (Word to the wise: Those "subject" lines don't work, and possibly, neither do the herbs.)

As long as your "subject" line is consistent with the content of your commercial email message, you will be fine.

9. How do I make sure I comply with the "opt-out mechanism" regulation?

All commercial email messages must include a clear and conspicuous opt-out mechanism that email recipients can use to tell the sender to stop sending future commercial email messages. This mechanism must be a reply email address or a link to a website; it *cannot* be a postal address, fax number, or phone number.

The sender must keep the opt-out mechanism available for at least 30 days after sending a commercial email message. If your opt-out mechanism suffers from technical difficulties, that alone will not protect you from being sued; however, you are protected so long as the opt-out problem was beyond your control and you corrected it within a reasonable time period.

CAN-SPAM's opt-out rights apply only to commercial email messages. You can continue to send transactional or relationship email messages to a recipient who submits an opt-out request, although that raises obvious customer relations issues.

Finally, CAN-SPAM allows you to present a *range* of opt-out choices in your opt-out mechanism, as long as one choice allows a recipient to opt-out of all of your commercial email messages. For example, a dealership could allow recipients to opt-out of messages advertising new models in stock but continue to receive messages delivering coupons related to parts and service.

There are certain things you cannot do in your opt-out mechanism, according to the FTC's CAN-SPAM Rule. In processing opt-out requests, you cannot charge a fee, require the recipient to provide any information other than email address and opt-out preferences, display additional advertising material, or require the person to do more than visit one web page or send a single email message.

10. What should I do with opt-out requests that I receive?

CAN-SPAM says you must process and honor opt-out requests within 10 business days after you receive the request. You can use a vendor, such as an email service provider, to do this for you. If it's taking longer than 10 business days to process your commercial email opt-out or suppression requests, you should delay sending new commercial email messages until your opt-out/suppression processing catches up.

CAN-SPAM also says that, beginning immediately after you receive an opt-out request, you must make sure that you do not sell, exchange, or otherwise release the email address of the recipient who submitted the request.

If you were not seriously managing your mailing list before, these email rules will require you to do so for email addresses, at least, to avoid liability. If a recipient submits an opt-out request and later gives you consent to resume sending commercial messages, you may do so. Otherwise, *opt-out requests last forever;* there is no expiration date.

11. How do I comply with required CAN-SPAM disclosures?

CAN-SPAM requires commercial email messages to include three disclosures.

- First, they must clearly and conspicuously identify that the commercial email message is an advertisement. The FTC says you don't have to announce "THIS IS AN AD!" at the beginning of the message, but it should be clear that the message is selling something. Do not hide that purpose.

- Second, the opt-out mechanism described above must be clear and conspicuous. The FTC seems to agree that it is OK to put this at the end of the message because that is what everybody does. It must be easy to find, however, and the notice of the mechanism must be clear. Don't make a puzzle out of it. The opt-out mechanism should say something like, "If you do not want to receive additional commercial messages from us, please reply to this message with the word 'Unsubscribe' in the 'subject' line."

- Third, commercial email messages must include the sender's "valid physical postal address." "Valid physical postal address" is not a common term. The street address of your location is good enough, as is a P.O. Box, according to the FTC.

12. Does CAN-SPAM regulate email messages in any other ways?

Yes. CAN-SPAM also addresses what it calls "aggravated violations." If you commit an aggravated violation (listed below) while also violating one of the provisions discussed previously, a court can triple your penalty. The aggravated violations are:

- Improperly "harvesting" email addresses from the Internet (using a software program that finds email addresses on the Internet and adds them to your recipient list);

- Engaging in "dictionary attacks" (sending email to a@xyz.com, b@xyz.com, c@xyz.com, etc.);

- Signing up for multiple email accounts using special software designed for that purpose (only spammers do this); and

- Routing your email through someone else's computer without their permission (only spammers do this, too).

CAN-SPAM also regulates sending commercial email messages containing adult content. If you're doing this to promote your dealership, you might want to try a different technique.

13. Does CAN-SPAM regulate forward-to-a-friend or viral marketing email messages?

Yes. In some cases, you can be on the hook if your original recipient forwards your email to his friends and the message he forwards does not comply with the law. Here's how it works:

CAN-SPAM says the original sender of a commercial email message (that's you) can be held responsible for violations if the sender pays someone else to send a message on the sender's behalf, whether we're talking about money or some other type of compensation. That means you're on the hook if you give people coupons for forwarding your commercial messages. On the other hand, if your recipient forwards your message without any encouragement from you, you're not responsible for what happens to the message after that.

It's OK for consumers to visit your website and give you the email addresses of leads as long as you make sure that none of these leads has sent you an opt-out request and that your messages otherwise comply with CAN-SPAM. (In other words, you need email list management.)

14. A detailing shop around the corner from my dealership wants to send out commercial messages that advertise both of our businesses. Is that allowed?

Dealing with commercial messages promoting more than one business is one of the trickier CAN-SPAM issues. The FTC has created a kind of safe harbor for these messages. This safe harbor requires one of the businesses to assume responsibility for CAN-SPAM compliance while giving the other businesses a free pass. This one business will be considered the only "sender" of the message if the business satisfies CAN-SPAM's "sender" definition, is listed in the message's "from" line, and otherwise complies with CAN-SPAM.

The law on this issue is complicated, so check with your lawyer before contributing to a commercial message promoting more than one business.

15. Let's say my email marketing violates the law. Who can come after me?

CAN-SPAM lets a lot of people sue you for violations. The only person who cannot sue you is the person who received your message. The federal government can sue you, state governments can sue you, and Internet service providers can sue you. And, all of these people have sued spammers for CAN-SPAM violations.

16. But I'm not a spammer. Is anyone really going to come after me if I break this law?

From the time CAN-SPAM enforcement began in 2004 until early in 2006, only blatant spammers had been sued. However, in the spring of 2006, the Federal Trade Commission sued Kodak for what was basically a technical glitch. That glitch resulted in a large number of email messages that were missing the disclosures required by CAN-SPAM. The FTC sued Kodak for that glitch, and the case settled for about $30,000.

That's not to say that you're going to get sued for every little mistake, but law enforcement is on the lookout for targets all the time. As always, the best way to avoid trouble is to implement a rigorous program of compliance, training, and quality control.

17. I use an email service provider (or another type of vendor) to send out my messages for me. Which one of us is responsible if the message violates CAN-SPAM?

CAN-SPAM says both you (as the business promoted in the message) and your service provider are responsible for violations. CAN-SPAM holds anyone directly involved in sending out a commercial email message responsible for making sure it complies with the law. Hiring a vendor to handle your email marketing does not give you a "get out of jail free" card under CAN-SPAM. You must monitor your service providers to make sure they follow the law.

18. My dealership likes to be on the cutting edge of marketing techniques. Does CAN-SPAM apply to text messages and other "non-traditional" marketing methods?

CAN-SPAM does apply to email messages sent directly to wireless devices like cell phones. Basically, if the device you're reaching has an Internet address, then the law applies. CAN-SPAM directed the Federal Communications Commission to write a regulation applying CAN-SPAM to these messages. The FCC's rule (available at www.dealerdeskbook.com/resources/internetcanspam/) is more restrictive than CAN-SPAM's regulation of other email messages because recipients often pay a per-message fee for messages sent directly to a wireless device.

The FCC's rule says commercial email messages to wireless devices are prohibited unless you have the recipient's advance permission. To make sure you don't accidentally send a commercial email message to a wireless device, the FCC has a web page that lists all domain names that service wireless devices. If you check this list before you send your messages, you can make sure you don't send any to a wireless device. (Again, email list management.)

When the FCC's Do-Not-Email Rule *does* allow you to send a commercial email message to a wireless device, you must identify yourself and provide an opt-out mechanism. This rule also addresses how to get advance permission to send commercial email messages to a recipient's wireless device. That permission is closely regulated by the FCC's Rule.

"Short message service" messages that are sent from one cell phone to another are not covered by CAN-SPAM. Telemarketing regulations, however, may apply.

19. If I get sued, what penalties can I face?

If the federal government sues you, a court can order you to pay up to $16,000 for each law violation. That means up to $16,000 per message. The feds can also seek criminal penalties (including jail) for the worst offenders. If you get sued by a state or an Internet service provider, the amount per violation goes way down, but it can still add up, again, because penalties are calculated per message.

20. What about state email marketing laws? Do I have to comply with them? Or does CAN-SPAM preempt state laws?

The federal CAN-SPAM Act preempts (or overrides) some state laws, but not all. Most people seem to agree that state laws that required you to put "ADV" or something similar in the "subject" line are thrown out by CAN-SPAM. There's less agreement on whether a state do-not-email list would be allowed or thrown out. State laws prohibiting fraud in email marketing are valid. The best way to handle this issue is to talk to your lawyer.

21. Are there any CAN-SPAM recordkeeping requirements?

No, CAN-SPAM does not include specific recordkeeping requirements. However, it's always advisable to keep copies of your marketing material and email list management procedures so you can show you comply with the law when asked to do so.

22. Are there any available defenses if I get sued?

Generally, no. However, there is a safe harbor if your mechanism for processing opt-out requests is taken out by a technical difficulty. Other than that, though, the FTC's Kodak case shows that other kinds of technical difficulties won't get you off the hook.

Chapter 17

Arbitration

By Thomas B. Hudson

Nine Things That Dealers Need to Know
About Arbitration

Many dealers have begun to use arbitration agreements as a first defense against class action lawsuits and as a way of avoiding an increasingly hostile court system. In addition to providing these protections to the dealer, arbitration can be a cost-efficient and customer-friendly way of resolving disputes.

Although arbitration offers several advantages to dealers, it may also offer some disadvantages as well. In some jurisdictions, plaintiffs' lawyers are beginning to take an "if you can't beat 'em, join 'em" approach and are actively using the arbitration process as a way of asserting their clients' claims. Some dealers have had some experience with arbitration and have observed that arbitration proceedings are more costly than court proceedings (although, we'll never know how many claims are never brought because plaintiffs' lawyers are discouraged by the presence of arbitration agreements). Dealers and dealers' lawyers should educate themselves on these issues before implementing an arbitration program.

Most states have arbitration laws, but most arbitration agreements in use today invoke the Federal Arbitration Act. There are some good reasons for doing so, not the least of which is the sizeable body of mostly pro-dealer and pro-creditor opinions that have been rendered over the years dealing with the federal law. The remainder of this discussion assumes that the Federal Arbitration Act applies.

1. *Where can I get an arbitration agreement?*

Some vendors offer arbitration agreements. Be sure to have any arbitration agreement you obtain from a vendor reviewed by your lawyer. As you'll notice later in this chapter, a poorly drafted arbitration agreement may not be enforceable. Also, if you are in a so-called "single document" state, where state law requires that all your agreements with your customer be incorporated into a single document, remember that you probably cannot use a stand-alone or addendum arbitration agreement.

2. *If I use an arbitration agreement, will I have to arbitrate my claims against my customer, such as the collection of my customer's bounced checks?*

If the arbitration agreement is crafted properly, no. The arbitration agreement should be worded in such a way that neither the dealer nor the customer is obligated to arbitrate unless the other party to the agreement requests arbitration. History so far suggests that customers very seldom ask for arbitration. If that trend continues, a dealer using an arbitration agreement can ignore it as long as the customer hasn't asked for arbitration and can proceed using the court system or any self-help remedies that he may have under state law.

3. *Why don't I just "carve out" of our requirement to arbitrate any disputes that we might have against the customer? And while I'm at it, why don't I provide in my arbitration clause that the customer cannot claim punitive damages in an arbitration proceeding?*

You can do those things, but chances are a court will not enforce your arbitration agreement, because it is too one-sided. You'll be more likely to have a court enforce your arbitration agreement if it is balanced and fair.

4. What should an arbitration agreement contain?

Test your arbitration agreement or clause to make sure that it

- Prohibits class arbitration—that is the main reason to use an arbitration agreement. So far, courts in most states have found that this prohibition is enforceable;

- Is not in a type size smaller than other important terms in the same document or in accompanying documents— bold type, capital letters, and other means of drawing attention to the arbitration clause or agreement are all good ideas;

- Is balanced in terms of who is required to arbitrate what claims—it shouldn't require the customer to arbitrate nearly everything and the dealer/finance company to arbitrate very little;

- Does not burden the customer with fees and costs that are so high or potentially high that the customer will be precluded from bringing a claim;

- Does not overreach in limiting the customer's claims for punitive or exemplary damages;

- Does not impose undue burdens, such as lengthy travel, on the customer;

- Does not limit the customer to just one arbitration service provider—it should list two or more providers or, if it lists one, should provide that the customer may choose another provider with the dealer/finance company's approval.

If your arbitration clause or agreement falls short in any of these areas, chances are it needs a legal checkup. Contact a knowledgeable lawyer for a review.

5. What do I do if the customer won't sign the arbitration agreement?

That's your call, but here's what we recommend. First, this should be a dealership policy decision. You are either going to require every buyer to agree to arbitration, or you're going to permit exceptions. Whichever way you decide to handle the issue, don't wait until it arises to make your choice. When you implement arbitration, train your staff that you do, or do not, permit exceptions. While you're at it, train your staff on how you would want them to respond to customer inquiries about what the arbitration agreement means.

We also recommend a strict "no exceptions" policy. Our experience with dealers indicates that few, if any, sales are lost by requiring every customer to arbitrate, and every exception is a potential class representative. So if the customer balks, thank her for shopping with you and give her the number of another store that sells what you sell. Our bet is that you won't lose the sale.

6. Why should my arbitration agreement provide that I will pay some part of my customer's costs of arbitration? Why should I pay someone to sue me?

The industry's experience so far is that customers do not often initiate arbitration, so the occasions that you will have to fork over arbitration costs will be rare. Remember that the principal reasons that you have an arbitration agreement are to protect against class action risk and to keep yourself out of hostile courts. Paying some part of the customer's arbitration costs can be a very reasonable price for achieving those results.

7. What happens if I have an arbitration clause in my buyer's order, and a different one in my retail installment sale contract?

You have a problem. Courts faced with this situation will often throw up their hands and refuse to enforce either arbitration clause. You could add language to one or both arbitration clauses to address the issue, or perhaps cross out one and have the customer initial the change. Talk to your lawyer for the best fix for this problem.

8. If I assign my retail installment sale contract to a sales finance company, can the sales finance company enforce the arbitration clause against the customer?

It depends. There are not any hard and fast rules about how arbitration clauses are constructed. Some arbitration clauses say that they apply only to disputes between the selling dealer and the customer. Others say that they bind any holder of the retail installment sale contract, and some even go so far as to say that they bind non-parties to the retail installment sale contract, such as providers of credit life insurance. You and your lawyer will need to read the terms of the arbitration clause and become familiar with its provisions and limitations.

9. My state prohibits arbitration clauses. What do I do?

Your state cannot prohibit you and your customer from agreeing to arbitrate under the Federal Arbitration Act. That's because of a legal doctrine called "federal preemption." In English, that means that federal law trumps state law. Under the Federal Arbitration Act, state laws that apply to all contracts (such as a provision that all consumer contracts have to be in at least 10-point type) can apply to arbitration agreements entered into under the FAA, but state laws expressly regulating only arbitration may not.

Typical State Laws: Retail Installment Sale and Lease Laws, Uniform Commercial Code Unfair and Deceptive Acts & Practices, Simple Language, Advertising, Discrimination, Credit Repair

By Thomas B. Hudson

Thirteen Things That Dealers Need to Know About State Laws

In earlier chapters, we noted that, generally, it is *state* law that regulates the substantive terms and conditions of vehicle sales, financing, and lease contracts, while *federal* law regulates how those terms and conditions must be disclosed.

It is also state law, generally, that regulates related dealership activities, such as advertising, facilities requirements, general contracting, and the like.

In this chapter, we will not attempt to recite all of the laws of all of the states regarding auto sales, financing, and leasing. Instead, we will describe the types of laws and regulations that typically can be found in each state to give you a feel for the general scope of state oversight of dealership activities. Getting through the maze of rules can be a little like crawling through a barbed wire fence; a dealership will suffer snags and cuts from every direction, but patience and diligence will see you to the other side.

1. What are the major sources of the rules that affect dealers?

State legislatures pass laws, or *statutes*. A state's laws are usually codified in such a way that all of the statutes regulating a particular activity can be found in one place. As an example, state dealership statutes will appear in the "Transportation Article" or in the "Motor Vehicle Code"—the names will vary by state. State departments and agencies will sometimes have "rulemaking power" and will promulgate (a big word that basically means "write and enact") *rules* or *regulations*. These rules or regulations usually have the force of law and usually appear in some sort of state code of regulations.

The departments or agencies may also dispense advice in more informal ways, such as by letter or in oral conversations. This informal advice sometimes does not have the force of law, and in those instances, it can be dangerous to rely on it. Finally, in nearly all states, courts render decisions that make up something called the "common law." A court case will guide how a law or regulation should be interpreted, unless that court case later is overruled.

Laws from all of these sources can affect dealers.

2. What state laws regulate the cash sale of a motor vehicle?

Many laws have an impact on a vehicle sale. Dealers are merchants. State laws that affect merchants generally will apply to dealers unless they are exempted from such laws. The Uniform Commercial Code's Article 2 (adopted in all states) governs the actions of merchants when they sell goods.

Many states will regulate dealership sales activities. State new car Lemon Laws are common. Some states have used car Lemon Laws, too. State common law (remember those court cases) about forming, interpreting, and enforcing contracts will also apply to sales of vehicles by dealers, because the sale involves a contract.

3. What state laws regulate the credit sale of a motor vehicle?

First, two quick observations: The laws that apply to the cash sale of a motor vehicle will also apply to credit sale of a motor vehicle. And, state Retail Installment Sales Acts tend to be more restrictive toward creditors than general interest and usury statutes.

Now, what are those laws? Most states have a "Retail Installment Sales Act" (or a "Motor Vehicle Retail Installment

Sales Act") that regulates the sale of motor vehicles on credit.

In some states, a version of the so-called "Uniform Consumer Credit Code," or "UCCC," contains provisions very similar to provisions that are found in other states' Retail Installment Sales Acts. We say "so-called" because the UCCC, originally intended to be uniform across states, varies, in part, from state to state, and only a few states have actually adopted a version of it. The Retail Installment Sales Act or the UCCC is the principal law in most states governing the credit sale of motor vehicles.

State Retail Installment Sales Acts usually regulate the key terms of the credit sale of a vehicle. Such laws will typically impose a maximum rate cap on finance charges, a maximum late charge, and a mandatory grace period before the late charge can be imposed. Typically, these laws also impose prohibitions on certain terms, such as balloon payments, and they will list permitted fees and charges that a selling dealer may impose. The problem is that not all state laws of this type will impose and permit these things.

State retail installment sales laws often contain traps for unwary dealers. Many contain provisions that reflect a concern for the ways in which "indirect lending" or "three-party paper" was done 40 years ago. Examples include:

- Finance charge rate caps expressed as "add-on" or "discount" rates instead of as simple finance charge rates;

- Definitions of concepts such as the "time sale price doctrine" that can make simple finance charge programs difficult and variable rate programs impossible; and

- Provisions that assume that finance charges on all transactions are "pre-computed" rather than assessed on a finance-charge bearing, or so-called "simple finance charge," basis.

Such laws often contain draconian provisions that render transactions void for failure to comply with disclosure terms, licensing provisions, or even requirements that sellers sign credit contracts. Like the hammered thumb, they become of intense interest once the damage is done. But also like that thumb, that attention to detail comes too late to avoid the pain. Some states have "simple language" laws that require that credit sale documents be written in everyday language or that impose a readability score on such documents.

Some states' laws mirror those at the federal level—an example would be a state version of the federal Equal Credit Opportunity Act. *And,* you shouldn't assume that you comply with state law if you meet federal standards; sometimes the state standards are more stringent. Nor should you assume that the state law is or is not preempted by the federal law. Check with your attorney if there is any question.

No review of state law would be complete without an analysis of the various Uniform Commercial Code, or "UCC" (not to be confused with the Uniform Consumer Credit Code, or "UCCC," discussed above), provisions that affect a dealer's forms and operations. The UCC has 11 chapters, or "Articles," that each deal with some substantive area of commercial law; for example, sales, negotiable instruments, fund transfers, warehouse receipts, and so on. Article 9, for example, is titled "Secured Transactions" and it controls the creation and perfection of security interests in things like the retail installment sale contracts that you sell to finance companies. It would also control the creation and perfection of security interests in motor vehicles sold on credit in a state that didn't address those issues in its titling scheme. Also, repossession rights of the debtor and creditor may, in some circumstances, fall within the provisions of UCC Article 9.

Some states have non-uniform versions of some provisions of the UCC, in order to add consumer protections not found in the UCC. Each state is permitted to enact any variations of these "uniform" laws that it likes. You know that only lawyers could call something "uniform" that can be subject to the whims of our 50 states.

4. What state laws regulate the lease of a motor vehicle?

Motor vehicle leases are usually regulated by UCC Article 2A. Article 2A's provisions, for the most part, may be varied by the parties; so, as a practical matter, lessors and lessees governed only by Article 2A have a great deal of freedom in determining the terms and conditions of a vehicle lease.

A few states have a "motor vehicle lease law" or a "consumer lease law" that often will also apply to a vehicle lease. Laws like these restrict leases in much the same way that a Retail Installment Sales Act restricts credit sales.

Such laws also frequently restrict fees and charges, limit late and other fees, regulate the maximum early termination liability of lessees, and impose disclosure requirements.

5. What state laws apply to dealer advertising?

Dealers need to look in at least four places to determine how the state regulates advertising.

First, many states will have an advertising law that applies to merchants generally. The dealer, as a merchant, must comply with those laws. It is possible that the state has enacted advertising laws that apply only to dealers, but such laws are not very common.

State regulatory bodies that oversee dealers (Motor Vehicle Administrators, DMVs, or the like) will often have regulations that address dealer advertising.

Most states have an "unfair and deceptive acts or practices" law that generally prohibits misrepresentations in advertising and other activities.

Finally, if your dealership is offering any sort of "game of chance," such as "if your key unlocks this car, you have won it," or a raffle as part of an advertising program, you should make sure that the state doesn't expressly regulate these activities. **Hint:** Don't forget to look in the state's criminal laws for these sorts of provisions.

If your state has a "credit repair organization" (CRO) law, you'll want to pay careful attention to the way that law defines a CRO. Sometimes your dealership's advertising can bring you within the definition of "credit repair organization" in a CRO law, making you subject to licensing and disclosure requirements and possibly providing your buyers with a right to get out of their deals.

6. Does my dealership need a license to sell vehicles on credit?

In most states, the answer is "no," but you really must nail this down with your lawyer. Although very few states require a license (other than the standard dealer's license) for dealers selling cars on credit, some do.

Many states require that entities purchasing installment sales contracts, usually referred to as "sales finance companies," be licensed to do so. The licensing statutes often contain annual licensing fee requirements, bonding requirements, recordkeeping requirements, and provisions for audits. Some statutory schemes also impose upon sales finance companies limitations and restrictions relating to refinancing and other transactions with the buyer. A "related finance company" that is affiliated with a "buy-here, pay-here" dealership would be a sales finance company regulated by such a statute.

State laws also may regulate (such as by requiring a license or merely requiring the dealer to register with a state office) the simple act of taking a credit application.

7. If my state has a "simple language" law, does that affect my forms?

Yes, it might. Some states have enacted "plain language" laws, mandating the form of consumer contracts. New Jersey, Delaware, and Connecticut, among others, have such statutes.

Such statutes often require words with everyday meanings, discourage Latin or "legalese," require certain type sizes, and require indices or tables of contents for contracts of a certain length.

At least one state, New Jersey, provides for (but does not require) regulatory review of a creditor's forms. Creditors electing to take advantage of this safe harbor can submit their forms (with a review fee) and receive the approval of the Attorney General's office. A form that has been so approved is thereafter immune from attack under the plain language law.

Even when not required by state law, it is usually a good business practice to have documents as readable as you can make them; incidentally, the requirements of these laws could be used as a "best practices" guide for any dealership.

8. What impact does a typical "unfair and deceptive acts and practices," or "UDAP," law have on my dealership?

Sometimes referred to as "mini-FTC laws," these state statutes prohibit a number of practices that state legislatures have deemed to be overreaching on the part of sellers and creditors. Most UDAP laws contain a very general *"don't do unfair and deceptive stuff"* provision; they typically also contain a laundry list of specific "bad acts" that are prohibited. For instance, such laws may prohibit "confessed judgment" clauses in consumer contracts—clauses that permit one party to obtain a judgment easily against the other without notice, because you've already obtained the consumer's written consent at closing. Note that federal regulations already prohibit this activity. However, if state law prohibits it also, that's another avenue through which an attack against you could be launched.

Plaintiffs' lawyers are particularly fond of UDAP laws and often make claims based on them. They like these laws for several reasons:

- The laws often use imprecise or broadly defined words like "unfair" to describe prohibited conduct. It is difficult to defend against such sweeping characterizations of conduct.

- UDAP laws often permit plaintiffs to recover some multiple (usually two or three times) of their actual damages, and some permit recovery of statutory damages or permit other relief, even when the plaintiff has no actual damages.

- Finally, UDAP laws typically provide that the customer may recover attorneys' fees and court costs.

9. My dealership sells credit life insurance. Are there laws we need to know about governing that activity?

Many dealers offer credit life insurance, credit accident and health insurance, and even credit unemployment insurance in connection with motor vehicle financing transactions. Such insurance coverage is heavily regulated by most states.

Licensing statutes sometimes require that those who offer such coverages be licensed as "agents" or as "enrollers."

States typically regulate insurance coverages that can be offered, and they mandate the disclosures that must be given to customers. Insurance regulators must approve the forms used to offer coverages (sometimes even including "election" provisions in creditors' contracts).

10. Are there state discrimination laws I need to worry about?

States often write laws to prohibit discrimination in the granting of credit. They often are similar to the antidiscrimination provisions contained in the federal Equal Credit Opportunity Act (discussed in Chapter 4).

You will need to examine such state "baby ECOA" statutes with care. While compliance with the federal ECOA will often constitute compliance with the similar state statutes (and some of the statutes expressly so state), this is not necessarily the case. Some of the statutes are not as broad as the federal act, but some are broader and must be followed. The additional breadth can take the form of additional protected classes (such as disabled persons, which are not a protected class under the ECOA), additional recordkeeping requirements, or additional notices or disclosures.

11. How about state privacy laws?

Many states have laws dealing with the privacy of consumers' financial information. Because dealers sell cars on credit and lease cars, they usually fall within the scope of these laws. Generally, compliance with federal laws and regulations will constitute compliance with state privacy laws. Your dealership should determine whether state laws impose any requirements beyond the federal ones.

One very frequent area that states have regulated recently is that of "data breach." Dealerships often maintain financial information on consumers. The data breach laws impose requirements on companies that maintain financial information on consumers. The requirements kick in when the data has been compromised in various ways, such as when the data has been lost, stolen, or "hacked." They often require you to notify the consumers whose personal information has been compromised and to cooperate with law enforcement.

12. OK, what other surprises are there in my state's law books?

State statutes relating to the collection of consumer debts can affect the forms and operations of dealers. Here are a few examples:

- In one state, repossession of collateral constitutes a felony, unless a specific form of consent to non-judicial repossession is contained in the credit document when the credit document is entered into.

- Another state statute prohibits setoff of a consumer debt against the consumer's deposit account, unless the consumer agrees to the setoff, but the statute does not say *when that agreement must be entered into!* The statute leaves open the question whether the consumer's consent may be included in the creditor's form document or if it must be obtained after the consumer's default.

• One western state enacted a used car sale provision requiring certain disclosures and buried the requirement in a bill amending the criminal code!

Many other aspects of a creditor's conduct may be regulated in such unexpected ways.

13. Where can I get help in understanding state law without spending a fortune on legal fees?

Contact your state Motor Vehicle Administration (or whatever your state agency is called that regulates dealers), and see if they have prepared explanatory materials designed to help dealers comply with the laws and regulations that they enforce.

Ask your state Auto Dealers Association or Independent Auto Dealers Association whether they have materials on any of the topics mentioned in this chapter.

Most states will have a "Consumer Protection Bureau" or similar agency that will provide helpful information.

These sources often have websites (although a few are so seldom updated that they are more accurately called "cobweb sites").

Finally, monitor your state Attorney General's website, paying particular attention to press releases and enforcement actions involving car dealers.

But, also, *also,* don't forget your lawyer. Yours is a very highly regulated business that involves many legal questions.

You should make sure that you share with your lawyer any "do-it-yourself" conclusions or documents you come up with, and you should look to your lawyer for guidance when you are not absolutely certain that you know what you are doing.

CHAPTER 18

The Dodd-Frank Wall Street Reform and Consumer Protection Act of 2010: The Federal Reregulation of Consumer Credit

By Thomas B. Hudson

Ten Things That Dealers Need to Know
About the Dodd-Frank Wall Street Reform and
Consumer Protection Act of 2010

On July 21, 2010, President Obama signed the Dodd-Frank Wall Street Reform and Consumer Protection Act (Pub. L. 111-203) into law. The law will effect sweeping reforms for every sector of the financial services industry. Car dealers are already feeling the direct and indirect force of federal regulation as they have never before experienced it.

1. Wait a minute! Aren't dealers exempted from the new law?

The new law was the subject of intense lobbying by the National Auto Dealers Association and other trade associations and entities. Most of the lobbying centered on whether dealers should be exempted from regulation by the Consumer Financial Protection Bureau (CFPB), the powerful, well-funded new federal agency created by the new law. The House bill's final version contained a dealer exemption. The Senate's version of the bill didn't, but the Senate agreed to a slightly modified version of the original House bill when the two sides met in conference to work out the differences between their versions of the proposed new law.

The result was a dealer exclusion for some dealers but not others. Dealers with servicing operations that sell their retail installment contracts to unaffiliated parties will enjoy an exemption. Dealers that do not service cars or that hold their own paper are not exempt.

What constitutes "servicing" for the purpose of determining whether a dealer enjoys an exclusion? What happens if a dealer ends up having to repurchase a single retail installment contract from a finance company, and thus "holds" some of its own paper? Will its exclusion from the CFPB's authority disappear?

As usual, Congress has left detailed questions like these to be answered by regulations to be issued by, among others, the new CFPB. As we write this, the CFPB is still in the process of getting organized and writing regulations that will answer these important questions. However, we still don't expect it to begin to address these or any of the other subjects they will need to address with proposed regulations any time soon as the Bureau has placed its initial focus on the mortgage and credit card markets.

If you are a car dealer, exempt or not, this legislation is the most significant federal law that you've seen since the Truth in Lending Act of the late 1960s. As noted above, the Act creates the Consumer Financial Protection Bureau, a very large regulatory and enforcement organization with vast powers and a huge annual budget.

2. What is this new "Bureau," anyway?

The CFPB was officially created as an independent federal agency on July 21, 2011. On January 4, 2012, the president appointed former Ohio Attorney General Richard Cordray as Bureau director through the end of 2013. Cordray's appointment was not confirmed by the Senate because the appointment was made while Congress was in recess. Controversy, and possible court challenges to the appointment, still swirls around the Bureau's first director who, by all accounts, is a zealous consumer advocate.

The Bureau's funding is provided by the Federal Reserve Board, with the ability to obtain more funding from Congress upon request. The Bureau's 2013 budget is about $450 million.

3. What has Congress told the new Bureau to do?

The Dodd-Frank Act outlines the Bureau's functions, which include research, the collection and tracking of complaints, and financial education. The Bureau will also collect, research, monitor, and publish information relevant to the consumer product and service market; supervise covered persons for compliance; and issue rules, orders, and guidance implementing the Act.

In drafting rules, the Bureau must consider the potential costs and benefits to consumers and covered persons, as well as the impact of the rules on consumers in rural areas.

The Bureau has established a complaint-handling capability and will receive, monitor, and follow up on consumer complaints. Just another reason to make sure you, the dealer, address consumer complaints as they arise.

The Bureau may prescribe registration requirements for covered persons. This registration information may be public. The Bureau must consult with state agencies in developing registration requirements. The Bureau may require reports and may conduct periodic exams to assess compliance, obtain information about activities and compliance systems, and detect and assess risks to consumers.

4. What will the Bureau do about arbitration agreements?

Congress has given the Bureau the authority to prohibit or impose conditions on the use of mandatory arbitration agreements with consumers and covered persons for future disputes, but has provided that the Bureau cannot restrict agreements to arbitrate entered into after a dispute has arisen.

5. What other rules will the Bureau issue?

It's still too soon to tell. The Act provides that the Bureau will issue rules to identify unfair, deceptive, or abusive acts or practices. The Federal Trade Commission has long had the authority to combat unfair and deceptive practices, but the addition of "abusive" to the Bureau's targeted practices list will create a great deal of uncertainty over the breadth of practices that the Bureau will be able to target. The Bureau's powers will apply to covered persons and to service providers, and the Bureau will have enforcement authority over violators.

6. Will the Bureau provide creditors with model forms?

The Bureau will have the authority to create model forms and disclosures, and the Act directs that such disclosures be in plain language, with clear format, design and font, and succinct explanations. The forms are to be validated through consumer testing. The Act provides a safe harbor for users of model forms.

7. So now we won't have to worry about state laws, right?

Nice try, but the answer is that dealers must also comply with applicable state laws. State Attorneys General may bring civil actions to enforce the Dodd-Frank Act and its implementing regulations.

8. What will the Bureau do other than issue regulations?

Plenty. The Bureau's powers will include the ability to conduct investigations to determine whether violation has occurred, conduct hearings and adjudication proceedings, issue cease and desist orders, and bring civil actions to impose civil penalties or to seek legal and equitable relief. The Bureau will be able to require rescission or reformation of contracts, refunds, restitution, unjust enrichment compensation, and damages or monetary relief. It also will be able to publish public notices of violations; impose limits on the activities of person; and impose civil penalties, injunctive relief, and costs.

Civil penalties will depend upon the Bureau's perceived severity of a violation, as follows:

- Tier 1: Any violation of law, rule, or Bureau order—$5,000 each day violation continues

- Tier 2: Reckless violation of federal consumer financial law—$25,000 each day violation continues

- Tier 3: Knowing violation of federal consumer financial law—$1 million each day violation continues

Don't be lulled into a false sense of security by the CFPB's slow start and by its ignoring the auto industry so far. To get a flavor for the Bureau's zest for penalizing violators, look at the settlement amounts in the Bureau's first actions. Deciding to target the credit card industry for its opening salvos, the Bureau has already assessed fines and consumer refunds totaling over $450 million. And that's over the span of just three months.

However, the Bureau will be able to consider mitigating factors when it imposes penalties. Such factors may include the financial resources and good faith of the person charged, the gravity of the violation or failure to pay, the severity of the consumer risk and loss, previous violations, and such other matters as justice may require.

9. Does the new law come with a statute of limitations?

Yes. The Bureau must bring an action within three years from the date of discovery of a violation. This statute of limitations doesn't apply, however, to claims arising solely out of enumerated consumer laws, such as the Truth in Lending Act or the Equal Credit Opportunity Act.

10. OK, but if my dealership is exempt, I'm free of all of this federal regulatory stuff, right?

Wishful thinking. Dealers who are exempt from the scope of the CFPB's powers will still be subject to the Federal Trade Commission's authority and the Federal Reserve Board's rulemaking authority for Regulations Z, M, and B. The FTC has primary enforcement authority for the Dodd-Frank Act, but the Bureau has secondary enforcement authority unless an entity is directly subject to Bureau authority. The Act requires the Bureau to consult with the FTC when drafting rules.

Postscript

By Thomas B. Hudson

CHAPTER 20

Well here we are, at the end.

We hope we delivered.

Consumer finance regulation keeps getting more complex. We promised you a guide, a desk book to help you understand the too many laws and regulations that affect financing and leasing cars. That was our goal with the *F&I Legal Desk Book.*

We wish the environment were simpler. But until it is, we'll keep producing **CARLAW®** and **Spot Delivery®** and maintaining **StateLaw Counselor™** and **CounselorLibrary** (www.CounselorLibrary.com), backed by one of the largest groups of attorneys in the country dedicated to the world of consumer finance (www.HudsonCook.com).

Who's behind your compliance? We are, the attorneys and staff of Hudson Cook. Thank you for letting us help.

Tom Hudson

CHAPTER 20

Auto Finance
Lexicon

APPENDIX 1

This book deals with the legal side of auto finance and leasing. In the chapters addressing the various subjects, we sometimes use shorthand references to legal terms. Here are some of the terms you will see from time to time and a short description of what they mean.

AG: stands for Attorney General. Every state has one, essentially the top legal officer in the state. AGs usually enforce consumer protection laws and regulations. When we are being cynical, we sometimes say the "AG" stands for "Aspiring Governor." We also sometimes say the same thing when we aren't being cynical.

CFPB: the Consumer Financial Protection Bureau. The CFPB, created by the Dodd-Frank Act, is a new federal agency charged with supervising certain providers of consumer finance products and enforcing certain consumer finance laws with respect to those providers. It is also the agency charged with writing and interpreting regulations implementing the ECOA (Reg. B), the CLA (Reg. M), TILA (Reg. Z), etc., as they apply to certain car dealers. The CFPB is the new consumer-friendly "federal cop" for these car dealers.

CLA: the Consumer Leasing Act. The CLA governs disclosures in consumer lease transactions. The CLA is actually Chapter 5 of TILA (the federal Truth in Lending Act), but it is usually referred to as if it is a separate piece of legislation.

Credit Practices Rule: a Federal Trade Commission rule that regulates certain creditor practices, such as the pyramiding of late charges, garnishing wages, notifying cosigners, and the like.

Dodd-Frank Act: we use this term to refer to the Dodd-Frank Wall Street Reform and Consumer Protection Act, sponsored by Senator Chris Dodd (D-CT) and Rep. Barney Frank (D-MA) and enacted on July 21, 2010. The Dodd-Frank Act was a sweeping reform of federal laws that deal with the regulation of regulating financial institutions. One of the principal parts of the Dodd-Frank Act created the Consumer Financial Protection Bureau.

ECOA: federal Equal Credit Opportunity Act. The ECOA prohibits credit discrimination on the basis of sex, race, marital status, etc.

F&I: finance and insurance. The "finance and insurance" department of a dealership is called the F&I department. That's where financing terms are arranged and various products such as credit insurance and extended warranties are sold.

FCRA: the federal Fair Credit Reporting Act. The "FACT Act" is a recent amendment to the FCRA. The FCRA regulates those who compile and use credit reports.

FRB: the Federal Reserve Board. The FRB is a federal agency that controls monetary policy in the United States and regulates certain banking institutions. Under the Dodd-Frank Act, the FRB retains rule writing authority for TILA (Reg. Z), the CLA (Reg. M), the ECOA (Reg. B), etc., as those laws apply to certain car dealers who are exempt from supervision and enforcement by the CFPB.

FTC: the Federal Trade Commission. The FTC is a federal agency that enforces several federal laws and regulations (including the TILA, the ECOA, and Regs. Z and B) with respect to certain car dealers exempt from the CFPB's enforcement authority. The FTC is a tough, consumer-friendly enforcement agency and is the "federal cop" for certain car dealers exempt from the CFPB's enforcement authority.

Gramm-Leach-Bliley (GLB) Act: a federal law, Title 5 of which deals with the privacy of personal financial information.

Green Pea: a brand new dealership sales employee.

Holder Rule: a shorthand reference to the Federal Trade Commission's Trade Regulation Rule titled "The Preservation of Consumer Claims and Defenses." The Holder Rule permits a buyer under a retail installment sale contract to assert against the holder of the contract certain claims and defenses the buyer has against the selling dealer.

Odometer Law: a federal law designed to curb abusive practices (rollbacks, for example) dealing with vehicle odometers.

OFAC, or the Office of Foreign Asset Control: a unit of the U.S. Treasury Department that maintains the so-called "Specially Designated Nationals" or "bad guy" list. It is illegal for U.S. citizens to do business with someone whose name is on the bad guy list, and dealers who do not wish to violate the law must check the list before engaging in any business with any person.

Magnuson-Moss Warranty Act: a federal law that regulates warranties.

Reg. B: a regulation of the FRB and the CFPB implementing the ECOA.

Reg. M: a regulation of the FRB and the CFPB implementing the CLA.

Reg. Z: a regulation of the FRB and the CFPB implementing TILA.

Reg. P: a regulation of the FTC, the CFPB, and the federal banking agencies, which in its various forms implements the Gramm-Leach-Bliley Act's privacy provisions.

RISA: refers to a "retail installment sales act." Nearly every state has a RISA. Some states (about half) have a special version of a RISA for motor vehicle financing and a separate RISA for other kinds of personal property financing. RISAs typically regulate finance charge rates, late charges, grace periods, bad check charges, disclosures, and the like in auto financing agreements between dealers and customers.

RISC: a retail installment sale contract. This document is used to document a credit sale from a dealer to a buyer. Then, the dealer usually sells the RISC to a finance company or bank. Buy-here, pay-here dealers hold RISCs and collect payments from buyers, unless they have created an affiliated finance company to assign them to. If you call a RISC a "loan," Spot (the Dalmatian mascot for our legal newsletter, *Spot Delivery*®), has instructions to bite you on the ankle.

TILA: the federal Truth in Lending Act. TILA governs disclosures in consumer credit transactions. This is the "granddaddy" of federal disclosure laws, dating from the late 1960s.

Tort: a tort is a "civil wrong." The actions that comprise a tort can also comprise a crime, but a tort is not necessarily a crime. Examples of torts are negligence, fraud, and defamation.

TRR: a Trade Regulation Rule. TRRs are issued by the FTC. The "Used Car Rule" requiring window stickers is a TRR.

UDAP: refers to unfair and deceptive acts and practices. The FTC has UDAP provisions, and the CFPB has its own UDAP provisions too. Only the FTC and the CFPB can enforce their respective versions—a consumer cannot bring a private lawsuit to enforce it. Most states have UDAP laws as well and many permit consumers to sue under them. UDAP laws are favorites of lawyers who sue dealers because they are very general in their prohibitions and usually provide for a multiple (two or three times) the consumer's actual damages, plus attorneys' fees.

USA PATRIOT Act: a federal law aimed at terrorism and specifically targeting money laundering.

Used Car Rule: the "Buyers Guide" rule issued by the FTC. It requires a Buyers Guide to be displayed on each used vehicle offered for sale and requires certain language regarding the Buyers Guide in the contract of sale.

A Quick Primer on Laws and Regulations

A word about laws and regulations: Laws are passed by legislatures. Congress passes federal laws, and state legislatures pass state laws. "Rules" (such as the FTC's Used Car Rule) are issued by agencies or other state or federal non-legislative bodies that have been given rule-making authority by the legislative body.

An attempt to change a law requires having Congress or the state legislature pass a new law, a process that can be very difficult. Changing a regulation also can be difficult, but it is usually not as difficult as changing a law. Sometimes regulatory authorities don't have the power to change regulations, because the laws they are administering won't permit the change. As an example, even if in 1995 the Federal Reserve Board had wanted to amend Reg. Z to apply to auto finance transactions in which the amount financed was more than $25,000, it could not have done so because TILA—an Act of Congress—provided that such transactions were not subject to TILA's disclosure requirements. That change required an act of Congress itself, a change Congress made in the Dodd-Frank Wall Street Reform Act of 2010.

Index